SIGNS

Complete Poetry and Language Skills
Leaving Certificate Ordinary Level

For examination in 2011 and onwards • SECOND EDITION

JOHN McCARTHY & ANNE CLANCY • GILL & MACMILLAN

Gill & Macmillan Ltd
Hume Avenue
Park West
Dublin 12
with associated companies throughout the world
www.gillmacmillan.ie

© John McCarthy & Anne Clancy 2009
978 07171 4532 4
Design and print origination in Ireland by Graham Thew Design

*The paper used in this book is made from the wood pulp of managed
forests. For every tree felled, at least one tree is planted, thereby
renewing natural resources.*

Photo Credits

For permission to reproduce photographs the author and publisher gratefully acknowledge the following:

ALAMY: 33B, 53, 121, 105, 100; ASSOCIATED PRESS: 5, 95; BLOODAXE/ BARBARA SAVAGE CHERSH: 101, 105;
CAMERA PRESS IRELAND: 3, 9, 45, 87, 114; CORBIS: 33T, 52, 54, 60, 73, 99, 137, 151; Courtesy of the Head of the
Department of Irish Folklore: 226BL; DEFENCE FORCES IRELAND: 222C; EDWIN MORGAN: 93; GETTY: 110, 96,
125, 152, 140, 141, 222T; IMAGEFILE: 66, 138; INPHOPHOTOGRAPHY: 233; IRISH IMAGE COLLECTION: 226TL,
226TR, 226CR, 226BR, 229CL; IRISH PICTURE LIBRARY: 226CL; IRISH TIMES: 19, 31, 97; JOHN SKELTON: 57
JOHN WHEATLEY: 135; KATE NEWMANN/ GALLERY PRESS: 41; KEVIN HONAN: 129; LEAPFROG PRESS: 107;
LEBRECHT: 43; MARK GERSON: 11; MARY EVANS PICTURE LIBRARY: 25, 119; MICHAEL MARKEE/ WILLIAM
STAFFORD ARCHIVES: 131; NATIONAL LIBRARY OF IRELAND: 222B; NATIONAL PORTRAIT GALLERY
LONDON: 89, 123; PA PHOTOS: 65; PACEMAKER PRESS INTERNATIONAL: 77; PETER SIRR: 149; PHOTOCALL:
61; REX FEATURES: 7, 75, 109, 229TR, 229BL; RTE: 229CR; SALMON POETRY: 91; SPORTSFILE: 233TL, 233TR,
233BR; TERESA OLSON: 39; TOM LAWLOR: 229TL; TOPFOTO: 69, 29, 133, 143; VASSAR COLLEGE LIBRARIES:
13; WRITER PICTURES: 59, 71.

The author and publisher have made every effort to trace all copyright holders, but if any has been inadvertently
overlooked we would be pleased to make the necessary arrangement at the first opportunity.

COURSE OVERVIEW
Poems Prescribed for Ordinary Level
June 2011 Examination

Boland
Child of Our Time (p.18)
Love (p.20)
This Moment (p.22)

Dickinson
I felt a Funeral, in my Brain (p.24)
I heard a Fly buzz — when I died (p.26)

Frost
The Tuft of Flowers (p.32)
Out, Out- (p.34)
Mending Wall (p.36)

Hopkins
Spring (p.52)
Inversnaid (p.54)

Kavanagh
Shancoduff (p.56)
A Christmas Childhood (p.58)

Rich
Aunt Jennifer's Tigers (p.114)
The Uncle Speaks in the Drawing Room (p.115)
Trying to Talk with a Man (p.116)

Wordsworth
She dwelt among the untrodden ways (p.142)
From The Prelude: Skating [ll 425–463] (p.144)
It is a beauteous evening, calm and free (p.146)

Yeats
The Wild Swans at Coole (p.150)
An Irish Airman Foresees His Death (p.152)

Adcock
For Heidi with Blue Hair (p.2)

Armitage
It Ain't What You Do, It's What It Does to You (p.6)

Auden
Funeral Blues (p.8)

Duffy
Valentine (p.28)

Durcan
Going Home to Mayo, Winter, 1949 (p.30)

Hardie
Daniel's Duck (p.40)

Herbert
The Collar (p.50)

Kennelly
A Glimpse of Starlings (p.60)

Levertov
What Were They Like? (p.72)

Monahan
All Day Long (p.90)

Morgan
Strawberries (p.92)

Muldoon
Anseo (p.94)

Murphy
Moonshine (p.96)

O'Callaghan
The Net (p.102)

Shuttle
Jungian Cows (p.124)

Wilbur
The Writer (p.136)

NOTE: Ordinary Level candidates sitting the exam in June 2011 may choose either the poems in the left-hand column or the poems in the right-hand column

Poems Prescribed for Ordinary Level
June 2012 Examination

Boland	Child of Our Time (p.18) Love (p.20) This Moment (p.22)
Frost	The Tuft of Flowers (p.32) Out, Out– (p.34) Mending Wall (p.36)
Heaney	A Constable Calls (p.44) A Call (p.46) The Underground (p.48)
Kavanagh	Shancoduff (p.56) A Christmas Childhood (p.58)
Kinsella	Thinking of Mr D. (p.64) Mirror in February (p.66)
Larkin	Ambulances (p.68) The Explosion (p.70)
Plath	Poppies in July (p.108) Child (p.110)
Rich	Aunt Jennifer's Tigers (p.114) The Uncle Speaks in the Drawing Room (p.115) Trying to Talk with a Man (p.116)

Angelou	Phenomenal Woman (p.4)
Durcan	Going Home to Mayo, Winter, 1949 (p.30)
Hardie	Daniel's Duck (p.40)
Hardy	When I set out for Lyonnesse (p.42)
Kennelly	A Glimpse of Starlings (p.60)
Levertov	What Were They Like? (p.72)
MacNeice	Meeting point (p.78)
McGough	Bearhugs (p.86)
Monahan	All Day Long (p.90)
Muldoon	Anseo (p.94)
Murphy	Moonshine (p.96)
Oliver	The Sun (p.104)
Shelley	Ozymandias (p.122)
Shuttle	Jungian Cows (p.124)
Stafford	Traveling through the Dark (p.130)
Wilbur	A Summer Morning (p.138)

NOTE: Ordinary Level candidates sitting the exam in June 2012 may choose either the poems in the left-hand column or the poems in the right-hand column

Poems Prescribed for Ordinary Level
June 2013 Examination

Bishop
The Fish (p.12)
The Filling Station (p.14)
The Prodigal (p.16)

Hopkins
Spring (p.52)
Inversnaid (p.54)

Kinsella
Thinking of Mr D. (p.64)
Mirror in February (p.66)

Mahon
Grandfather (p.80)
After the Titanic (p.82)
Antarctica (p.84)

Plath
Poppies in July (p.108)
Child (p.110)
The Arrival of the Bee Box (p.112)

Rich
Aunt Jennifer's Tigers (p.114)
The Uncle Speaks in the Drawing Room (p.115)

Shakespeare
Sonnet 18: Shall I compare thee … (p.118)
Sonnet 60: Like as the waves … (p.120)

Wordsworth
She dwelt among the untrodden ways (p.142)
From The Prelude: Skating [ll 425–463] (p.144)
It is a beauteous evening, calm and free (p.146)

Adcock
For Heidi with Blue Hair (p.2)

Gallagher
The Hug (p.38)

Hardie
Daniel's Duck (p.40)

Kennelly
Night Drive (p.62)

Longley
Badger (p.76)

Milton
When I Consider (p.88)

Muldoon
Anseo (p.94)

O'Callaghan
Problems (p.100)

Oliver
The Sun (p.104)

Piercy
Will We Work Together? (p.106)

Shuttle
Jungian Cows (p.124)

Sirr
Madly Singing in the City (p.128)

Stafford
Traveling through the Dark (p.130)

Thomas
Do Not Go Gentle into That Good Night (p.132)

Wheatley
Chronicle (p.134)

Wilbur
A Summer Morning (p.138)

NOTE: Ordinary Level candidates sitting the exam in June 2013 may choose either the poems in the left-hand column or the poems in the right-hand column

Poems Prescribed for Ordinary Level
June 2014 Examination

Bishop
The Fish (p.12)
The Filling Station (p.14)
The Prodigal (p.16)

Dickinson
I felt a Funeral, in my Brain (p.24)
I heard a Fly buzz — when I died (p.26)

Heaney
A Constable Calls (p.44)
A Call (p.46)
The Underground (p.48)

Kinsella
Thinking of Mr D. (p.64)
Mirror in February (p.66)

Larkin
Ambulances (p.68)
The Explosion (p.70)

Mahon
Grandfather (p.80)
After the Titanic (p.82)
Antarctica (p.84)

Plath
Poppies in July (p.108)
Child (p.110)
The Arrival of the Bee Box (p.112)

Yeats
The Wild Swans at Coole (p.150)
An Irish Airman Foresees His Death (p.152)

Beer
The Voice (p.10)

Duffy
Valentine (p.28)

Herbert
The Collar (p.50)

Gallagher
The Hug (p.38)

Hardie
Daniel's Duck (p.40)

Kennelly
Night Drive (p.62)

Lochhead
Kidspoem/Bairnsang (p.74)

Nemerov
Wolves in the Zoo (p.98)

O'Callaghan
The Net (p.102)

Piercy
Will We Work Together? (p.106)

Shuttle
Zoo Morning (p.126)

Sirr
Madly Singing in the City (p.128)

Thomas
Do Not Go Gentle into That Good Night (p.132)

Wheatley
Chronicle (p.134)

Williams
This Is Just to Say (p.140)

Wyley
Poems for Breakfast (p.148)

NOTE: Ordinary Level candidates sitting the exam in June 2014 may choose either the poems in the left-hand column or the poems in the right-hand column

CONTENTS

POETRY
Poems, Biographies, Explorations

Fleur Adcock (1934–)
For Heidi with Blue Hair (2011 & 2013)   2

Maya Angelou (1928–)
Phenomenal Woman (2012)   4

Simon Armitage (1963–)
It Ain't What You Do, It's What It
    Does to You (2011)   6

W. H. Auden (1907–1973)
Funeral Blues (2011)   8

Patricia Beer (1924–1999)
The Voice (2014)   10

Elizabeth Bishop (1911–1979)
The Fish (2013 & 2014)   12
The Filling Station (2013 & 2014)   14
The Prodigal (2013 & 2014)   16

Eavan Boland (1944–)
Child of Our Time (2011 & 2012)   18
Love (2011 & 2012)   20
This Moment (2011 & 2012)   22

Emily Dickinson (1830–1886)
I felt a Funeral, in my Brain
    (2011 & 2014)   24
I heard a Fly buzz – when I died
    (2011 & 2014)   26

Carol Ann Duffy (1955–)
Valentine (2011 & 2014)   28

Paul Durcan (1944–)
Going Home to Mayo, Winter, 1949
    (2011 & 2012)   30

Robert Frost (1874–1963)
The Tuft of Flowers (2011 & 2012)   32
Out, Out– (2011 & 2012)   34
Mending Wall (2011 & 2012)   36

Tess Gallagher (1943–)
The Hug (2013 & 2014)   38

Kerry Hardie (1951–)
Daniel's Duck (2011 & 2012 & 2013
    & 2014)   40

Thomas Hardy (1840–1928)
When I set out for Lyonnesse (2012)   42

Seamus Heaney (1939–)
A Constable Calls (2012 & 2014)   44
A Call (2012 & 2014)   46
The Underground (2012 & 2014)   48

George Herbert (1593–1633)
The Collar (2011 & 2014)   50

**Gerard Manley Hopkins
(1844–1889)**
Spring (2011 & 2013)   52
Inversnaid (2011 & 2013)   54

Patrick Kavanagh (1904–1967)
Shancoduff (2011 & 2012)   56
A Christmas Childhood (2011 & 2012)   58

Brendan Kennelly (1936–)
A Glimpse of Starlings (2011 & 2012)   60
Night Drive (2013 & 2014)   62

Thomas Kinsella (1928–)
Thinking of Mr D. (2012 & 2013 & 2014)   64
Mirror in February (2012 & 2013
    & 2014)   66

Philip Larkin (1922–1985)
Ambulances (2012 & 2014)   68
The Explosion (2012 & 2014)   70

Denise Levertov (1923–1997)
What Were They Like? (2011 & 2012)   72

Liz Lochhead (1947–)
Kidspoem/Bairnsang (2014)   74

Michael Longley (1939–)
Badger (2013)   76

Louis MacNeice (1907–1963)
Meeting point (2012)   78

Derek Mahon (1941–)
Grandfather (2013 & 2014)   80
After the Titanic (2013 & 2014)   82
Antarctica (2013 & 2014)   84

Roger McGough (1937–)
Bearhugs (2012)   86

John Milton (1608–1674)
When I Consider (2013)   88

Noel Monahan
All Day Long (2011 & 2012)   90

Edwin Morgan (1920–)
Strawberries (2011)   92

Paul Muldoon (1951–)
Anseo (2011 & 2012 & 2013)   94

Richard Murphy (1927–)
Moonshine (2011 & 2012)   96

Howard Nemerov (1920–1991)
Wolves in the Zoo (2014)   98

Julie O'Callaghan (1954–)
Problems (2013)   100
The Net (2011 & 2014)   102

Mary Oliver (1935–)
The Sun (2012 & 2013)   104

Marge Piercy (1936–)
Will We Work Together? (2013 & 2014)   106

Sylvia Plath (1932–1963)
Poppies in July (2012 & 2013 & 2014)   108
Child (2012 & 2013 & 2014)   110
The Arrival of the Bee Box
    (2013 & 2014)   112

Adrienne Rich (1929–)
Aunt Jennifer's Tigers (2011 & 2012
    & 2013)   114
The Uncle Speaks in the Drawing
    Room (2011 & 2012 & 2013)   115
Trying to Talk with a Man (2011
    & 2012)   116

William Shakespeare (1564–1616)
Sonnet 18: Shall I compare thee …
    (2013)   118
Sonnet 60: Like as the waves … (2013)   120

Percy Bysshe Shelley (1792–1822)
Ozymandias (2012)   122

Penelope Shuttle (1947–)
Jungian Cows (2011 & 2012 & 2013)   124
Zoo Morning (2014)   126

Peter Sirr (1960–)
Madly Singing in the City (2013
    & 2014)   128

William Stafford (1914–1993)
Traveling through the Dark (2012 & 2013)   130

Dylan Thomas (1914–1953)
Do Not Go Gentle into That Good Night (2013 & 2014)   132

David Wheatley (1970–)
Chronicle (2013 & 2014)   134

Richard Wilbur (1921–)
The Writer (2011)   136
A Summer Morning (2012 & 2013)   138

William Carlos Williams (1883–1963)
This Is Just To Say (2014)   140

William Wordsworth (1770–1850)
She dwelt among the untrodden ways (2011 & 2013)   142
From The Prelude: Skating ... *(2011 & 2013)*   144
It is a beauteous evening, calm and free (2011 & 2013)   146

Enda Wyley (1966–)
Poems for Breakfast (2014)   148

W. B. Yeats (1865–1939)
The Wild Swans at Coole (2011 & 2014)   150
An Irish Airman Foresees His Death (2011 & 2014)   152

POETRY NOTES

For Heidi with Blue Hair *(2011 & 2013)*   156

Phenomenal Woman *(2012)*   156

It Ain't What You Do, It's What It Does to You *(2011)*   157

Funeral Blues *(2011)*   158

The Voice *(2014)*   158

The Fish *(2013 & 2014)*   159

The Filling Station *(2013 & 2014)*   160

The Prodigal *(2013 & 2014)*   160

Child of Our Time *(2011 & 2012)*   161

Love *(2011 & 2012)*   162

This Moment *(2011 & 2012)*   162

I felt a Funeral, in my Brain *(2011 & 2014)*   163

I heard a Fly buzz — when I died *(2011 & 2014)*   163

Valentine *(2011 & 2014)*   163

Going Home to Mayo, Winter, 1949 *(2011 & 2012)*   164

The Tuft of Flowers *(2011 & 2012)*   165

Out, Out– *(2011 & 2012)*   166

Mending Wall *(2011 & 2012)*   167

The Hug *(2013 & 2014)*   167

Daniel's Duck (2011 & 2012 & 2013 & 2014) — 168

When I set out for Lyonnesse (2012) — 168

A Constable Calls (2012 & 2014) — 169

A Call (2012 & 2014) — 169

The Underground (2012 & 2014) — 170

The Collar (2011 & 2014) — 171

Inversnaid (2011 & 2013) — 171

Spring (2011 & 2013) — 171

Shancoduff (2011 & 2012) — 172

A Christmas Childhood (2011 & 2012) — 174

A Glimpse of Starlings (2011 & 2012) — 175

Night Drive (2013 & 2014) — 176

Thinking of Mr D. (2012 & 2013 & 2014) — 176

Mirror in February (2012 & 2013 & 2014) — 177

Ambulances (2012 & 2014) — 178

The Explosion (2012 & 2014) — 178

What Were They Like? (2011 & 2012) — 179

Kidspoem/Bairnsang (2014) — 180

Badger (2013) — 180

Meeting point (2012) — 181

Grandfather (2013 & 2014) — 181

After the Titanic (2013 & 2014) — 182

Antarctica (2013 & 2014) — 183

Bearhugs (2012) — 183

When I Consider (2013) — 184

All Day Long (2011 & 2012) — 184

Strawberries (2011) — 185

Anseo (2011 & 2012 & 2013) — 185

Moonshine (2011 & 2012) — 186

Wolves in the Zoo (2014) — 187

Problems (2013) — 187

The Net (2011 & 2014) — 187

The Sun (2012 & 2013) — 188

Will We Work Together? (2013 & 2014) — 189

Poppies in July (2012 & 2013 & 2014) — 189

Child (2012 & 2013 & 2014) — 190

The Arrival of the Bee Box (2013 & 2014) — 191

Sonnet 18: Shall I compare thee … (2013) — 192

Sonnet 60: Like as the waves … (2013) — 192

Ozymandias (2012) — 193

Jungian Cows (2011 & 2012 & 2013) — 193

Zoo Morning (2014) — 194

Madly Singing in the City (2013 & 2014)   194

Traveling through the Dark (2012 & 2013)   195

Do Not Go Gentle into That Good Night (2013 & 2014)   195

Chronicle (2013 & 2014)   196

The Writer (2011)   197

A Summer Morning (2012 & 2013)   197

This Is Just To Say (2014)   198

She dwelt among the untrodden ways (2011 & 2013)   198

From The Prelude: Skating ... (2011 & 2013)   199

It is a beauteous evening, calm and free (2011 & 2013)   199

Poems for Breakfast (2014)   200

The Wild Swans at Coole (2011 & 2014)   200

An Irish Airman Foresees His Death (2011 & 2014)   201

Approaching the unseen poem   202

LANGUAGE SKILLS

Criteria for assessment   205

Approaching the exam paper   205

Writing Skills   205
   letter-writing   206
   writing instructions   211
   writing a speech or debate   212
   describing an image or picture   212
   writing a diary   213
   creative writing   213
   summarising and paraphrasing   214
   writing a newspaper article   215
   writing a review   216
   writing a personal opinion piece   217
   writing a commentary piece   218
   writing an interview or a question-and-answer piece   218

Questions based on exam papers   219

Comprehension samples and questions   220

Important words and terms   234

Past Examination Questions   237

Acknowledgments   241

For Heidi with Blue Hair *Fleur Adcock*

*Prescribed for the **Ordinary Level** exams in **2011** and **2013***

When you dyed your hair blue
(or, at least, ultramarine
for the clipped sides, with a crest
of jet-black spikes on top)
you were sent home from school   5

because, as the headmistress put it,
although dyed hair was not
specifically forbidden, yours
was, apart from anything else,
not done in the school colours.   10

Tears in the kitchen, telephone-calls
to school from your freedom-loving father:
'She's not a punk in her behaviour;
it's just a style.' (You wiped your eyes,
also not in a school colour.)   15

'She discussed it with me first –
we checked the rules.' 'And anyway, Dad,
it cost twenty-five dollars.
Tell them it won't wash out –
not even if I wanted to try.'   20

It would have been unfair to mention
your mother's death, but that
shimmered behind the arguments.
The school had nothing else against you;
the teachers twittered and gave in.   25

Next day your black friend had hers done
in grey, white and flaxen yellow –
the school colours precisely:
an act of solidarity, a witty
tease. The battle was already won.   30

GLOSSARY

ULTRAMARINE: Deep bright blue
CLIPPED: Cut short
PUNK: Follower of rebellious, outrageous rock music
(sometimes violent and aggressive)

SHIMMERED: Shone in a soft, quivering light
TWITTERED: Made silly bird-like sounds of laughter
FLAXEN: Pale yellow
SOLIDARITY: Act of unity

FLEUR ADCOCK • BORN 1934 IN NEW ZEALAND • LEFT NEW ZEALAND. SPENT MUCH OF HER LIFE IN ENGLAND • FEMINIST POET • THIS POEM IS FROM *THE INCIDENT ROOM*, WHICH IS DEDICATED TO HER GODCHILD, HEIDI JACKSON • COLLECTIONS: *THE EYE OF THE HURRICANE*, 1964; *TIGERS*, 1967; *HIGH TIDE IN THE GARDEN*, 1971; *THE INNER HARBOUR*, 1979; *THE INCIDENT ROOM*, 1986; *TIME ZONES*, 1991

■ **Pre**Reading

1 When you read the title, what kind of person do you expect Heidi to be?
2 Describe what you think of when you hear someone has blue hair.
3 What do you think is the relationship between the poet and Heidi?

● **1st**Reading

4 Why did the headmistress send Heidi home from school if having dyed hair was not against the rules?
5 Describe Heidi's hairstyle.
6 Describe the scene in Heidi's house when she arrives home.
7 How does Heidi react? Does her reaction change? Is it what you would expect from a teenage girl?
8 Describe the headmistress and the teachers. Write down every sentence in which they are mentioned and then describe the image that is portrayed.
9 Why does Heidi's friend get her hair dyed?
10 Describe her hairstyle.

●● **2nd**Reading

11 Describe Heidi's father. Is he strict, supportive, typical, modern, old-fashioned?
12 Describe the relationship between Heidi and her father.

●●● **3rd**Reading

13 Discuss the tone each character would use when speaking: headmistress, teachers, father, Heidi, Heidi's friend.
14 Explain why the poet uses the word 'shimmered' when discussing Heidi's mother's death.
15 Why is Heidi's mother's death even mentioned?
16 Why do you think Heidi dyed her hair in the first place? Is she a typical teenager? Describe a typical teenager. (Stereotyping is when you generalise or standardise a character or idea.)
17 What is the theme of this poem? Is there more than one theme?
18 What do you think the poet means in the last line when she says 'The battle was already won'?

▼ **Link**to**Language**

19 Write a letter to the headmistress from Heidi's father outlining what he sees as the main problem.
20 Imagine you are Heidi. Write a letter to your aunt, Fleur Adcock, telling her about your new hair colour and your suspension from school.

Phenomenal Woman *Maya Angelou*

*Prescribed for the **Ordinary Level** exam in **2012***

Pretty women wonder where my secret
   lies.
I'm not cute or built to suit a fashion
   model's size
But when I start to tell them,
They think I'm telling lies.
I say,   5
It's in the reach of my arms
The span of my hips
The stride of my step,
The curl of my lips.
I'm a woman   10
Phenomenally.
Phenomenal woman,
That's me.

I walk into a room
Just as cool as you please,   15
And to a man,
The fellows stand or
Fall down on their knees.
Then they swarm around me,
A hive of honey bees.   20
I say,
It's the fire in my eyes,
And the flash of my teeth,
The swing in my waist,
And the joy in my feet.   25
I'm a woman
Phenomenally.
Phenomenal woman,
That's me.

Men themselves have wondered 30
What they see in me.
They try so much
But they can't touch
My inner mystery.
When I try to show them   35
They say they still can't see.
I say,
It's in the arch of my back,
The sun of my smile,
The ride of my breasts,   40
The grace of my style.
I'm a woman
Phenomenally.
Phenomenal woman,
That's me.   45

Now you understand
Just why my head's not bowed.
I don't shout or jump about
Or have to talk real loud.
When you see me passing   50
It ought to make you proud.
I say,
It's in the click of my heels,
The bend of my hair,
The palm of my hand,   55
The need of my care,
'Cause I'm a woman
Phenomenally.
Phenomenal woman,
That's me.   60

MAYA ANGELOU

• BORN 1928 IN ST LOUIS, MISSOURI, USA • REARED IN SEGREGATED RURAL ARKANSAS • RAPED AT THE AGE OF EIGHT AND BECAME MUTE FOR A TIME • WORKED AS A POET, EDUCATOR, HISTORIAN, ACTRESS, DANCER, PLAYWRIGHT, CIVIL RIGHTS ACTIVIST, PRODUCER AND DIRECTOR • WAS ALSO A POLITICAL CO-ORDINATOR FOR MARTIN LUTHER KING • AUTOBIOGRAPHY: *I KNOW WHY THE CAGED BIRD SINGS*, 1969 • WROTE PRESIDENT CLINTON'S 1993 INAUGURATION POEM • WRITES FOR 'THE BLACK VOICE AND FOR ANY EAR WHICH CAN HEAR IT'

■ **Pre**Reading

1 Use the dictionary or thesaurus to find out the meaning of the word 'phenomenal'.
2 Describe the image that the title 'Phenomenal Woman' suggests to you.

● **1st**Reading

3 Having read the poem through, what is your impression of the speaker? Do you like her? Describe her in five or six words.
4 In the poem the speaker is constantly promoting herself and presenting herself in a positive light. What words or phrases stand out to support this statement?
5 What reaction does the speaker get from the 'pretty women'?
6 What reaction does the speaker get from the men?
7 How does the speaker behave around men and women she comes into contact with?

●● **2nd**Reading

8 Why do you think the poet repeats the lines 'I'm a woman / Phenomenally. / Phenomenal woman / That's me.'?
9 What, in the poet's view, does she possess to make her a 'phenomenal woman'?

10 It has been said that the poetry of Maya Angelou 'reminds us of where we are as women at the dawn of a new century'.
Do you agree that this poem is a true representation of women in the twenty-first century?
11 Maya Angelou is celebrating her womanhood in this poem. Where in particular do we see this? Go through the poem verse by verse and pick out the words and phrases in which she delights in womanhood.
12 Are we seeing the real person or is this all an act or show of pride and courage? Is it realistic? Do you know anyone like this?

▼ **Link**to**Language**

13 Maya Angelou has appeared on many chat shows in America, most notably *The Oprah Winfrey Show*. Write out the answer you imagine she might give to the question: 'What does being a woman mean to you?'.

It Ain't What You Do, It's What It Does to You *Simon Armitage*

*Prescribed for the **Ordinary Level** exam in **2011***

I have not bummed across America
with only a dollar to spare, one pair
of busted Levi's and a bowie knife.
I have lived with thieves in Manchester.

I have not padded through the Taj Mahal,   5
barefoot, listening to the space between
each footfall picking up and putting down
its print against the marble floor. But I

skimmed flat stones across Black Moss on a day
so still I could hear each set of ripples   10
as they crossed. I felt each stone's inertia
spend itself against the water; then sink.

I have not toyed with a parachute cord
while perched on the lip of a light-aircraft;
but I held the wobbly head of a boy   15
at the day centre, and stroked his fat hands.

And I guess that the tightness in the throat
and the tiny cascading sensation
somewhere inside us are both part of that
sense of something else. That feeling, I mean.   20

SIMON ARMITAGE

- **BORN 1963 IN HUDDERSFIELD, ENGLAND**
- **WORKED AS A SOCIAL WORKER**
- **COLLECTIONS:** *KID*, 1992; *ZOOM!*, 1989

■ **Pre**Reading

1 What usually comes after the line 'It ain't what you do'? Would it have the same effect?

● **1st**Reading

2 There are three things that the poet has not done and three things that he has. Compare them. Which is the more attractive to you?

3 What emotion does he get from living with thieves? How would this compare with the feeling that he would get if he was hiking across America?

4 How does he justify comparing a lake in Manchester with one of the seven wonders of the world?

5 How does helping a boy at the day care centre make the poet feel?

6 Describe how the boy might feel.

●● **2nd**Reading

7 Have you ever experienced the sensation that the poet describes in the final verse? When? Describe it.

●●● **3rd**Reading

8 How does the poet use repetition in the poem? Why does he use repetition?

●●●● **4th**Reading

9 Is the last sentence in the poem completely necessary?

10 What type of person do you think the poet is?

▼ **Link**to**Language**

11 Write an essay based on the theme 'Live life to its fullest'.

Funeral Blues W. H. Auden

*Prescribed for the **Ordinary Level** exam in **2011***

Stop all the clocks, cut off the telephone,
Prevent the dog from barking with a juicy bone,
Silence the pianos and with muffled drum
Bring out the coffin, let the mourners come.

Let aeroplanes circle moaning overhead   5
Scribbling on the sky the message He Is Dead,
Put the crêpe bows round the white necks of the public doves,
Let the traffic policemen wear black cotton gloves.

He was my North, my South, my East and West,
My working week and my Sunday rest,   10
My noon, my midnight, my talk, my song;
I thought that love would last for ever: I was wrong.

The stars are not wanted now: put out every one;
Pack up the moon and dismantle the sun;
Pour away the ocean and sweep up the wood.   15
For nothing now can ever come to any good.

GLOSSARY
MUFFLED: Not a clear sound — a dull sound
CRÊPE: Fabric with a wrinkled surface
DISMANTLE: Take to pieces

W. H. AUDEN
• WYSTAN HUGH AUDEN, BORN 1907 IN YORK, ENGLAND • EDUCATED AT CHRIST CHURCH COLLEGE, OXFORD, AND IN BERLIN • BECAME AN AMERICAN CITIZEN IN 1946 • ALSO WROTE PROSE AND DRAMA • PROFESSOR OF POETRY AT OXFORD FROM 1956 TO 1960 • MAIN THEMES OF HIS POETRY ARE POLITICAL AND SOCIAL ISSUES OF HIS TIME. THIS MADE HIM ONE OF THE MOST IMPORTANT POETS OF THE 1930S • PROLIFIC WRITER • DIED IN 1973

■ PreReading

1 What do you think the poet means by 'Blues'?
2 Describe the usual procedure of mourning and the feelings of mourners at a funeral. Are there different types of mourner? Examine why people go to funerals. What images do you usually associate with a funeral?
3 List the feelings experienced at the death of a loved one.

● 1stReading

4 How does the speaker feel?
5 What does the speaker want to do to mourn the death of his loved one?
6 As part of the speaker's mourning he wants to stop the clocks, cut off the phone and stop the dog from barking. Examine these first three images put forward by the speaker and say how each one affects him.
7 Is this a realistic reaction to the death of a loved one?
8 Which images dominate this poem?

●● 2ndReading

9 Why does the speaker no longer need the stars, moon, sun, ocean and wood? What does he suggest be done with them?
10 The speaker wants all sources of light to be cut off. What are these and why does he want them cut off?
11 What evidence is there to show that the speaker and the deceased were very close?
12 In line 12 the poet says 'I thought that love would last forever: I was wrong.' Describe the speaker's state of mind at this stage of the poem.
13 Is it realistic for the speaker to ask for all of these various things to be done?
14 Explain what the poet means in the final line when he says 'For nothing now can ever come to any good'.

●●● 3rdReading

15 How do you feel (i) about the poem, (ii) about the speaker?
16 What do you think the future has in store for the speaker?

●●●● 4thReading

17 Is this a poem that you will remember? Why?
18 This poem can be seen as a deeply personal poem or a poem about universal mourning. Discuss.
19 Is this a love poem or a satirical attack on the self-importance of people in public life? How would you like to read it?
20 Do you think the poet is exaggerating the mourning and love? Why would he do this? Is there a need for public displays of grief?
21 Describe the tone of the poem.
22 The poet wants everyone to know that this person, 'he', is dead. How does he suggest doing this?
23 What did the dead person mean to the speaker? Where do you find evidence of this?

The Voice *Patricia Beer*

*Prescribed for the **Ordinary Level** exam in 2014*

When God took my aunt's baby boy, a merciful neighbour
Gave her a parrot. She could not have afforded one
But now bought a new cage as brilliant as the bird,
And turned her back on the idea of other babies.

He looked unlikely. In her house his scarlet feathers   5
Stuck out like a jungle, though his blue ones blended
With the local pottery which carried messages
Like 'Du ee help yerself to crame, me handsome.'

He said nothing when he arrived, not a quotation
From pet-shop gossip or a sailor's oath, no sound   10
From someone's home: the telephone or car-door slamming,
And none from his: tom-tom, war-cry or wild beast roaring.

He came from silence but was ready to become noise.
My aunt taught him nursery rhymes morning after morning.
He learnt Miss Muffett, Jack and Jill, Little Jack Horner,   15
Including her jokes; she used to say turds and whey.

A genuine Devon accent is not easy. Actors
Cannot do it. He could though. In his court clothes
He sounded like a farmer, as her son might have.
He sounded like our family. He fitted in.   20

Years went by. We came and went. A day or two
Before he died, he got confused, and muddled up
His rhymes. Jack Horner ate his pail of water.
The spider said what a good boy he was. I wept.

He had never seemed puzzled by the bizarre events   25
He spoke of. But that last day he turned his head towards us
With the bewilderment of death upon him. Said
'Broke his crown' and 'Christmas pie'. And tumbled after.

My aunt died the next winter, widowed, childless, pitied
And patronised. I cannot summon up her voice at all.   30
She would not have expected it to be remembered
After so long. But I can still hear his.

PATRICIA BEER • BORN 1924 IN EXMOUTH, DEVON, ENGLAND • EDUCATED AT EXETER UNIVERSITY AND ST HUGH'S COLLEGE, OXFORD • LIVED IN ITALY FROM 1946 TO 1953 • TAUGHT AT GOLDSMITHS COLLEGE, LONDON, FROM 1962 TO 1968 • HER FAVOURED THEMES WERE MORTALITY AND RELIGIOUS FAITH • DIED IN 1999

● 1st Reading

1 Why did the neighbour give the parrot to the aunt?
2 Did it have the effect that the neighbour wished?
3 Describe the parrot.
4 How did the aunt teach him to talk?
5 Why did she do it this way?
6 How successful was she?
7 What happened to him before he died?
8 Why can the poet still hear the parrot's voice?

●● 2nd Reading

9 What is your favourite image in the poem?
10 What tone does the poet use in the poem?
11 How does she create this?

●●● 3rd Reading

12 Describe the parrot's character.
13 Do you see any hints of humour in the poem?
14 Describe the aunt's character.

●●●● 4th Reading

15 What did the poet think of the aunt?
16 How do you think the aunt felt in her last few years?
17 What do we learn about the poet from this poem?

The Fish *Elizabeth Bishop*

*Prescribed for the **Ordinary Level** exams in **2013** and **2014***

I caught a tremendous fish
and held him beside the boat
half out of water, with my hook
fast in a corner of his mouth.
He didn't fight. 5
He hadn't fought at all.
He hung a grunting weight,
battered and venerable
and homely. Here and there
his brown skin hung in strips 10
like ancient wallpaper,
and its pattern of darker brown
was like wallpaper:
shapes like full-blown roses
stained and lost through age. 15
He was speckled with barnacles,
fine rosettes of lime,
and infested
with tiny white sea-lice,
and underneath two or three 20
rags of green weed hung down.
While his gills were breathing in
the terrible oxygen
– the frightening gills,
fresh and crisp with blood, 25
that can cut so badly –
I thought of the coarse white flesh
packed in like feathers,
the big bones and the little bones,
the dramatic reds and blacks 30
of his shiny entrails,
and the pink swim-bladder
like a big peony.
I looked into his eyes
which were far larger than mine 35
but shallower, and yellowed,
the irises backed and packed
with tarnished tinfoil

seen through the lenses
of old scratched isinglass. 40
They shifted a little, but not
to return my stare.
– It was more like the tipping
of an object toward the light.
I admired his sullen face, 45
the mechanism of his jaw,
and then I saw
that from his lower lip
– if you could call it a lip –
grim, wet, and weaponlike, 50
hung five old pieces of fish-line,
or four and a wire leader
with the swivel still attached,
with all their five big hooks
grown firmly in his mouth. 55
A green line, frayed at the end
where he broke it, two heavier lines,
and a fine black thread
still crimped from the strain and snap
when it broke and he got away. 60
Like medals with their ribbons
frayed and wavering,
a five-haired beard of wisdom
trailing from his aching jaw.
I stared and stared 65
and victory filled up
the little rented boat,
from the pool of bilge
where oil had spread a rainbow
around the rusted engine 70
to the bailer rusted orange,
the sun-cracked thwarts,
the oarlocks on their strings,
the gunnels – until everything
was rainbow, rainbow, rainbow! 75
and I let the fish go.

ELIZABETH BISHOP

• BORN 1911 IN WORCESTER, MASSACHUSETTS, USA • HER FATHER, A WEALTHY BUILDING CONTRACTOR, DIED WHEN SHE WAS EIGHT MONTHS OLD • HER MOTHER WAS A REGULAR PATIENT IN MENTAL HOSPITALS AND ELIZABETH LAST SAW HER IN 1916 WHEN SHE WAS FINALLY INSTITUTIONALISED • REARED BY HER GRANDPARENTS IN NOVA SCOTIA IN A SMALL RURAL VILLAGE • GRADUATED FROM AN EXCLUSIVE NEW YORK UNIVERSITY, VASSAR, IN ENGLISH LITERATURE • PUBLISHED POETRY AND PROSE SINCE HER COLLEGE DAYS • TRAVELLED EXTENSIVELY THROUGH EUROPE, SOUTH AMERICA AND NORTH AFRICA • WON THE PULITZER PRIZE IN 1956 • HER POETRY ENCOURAGES THE READER TO LOOK DEEPER AT HER SUBJECTS AND DELVE BENEATH THE FAÇADE • DIED IN 1979

■ Pre Reading

1 What would a fisherman consider a successful fishing trip?
2 Is fishing about sitting waiting for the 'bite' or about catching a fish?

● 1st Reading

3 Describe the fish.
4 How does the fish behave on being caught?
5 What kind of person is the fisher?

●● 2nd Reading

6 The fish's skin is described as 'ancient wallpaper'. Why?
7 Describe the fish's appearance.
8 Describe how the poet imagines the fish internally.
9 The fish's gills are frightening. How does the poet create this feeling?

●●● 3rd Reading

10 There are two comparisons to flowers. What are they and why does the poet use them?

11 The poet looks into the fish's eyes. What does she see? Does the fish look back?
12 The five pieces of fishing line hanging from the fish's mouth were 'like medals'. Why does the poet compare them to medals?
13 Why does everything become 'a rainbow'?
14 Why does the poet let the fish go? Has the fish's history anything to do with his release?
15 What does the poet feel about the fish?
16 The poet has a moment of insight or epiphany. Discuss.
17 The poet was a painter as well as a poet. In what way is this poem like a painting? Describe the painting the poet might paint depicting this scene.

▼ Link to Language

18 Write Elizabeth Bishop's diary extract telling of her fishing experience. Remember that a diary is an outpouring of a person's innermost feelings. Outline how the poet felt on catching the fish, examining him and on releasing him.

The Filling Station *Elizabeth Bishop*

*Prescribed for the **Ordinary Level** exams in **2013** and **2014***

Oh, but it is dirty!
– this little filling station,
oil-soaked, oil-permeated
to a disturbing, over-all
black translucency.   5
Be careful with that match!

Father wears a dirty,
oil-soaked monkey suit
that cuts him under the arms,
and several quick and saucy   10
and greasy sons assist him
(it's a family filling station),
all quite thoroughly dirty.

Do they live in the station?
It has a cement porch   15
behind the pumps, and on it
a set of crushed and grease-
impregnated wickerwork;
on the wicker sofa
a dirty dog, quite comfy.   20

Some comic books provide
the only note of color –
of certain color. They lie
upon a big dim doily
draping a taboret   25
(part of the set), beside
a big hirsute begonia.

Why the extraneous plant?
Why the taboret?
Why, oh why, the doily?   30
(Embroidered in daisy stitch
with marguerites, I think,
and heavy with gray crochet.)

Somebody embroidered the doily.
Somebody waters the plant,   35
or oils it, maybe. Somebody
arranges the rows of cans
so that they softly say:
ESSO-SO-SO-SO
to high-strung automobiles.   40
Somebody loves us all.

GLOSSARY

PERMEATED: Seeped through, soaked through
TRANSLUCENCY: Shininess, allows light to shine through
MONKEY SUIT: Man's evening suit
GREASE-IMPREGNATED: Saturated with grease
WICKERWORK: Furniture made from woven cane
DOILY: Small, lacy, ornamental piece of material

TABORET: Low seat
HIRSUTE: Untrimmed, hairy
BEGONIA: Plant with bright leaves and flowers
EXTRANEOUS: Not fitting in, not belonging
MARGUERITES: Large daisies
CROCHET: Knitting done with a hooked needle
EMBROIDERED: Sewn ornamentally

■ PreReading

1 Jot down all the words that come to mind when you think of a petrol station.

● 1stReading

2 What images of the filling station stand out after your first reading of the poem?

3 Is the poet a character in the poem?

4 Would living in this filling station appeal to you? Why?

●● 2ndReading

5 'Oh, but it is dirty!' Describe, using quotations from the poem, just how dirty the filling station is.

6 In this poem, the father and sons have a lot in common. Discuss.

7 Describe the filling station.

8 'Somebody' makes an effort to make the place pretty; what details has this person added?

●●● 3rdReading

9 There are two exclamation marks in the first verse. Why? What do they add to the poem?

10 The tone changes as the poem progresses. Identify the different tones.

11 On the surface the filling station looks 'oil-soaked, oil-permeated' and 'grease-impregnated', but what lies beneath?

12 Discuss the musical qualities of this poem — alliteration, onomatopoeia, rhyme and assonance.

13 The poem ends with an unexpected 'Somebody loves us all'. Where does this idea originate in the poem?

14 Imagine this poem as a painting or series of paintings. What colours and images dominate?

▼ LinktoLanguage

15 Write character sketches of (i) the father, (ii) the sons. Remember a good character should have a name, an appearance and a personality.

The Prodigal *Elizabeth Bishop*

*Prescribed for the **Ordinary Level** exams in **2013** and **2014***

The brown enormous odor he lived by
was too close, with its breathing and thick hair,
for him to judge. The floor was rotten; the sty
was plastered halfway up with glass-smooth dung.
Light-lashed, self-righteous, above moving snouts,   5
the pigs' eyes followed him, a cheerful stare –
even to the sow that always ate her young –
till, sickening, he leaned to scratch her head.
But sometimes mornings after drinking bouts
(he hid the pints behind a two-by-four),   10
the sunrise glazed the barnyard mud with red;
the burning puddles seemed to reassure.
And then he thought he almost might endure
his exile yet another year or more.

But evenings the first star came to warn.   15
The farmer whom he worked for came at dark
to shut the cows and horses in the barn
beneath their overhanging clouds of hay,
with pitchforks, faint forked lightnings, catching light,
safe and companionable as in the Ark.   20
The pigs stuck out their little feet and snored.
The lantern – like the sun, going away –
laid on the mud a pacing aureole.
Carrying a bucket along a slimy board,
he felt the bats' uncertain staggering flight,   25
his shuddering insights, beyond his control,
touching him. But it took him a long time
finally to make up his mind to go home.

GLOSSARY

PRODIGAL: Wasteful and extravagant
The biblical story of 'The Prodigal Son' tells of a rich man and his two sons. The younger son asks for his inheritance and spends it unwisely on drink and wild living, while the elder son remains at home, obedient and loyal. The younger son — The Prodigal — is forced to work as a swineherd to save himself from starving, now that he is penniless. After a time, he realises the error of his ways and returns home to beg his father's forgiveness. His father is delighted at the return of his errant son and welcomes him with open arms. The older son is resentful and bitter. Often in the telling of this story the emphasis is placed on the homecoming and forgiveness. In this poem Bishop concentrates on the hardships endured by 'The Prodigal' during his years of self-exile.
ODOR: Smell
SELF-RIGHTEOUS: smug and self-assured
TWO-BY-FOUR: a piece of wood measuring two units by four units
AUREOLE: halo

■ PreReading

1 What do you remember of the story of the Prodigal Son?

● 1stReading

2 Who are the main characters in the poem?

3 What is your initial impression of the Prodigal's life? What images dominate?

4 Is the Prodigal happy with his life? What does the future hold for him?

5 Is the image of the Prodigal's life an attractive one in any way? Is it disgusting? Do you feel that the Prodigal accepts his lot?

●● 2ndReading

6 Which senses are appealed to in the poem? Examine the poem for images appealing to all the senses.

7 Are the 'drinking bouts' negative or positive for the Prodigal? Explain.

8 Does the Prodigal live with the pigs? Does he have anything else in his life?

9 Describe the farmer and his job in the barn. How does it differ from the Prodigal and his job?

●●● 3rdReading

10 Why did it take the Prodigal a long time 'to decide to go home'?

11 Is there beauty in the poem? Where?

12 What is your impression of the pigs? Describe the Prodigal's relationship with them.

13 What are the 'shuddering insights' referred to in line 26?

14 How do you feel about the Prodigal? What do you hope happens to him in the future?

▼ LinktoLanguage

15 'Families — the basis of a happy life.' Write a personal account of what family means to you.

Or

Imagine you are the Prodigal or the Prodigal's father. Write three diary entries describing how you feel as time passes and there seems to be no sign of a reunion.

Child of Our Time *Eavan Boland*

For Aengus

*Prescribed for the **Ordinary Level** exams in **2011** and **2012***

Yesterday I knew no lullaby
But you have taught me overnight to order
This song, which takes from your final cry
Its tune, from your unreasoned end its reason;
Its rhythm from the discord of your murder   5
Its motive from the fact you cannot listen.

We who should have known how to instruct
With rhymes for your waking, rhythms for your sleep,
Names for the animals you took to bed,
Tales to distract, legends to protect   10
Later an idiom for you to keep
And living, learn, must learn from you dead,

To make our broken images, rebuild
Themselves around your limbs, your broken
Image, find for your sake whose life our idle   15
Talk has cost, a new language. Child
Of our time, our times have robbed your cradle.
Sleep in a world your final sleep has woken.

GLOSSARY

IDIOM: Mode of expression

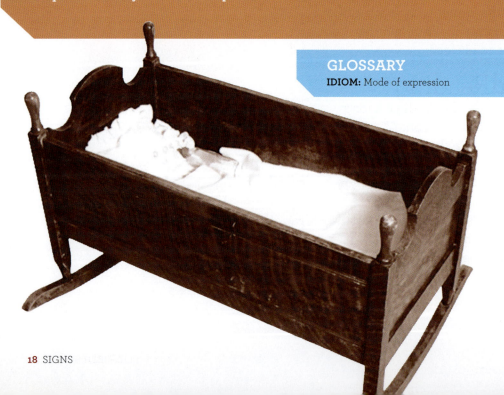

EAVAN BOLAND • BORN 1944 IN DUBLIN • EDUCATED IN LONDON, WHERE HER FATHER WAS THE IRISH AMBASSADOR • LATER STUDIED AT TRINITY COLLEGE, DUBLIN • LECTURED FOR A WHILE, BUT GAVE UP TO BECOME A FULL-TIME POET • WRITES ABOUT IRISH HISTORY AND THE POSITION OF WOMEN IN CONTEMPORARY IRISH SOCIETY • COLLECTION: *OUTSIDE HISTORY*, 1990

●1stReading

1 What has happened to the child?
2 Why does the poet write this poem?
3 What type of poem does she want to write?
4 How can she 'learn from you dead'?

●●2ndReading

5 How does the poet see the death of the child?
6 What does the poet mean by the phrase 'our times have robbed your cradle'?

●●●3rdReading

7 Does the poet find any signs of hope from the death of this child?
8 What sounds help to create the mood of the poem?
9 Children have a purity that is only disturbed by interfering adults. From your reading of this poem, do you think the poet might agree?

▼LinktoLanguage

10 Write a newspaper article about a bombing which has left a child dead.

Love *Eavan Boland*

*Prescribed for the **Ordinary Level** exams in **2011** and **2012***

Dark falls on this mid-western town
where we once lived when myths collided.
Dusk has hidden the bridge in the river
which slides and deepens
to become the water   5
the hero crossed on his way to hell.

Not far from here is our old apartment.
We had a kitchen and an Amish table.
We had a view. And we discovered there
love had the feather and muscle of wings   10
and had come to live with us,
a brother of fire and air.

We had two infant children one of whom
was touched by death in this town
and spared; and when the hero   15
was hailed by his comrades in hell
their mouths opened and their voices failed and
there is no knowing what they would have asked
about a life they had shared and lost.

I am your wife.   20
It was years ago.
Our child was healed. We love each other still.
Across our day-to-day and ordinary distances
we speak plainly. We hear each other clearly.

And yet I want to return to you   25
on the bridge of the Iowa river as you were,
with snow on the shoulders of your coat
and a car passing with its headlights on:

I see you as a hero in a text —
the image blazing and the edges gilded —   30
and I long to cry out the epic question
my dear companion:
Will we ever live so intensely again?
Will love come to us again and be
so formidable at rest it offered us ascension   35
even to look at him?

But the words are shadows and you cannot hear me.
You walk away and I cannot follow.

■PreReading

1. What does the title suggest to you?
2. What do you expect from a love poem?

●1stReading

3. Where is the poem set?
4. At what time of the day is it set?
5. What is the significance of this?
6. Who is the poet addressing?
7. What has happened to their child?

●●2ndReading

8. What tense is the poem written in?
9. What is the significance of this?
10. The poet changes tense in stanza four. Why does she do this?
11. What effect does it have on the reader?

●●●3rdReading

12. Do you think the relationship between wife and husband has changed?
13. How does the poet see her husband?
14. How does she see their relationship?

●●●●4thReading

15. How does the poet use the myth of Aeneas to illustrate her feelings?
16. What does this poem teach us about strength in times of difficulty?

▼LinktoLanguage

17. Write a letter to an old friend reminiscing about a difficult time for both of you.

This Moment Eavan Boland

*Prescribed for the **Ordinary Level** exams in **2011** and **2012***

A neighbourhood.
At dusk.

Things are getting ready
to happen
out of sight.   5

Stars and moths.
And rinds slanting around fruit.

But not yet.

One tree is black.
One window is yellow as butter.   10

A woman leans down to catch a child
who runs into her arms
this moment.

Stars rise.
Moths flutter.   15
Apples sweeten in the dark.

● **1st**Reading

1 List the visual images that can be seen in this scene.
2 What different senses are used in the poem?
3 What does each sense do?
4 Describe the action in the poem.

●● **2nd**Reading

5 What happens 'out of sight'?
6 What do the images in the third and final verses suggest to you?
7 Which image is your favourite? Why?

●●● **3rd**Reading

8 What effect do the short verses have on the overall poem?
9 Would you agree that there is a sense of mystery in this poem?
10 How is this created?

▼ **Link**to**Language**

11 Write a short story beginning with the line 'Things were getting ready to happen'.

I felt a Funeral, in my Brain
Emily Dickinson

*Prescribed for the **Ordinary Level** exams in **2011** and **2014***

I felt a Funeral in my Brain,
And Mourners to and fro
Kept treading — treading — till it seemed
That Sense was breaking through —

And when they all were seated,   5
A Service, like a Drum —
Kept beating — beating — till I thought
My Mind was going numb —

And then I heard them lift a Box
And creak across my Soul   10
With those same Boots of Lead, again,
Then Space — began to toll,

As all the Heavens were a Bell,
And Being, but an Ear,
And I, and Silence, some strange Race   15
Wrecked, solitary, here —

And then a Plank in Reason, broke,
And I dropped down, and down —
And hit a World, at every plunge,
And Finished knowing — then —   20

EMILY DICKINSON • BORN 1830 IN AMHERST, MASSACHUSETTS, USA • BECAME A RECLUSE AROUND 1854, POSSIBLY AS A RESULT OF AN UNHAPPY LOVE AFFAIR • COMPLETELY IMMERSED HERSELF IN COMPOSING FOR THE REST OF HER LIFE • WROTE 1,775 POEMS IN HER LIFETIME • DIED 1886

■**Pre**Reading

1 Make a list of the distinctive features of a funeral.

●**1st**Reading

2 How many of the distinctive features of a funeral listed in Question 1 are obvious in this poem? Highlight them.

3 What do you think this poem is about? Is the poet discussing a real funeral or is she remembering a memory or possibly a nightmare?

4 What do you think the poet means when she says 'I felt a Funeral, in my Brain'?

5 What role is the poet playing in the funeral? Is she a mourner, the deceased or is she an onlooker?

●●**2nd**Reading

6 Discuss why you think the poet uses repetition in line three 'treading — treading' and in line seven 'beating — beating'.

7 Make a list of all the things the poet hears in this poem.

8 Make a list of the poet's feelings stanza by stanza.

9 Why do you think the poet uses capital letters for some words in the poem?

●●●**3rd**Reading

10 Examine the slow, steady rhythm of the poem. What does the poet hope to achieve?

11 The speaker refers to herself as 'I', 'my Brain', 'my Mind', 'my Soul' throughout the poem. Do these all refer to the same thing/sense of being or are there subtle differences?

12 Is this poem interesting or darkly depressing? Discuss your answer.

13 Examine the tone of the poem. Does it change as the poem progresses?

●●●●**4th**Reading

14 Is there evidence in the poem that perhaps the poet is not discussing death or the state of being dead, but is, instead, using the funeral as a metaphor to discuss mental decay and breakdown? Examine.

15 What happens in the final stanza? What breaks? What does the poet mean by 'I dropped down, and down'?

16 Consider alternative titles for this poem and explain your choices.

▼**Link**to**Language**

17 Write out the text of an interview with a famous person in which you discuss life and making the most of the opportunities available.

I heard a Fly buzz — when I died
Emily Dickinson

*Prescribed for the **Ordinary Level** exams in **2011** and **2014***

I heard a Fly buzz — when I died —
The Stillness in the Room
Was like the Stillness in the Air —
Between the Heaves of Storm —

The Eyes around — had wrung them dry —   5
And Breaths were gathering firm
For that last Onset — when the King
Be witnessed — in the Room —

I willed my Keepsakes — Signed away
What portion of me be   10
Assignable — and then it was
There interposed a Fly —

With Blue — uncertain stumbling Buzz —
Between the light — and me —
And then the Windows failed — and then   15
I could not see to see.

GLOSSARY

HEAVES: Great efforts in a raging storm
ONSET: Beginning of the attack or assault
KING: Christ, Death
KEEPSAKES: Mementos, something to help one remember

ASSIGNABLE: Allocated, distributed
INTERPOSED: Insert, intervene
WINDOWS: Possibly referring to the eyes — 'windows to the soul'

■ **Pre**Reading

1 Describe what you imagine would be the activity in the room of a dying person.
2 Imagine a fly buzzing around a silent room. Describe its sounds and movements.

● **1st**Reading

3 Who is the speaker in the poem?
4 Are there others in the scene? Who are they? Describe them.
5 Describe the presence of the fly and his impact on the scene.

●● **2nd**Reading

6 Describe the room.
7 There is a sense of anticipation / waiting in the poem. For what are they waiting?
8 How did the speaker prepare for her death?
9 Is the arrival of the fly a good or a bad thing?

●●● **3rd**Reading

10 Describe the moment of death as the speaker in this poem experiences it.
11 The fly comes between the speaker and the light in line 12. What does she mean here? Is there more than one possible answer?
12 The speaker tells us that at the moment of her death she heard a fly buzz. Is this unusual or strange? Why?

▼ **Link**to**Language**

13 'And then at the crucial moment I was distracted by a buzzing fly.'
Write a short story suggested by the above phrase.

Valentine *Carol Ann Duffy*

*Prescribed for the **Ordinary Level** exams in **2011** and **2014***

Not a red rose or a satin heart.

I give you an onion.
It is a moon wrapped in brown paper.
It promises light
like the careful undressing of love.   5

Here.
It will blind you with tears
like a lover.
It will make your reflection
a wobbling photo of grief.   10

I am trying to be truthful.

Not a cute card or a kissogram.

I give you an onion.
Its fierce kiss will stay on your lips,
possessive and faithful   15
as we are,
for as long as we are.

Take it.
Its platinum loops shrink to a wedding-ring,
if you like.   20
Lethal.
Its scent will cling to your fingers,
cling to your knife.

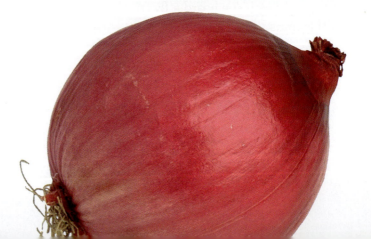

CAROL ANN DUFFY
• BORN 1955 IN GLASGOW, SCOTLAND, RAISED IN STAFFORDSHIRE, ENGLAND • STUDIED AT UNIVERSITY OF LIVERPOOL • ALSO WRITES FOR CHILDREN • COLLECTIONS: *SELLING MANHATTAN*, 1987; *MEAN TIME*, 1993

■ **Pre**Reading
1 What do you associate with Valentine's Day?

● **1st**Reading
2 Are the effects that the onion has on the lover positive or negative?
3 How is the onion personified?
4 The onion is given four times. What does this indicate?

●● **2nd**Reading
5 How long will the taste of onion stay on the lover's lips? How long will the couple last?
6 What type of relationship does the couple have? Have they been in love for long?
7 How does the onion promise light?

●●● **3rd**Reading
8 How would you feel if you were given an onion for Valentine's Day?
9 The poet uses very short lines regularly in the poem. What effect do these short lines have?
10 Describe each metaphor that the speaker uses to describe the onion.

●●●● **4th**Reading
11 Read 'My Mistress's Eyes . . .' by William Shakespeare and compare it with this poem.
12 This poem manages to be 'cold and passionate'. How?
13 Do you think that this is a good love poem? What makes it good or bad?
14 Love is particular to individuals and cannot be represented by love hearts and teddy bears. Does the poet agree? Do you?

▼ **Link**to**Language**
15 Write the lover's response to this unusual gift.

Going Home to Mayo, Winter, 1949
Paul Durcan

*Prescribed for the **Ordinary Level** exams in **2011** and **2012***

Leaving behind us the alien, foreign city of Dublin
My father drove through the night in an old Ford Anglia,
His five-year-old son in the seat beside him,
The rexine seat of red leatherette,
And a yellow moon peered in through the windscreen.   5
'Daddy, Daddy,' I cried, 'pass out the moon,'
But no matter how hard he drove he could not pass out the moon.
Each town we passed through was another milestone
And their names were magic passwords into eternity:
Kilcock, Kinnegad, Strokestown, Elphin,   10
Tarmonbarry, Tulsk, Ballaghaderreen, Ballavarry;
Now we were in Mayo and the next stop was Turlough,
The village of Turlough in the heartland of Mayo,
And my father's mother's house, all oil-lamps and women,
And my bedroom over the public bar below,   15
And in the morning cattle-cries and cock-crows:
Life's seemingly seamless garment gorgeously rent
By their screeches and bellowings. And in the evenings
I walked with my father in the high grass down by the river
Talking with him – an unheard-of thing in the city.   20

But home was not home and the moon could be no more outflanked
Than the daylight nightmare of Dublin City:
Back down along the canal we chugged into the city
And each lock-gate tolled our mutual doom;
And railings and palings and asphalt and traffic lights,   25
And blocks after blocks of so-called 'new' tenements –
Thousands of crosses of loneliness planted
In the narrowing grave of the life of the father;
In the wide, wide cemetery of the boy's childhood.

GLOSSARY

ALIEN: Unfamiliar, not part of what you know or understand
REXINE: Fake leather, plastic
MILESTONE: Stone showing distance to or from a certain place; an important stage reached
SEAMLESS: No beginning, no end; no seams or joins
RENT: Torn apart
OUTFLANKED: Outrun, got in front of

CHUGGED: Moved with dull, short, repeated sounds
TOLLED: Stroke of a ringing bell (especially to mark death)
MUTUAL: Felt or done by both
ASPHALT: Black tar and gravel road surface
TENEMENTS: Large houses or buildings divided into apartments for those who cannot afford a full house

PAUL DURCAN • BORN 1944 IN DUBLIN TO COUNTRY PARENTS FROM CO. MAYO • SPENT HIS SUMMER HOLIDAYS WITH HIS RELATIONS IN MAYO • EDUCATED AT GONZAGA COLLEGE AND STUDIED MEDIEVAL HISTORY AND ARCHAEOLOGY AT UNIVERSITY COLLEGE, CORK • A REGULAR GUEST ON THE PAT KENNY RADIO SHOW • A POPULAR POET, MUCH QUOTED AND RECOGNISED IN IRISH SOCIETY

■ Pre Reading

1 Where do you call home? Why do you call this place home? What makes a place a home?

● 1st Reading

2 How does the boy feel at the beginning of the poem?
3 What game do the father and son play on their journey westwards?
4 Describe the relationship between father and son in the car on the journey to Mayo.
5 Mayo is attractive and homely to the poet. What images stand out to make it so?
6 The father and son go walking in the high grass. Why does this image stand out? Why is it important to the poet?

●● 2nd Reading

7 Describe the journey to Mayo in terms of the images and mood of the poem.
8 Describe the stay in Mayo in terms of the images and mood of the poem.
9 Describe the journey back to Dublin in terms of the images and mood of the poem.
10 Durcan was five years old when he took this journey to Mayo. Was this his first journey to Mayo? What evidence is there to support your answer?

●●● 3rd Reading

11 Durcan's writing is very detailed. Why does he include so much detail?
12 Why is Dublin described as an 'alien, foreign city'?
13 This poem is divided between lines 1–20 and 21–29. Why is there a division? Why is the first section twice as long as the second? What are the main differences between the sections?
14 Is there a sense that Durcan is trying to resist reality and escape from real life in Dublin? Where do you see this?
15 Describe Durcan's relationship with his father as outlined in the poem. Are there any high points or low points in the relationship?
16 The last three lines present us with images of death. What are they? What do they mean in the context of the poem?
17 Is this a child's view of an event or an adult looking back on an event in his childhood? Support your answer with evidence from the poem.

▼ Link to Language

18 Paul Durcan is widely acclaimed as a popular modern Irish poet. Research his life, influences and works and prepare a report on his life and works.

The Tuft of Flowers Robert Frost

Prescribed for the **Ordinary Level** exams in **2011** and **2012**

I went to turn the grass once after one
Who mowed it in the dew before the sun.

The dew was gone that made his blade so keen
Before I came to view the levelled scene.

I looked for him behind an isle of trees;   5
I listened for his whetstone on the breeze.

But he had gone his way, the grass all mown,
And I must be, as he had been, — alone,

'As all must be,' I said within my heart,
'Whether they work together or apart.'   10

But as I said it, swift there passed me by
On noiseless wing a bewildered butterfly,

Seeking with memories grown dim o'er night
Some resting flower of yesterday's delight.

And once I marked his flight go round and round,   15
As where some flower lay withering on the ground.

And then he flew as far as eye could see,
And then on tremulous wing came back to me.

I thought of questions that have no reply,
And would have turned to toss the grass to dry;   20

But he turned first, and led my eye to look
At a tall tuft of flowers beside a brook,

A leaping tongue of bloom the scythe had spared
Beside a reedy brook the scythe had bared.

I left my place to know them by their name,   25
Finding them butterfly weed when I came.

The mower in the dew had loved them thus,
By leaving them to flourish, not for us,

Nor yet to draw one thought of ours to him,
But from sheer morning gladness at the brim.   30

The butterfly and I had lit upon,
Nevertheless, a message from the dawn,

That made me hear the wakening birds around,
And hear his long scythe whispering to the ground,

And feel a spirit kindred to my own;
So that henceforth I worked no more alone;

But glad with him, I worked as with his aid,
And weary, sought at noon with him the shade;

And dreaming, as it were, held brotherly speech
With one whose thought I had not hoped to reach.

'Men work together,' I told him from the heart,
'Whether they work together or apart.'

35

40

ROBERT FROST • BORN 1874 IN SAN FRANCISCO, USA • EDUCATED AT DARTMOUTH AND HARVARD • WORKED AS A FARMER • LIVED IN ENGLAND • RETURNED TO THE USA AND TAUGHT AT AMHERST COLLEGE • COLLECTIONS: *NORTH OF BOSTON*, 1914; *THE CLEARING*, 1962 • DIED 1963

•PreReading

1 What does the word 'tuft' suggest to you? Think about the sound of the word.

•1stReading

2 What does the speaker in the poem set out to do?
3 When does he do it?
4 Where is the second man in the poem?
5 What did he do?
6 What is the relationship between the two men at the start of the poem?
7 What does the butterfly do?
8 How did the speaker react to the butterfly?

••2ndReading

9 What does the poet mean by the phrase 'a message from the dawn'?
10 How does this message affect him?
11 How does the relationship between the two men change?

•••3rdReading

12 Comment on the versification.
13 Comment on the rhyming scheme.

••••4thReading

14 Examine the two quotes in the poem (lines 9 and 10 and lines 41 and 42).
15 What do the flowers symbolise?
16 What has changed between them?
17 This poem is about a shared spiritual experience. Do you agree?

Out, Out– *Robert Frost*

Prescribed for the **Ordinary Level** exams in **2011** and **2012**

The buzz-saw snarled and rattled in the yard
And made dust and dropped stove-length sticks of wood,
Sweet-scented stuff when the breeze drew across it.
And from there those that lifted eyes could count
Five mountain ranges one behind the other   5
Under the sunset far into Vermont.
And the saw snarled and rattled, snarled and rattled,
As it ran light, or had to bear a load.
And nothing happened: day was all but done.
Call it a day, I wish they might have said   10
To please the boy by giving him the half hour
That a boy counts so much when saved from work.
His sister stood beside them in her apron
To tell them 'Supper'. At the word, the saw,
As if to prove saws knew what supper meant,   15
Leaped out at the boy's hand, or seemed to leap –
He must have given the hand. However it was,
Neither refused the meeting. But the hand!
The boy's first outcry was a rueful laugh,
As he swung toward them holding up the hand   20
Half in appeal, but half as if to keep
The life from spilling. Then the boy saw all –
Since he was old enough to know, big boy
Doing a man's work, though a child at heart –
He saw all spoiled. 'Don't let him cut my hand off –   25
The doctor, when he comes. Don't let him, sister!'
So. But the hand was gone already.
The doctor put him in the dark of ether.
He lay and puffed his lips out with his breath.
And then – the watcher at his pulse took fright.   30
No one believed. They listened at his heart.
Little – less – nothing! – and that ended it.
No more to build on there. And they, since they
Were not the one dead, turned to their affairs.

● 1st Reading

1 Write a brief paragraph describing the action of the poem.
2 Describe the initial setting for the poem.
3 What impression do you have of the boy's life up until this day?
4 How does the setting change as the poem goes on?
5 What is the boy thinking to himself as the action of the poem develops?
6 How does the poet give life to inanimate objects in the poem?

●● 2nd Reading

7 At what exact point does the poem change?
8 What happens to the pace of the poem?
9 Which sounds dominate the beginning of the poem? Read the poem out loud to make sure. Why do you think the poet included those sounds?
10 How do the sounds in the poem change? What sounds dominate later in the poem?

●●● 3rd Reading

11 Write about the importance of these phrases:
'day was all but done.' (line 9)
'Neither refused the meeting.' (line 18)
'He saw all spoiled.' (line 25)
'So.' (line 27)
'Little – less – nothing!' (line 32)
12 What part is played by other people in the poem?

●●●● 4th Reading

13 How does the poet feel about the incident?
14 This poem is about the cruelty of life. Do you agree?

▼ Link to Language

15 Write the doctor's report after the boy died.

Mending Wall *Robert Frost*

*Prescribed for the **Ordinary Level** exams in **2011** and **2012***

Something there is that doesn't love a wall,
That sends the frozen-ground-swell under it,
And spills the upper boulders in the sun;
And makes gaps even two can pass abreast.
The work of hunters is another thing: 5
I have come after them and made repair
Where they have left not one stone on a stone,
But they would have the rabbit out of hiding,
To please the yelping dogs. The gaps I mean,
No one has seen them made or heard them made,   10
But at spring mending-time we find them there.
I let my neighbour know beyond the hill;
And on a day we meet to walk the line
And set the wall between us once again.
We keep the wall between us as we go.   15
To each the boulders that have fallen to each.
And some are loaves and some so nearly balls
We have to use a spell to make them balance:
'Stay where you are until our backs are turned!'
We wear our fingers rough with handling them.   20
Oh, just another kind of out-door game,
One on a side. It comes to little more:
There where it is we do not need the wall:
He is all pine and I am apple orchard.
My apple trees will never get across   25
And eat the cones under his pines, I tell him.
He only says, 'Good fences make good neighbours.'
Spring is the mischief in me, and I wonder
If I could put a notion in his head:
'*Why* do they make good neighbours? Isn't it   30
Where there are cows? But here there are no cows.
Before I built a wall I'd ask to know
What I was walling in or walling out,
And to whom I was like to give offence.
Something there is that doesn't love a wall,   35
That wants it down.' I could say 'Elves' to him,
But it's not elves exactly, and I'd rather

He said it for himself. I see him there
Bringing a stone grasped firmly by the top
In each hand, like an old-stone savage armed.   40
He moves in darkness as it seems to me,
Not of woods only and the shade of trees.
He will not go behind his father's saying,
And he likes having thought of it so well
He says again, 'Good fences make good neighbours.'   45

●1stReading

1 What is the poet doing?
2 What is his procedure?
3 Why does he have to do it?
4 How are the gaps made?
5 When do they mend the wall?
6 Why would they mend the wall at that time?

●●2ndReading

7 What does the poet mean in line 18 by the word 'spell'?
8 Who does the poet think 'that doesn't love a wall'?
9 What does the poet think about doing?

●●●3rdReading

10 Do they need a wall?
11 Describe the neighbour's movements.
12 Is the phrase 'an old-stone savage' meant as an insult or a compliment? Explain.

●●●●4thReading

13 Does the poet have a change of heart about the wall?
14 How does something that is meant to keep them apart bring the two men closer together?

▼LinktoLanguage

15 Write a diary entry that you would write after your first day at work in a new job.

*Prescribed for the **Ordinary Level** exams in **2013** and **2014***

A woman is reading a poem on the street
and another woman stops to listen. We stop too,
with our arms around each other. The poem
is being read and listened to out here
in the open. Behind us   5
no one is entering or leaving the houses.

Suddenly a hug comes over me and I'm
giving it to you, like a variable star shooting light
off to make itself comfortable, then
subsiding. I finish but keep on holding   10
you. A man walks up to us and we know he hasn't
come out of nowhere, but if he could, he
would have. He looks homeless because of how
he needs. 'Can I have one of those?' he asks you,
and I feel you nod. I'm surprised,   15
surprised you don't tell him how
it is – that I'm yours, only
yours, etc., exclusive as a nose to
its face. Love – that's what we're talking about, love
that nabs you with 'for me   20
only' and holds on.

So I walk over to him and put my
arms around him and try to
hug him like I mean it. He's got an overcoat on
so thick I can't feel   25
him past it. I'm starting the hug
and thinking, 'How big a hug is this supposed to be?
How long shall I hold this hug?' Already
we could be eternal, his arms falling over my
shoulders, my hands not   30
meeting behind his back, he is so big!

I put my head into his chest and snuggle
in. I lean into him. I lean my blood and my wishes
into him. He stands for it. This is his
and he's starting to give it back so well I know he's   35

getting it. This hug. So truly, so tenderly
we stop having arms and I don't know if
my lover has walked away or what, or
if the woman is still reading the poem, or the houses –
what about them? – the houses.   40

Clearly, a little permission is a dangerous thing.
But when you hug someone you want it
to be a masterpiece of connection, the way the button
on his coat will leave the imprint of
a planet in my cheek   45
when I walk away. When I try to find some place
to go back to.

TESS GALLAGHER · BORN 1943 IN PORT ANGELES, WASHINGTON,
USA · POET, ESSAYIST, NOVELIST AND PLAYWRIGHT · POETRY COLLECTIONS
INCLUDE *MOON CROSSING BRIDGE* AND *DEAR GHOSTS*.

■Pre Reading

1 Who do you usually hug?
2 What does a hug signify?
3 Think about the sound of the word 'hug', does it sound affectionate?

●1st Reading

4 Describe the scene at the start of the poem. What effect does the poetry reading have on the couple?
5 Describe the man who approaches them.
6 What does he want?
7 Why does the woman hesitate?

●●2nd Reading

8 What happens to her and the stranger she hugs?
9 What happens to her partner?
10 What does she mean by the phrase 'a masterpiece of connection'? (line 43)

●●●3rd Reading

11 How did this poem make you feel?
12 Would you do what the poet did?

▼Link to Language

13 Write a diary entry for a day in the life of a homeless person.

Daniel's Duck *Kerry Hardie*

Prescribed for the **Ordinary Level** *exams in* **2011, 2012, 2013** *and* **2014**

I held out the shot mallard, she took it from me,
looped its neck-string over a drawer of the dresser.
The children were looking on, half-caught.
Then the kitchen life — warm, lit, glowing —
moved forward, taking in the dead bird,   5
and its coldness, its wildness, were leaching away.

The children were sitting to their dinners.
Us too — drinking tea, hardly noticing
the child's quiet slide from his chair,
his small absorbed body before the duck's body,   10
the duck changing — feral, live —
arrowing up out of black sloblands
with the gleam of a river
falling away below.

Then the duck — dead again — hanging from the drawer-knob,   15
the green head, brown neck running into the breast,
the intricate silvery-greyness of the back;
the wings, their white bars and blue flashes,
the feet, their snakey, orange scaliness, small claws, piteous
  webbing,
the yellow beak, blooded,   20
the whole like a weighted sack —
all that downward-dragginess of death.

He hovered, took a step forward, a step back,
something appeared in his face, some knowledge
of a place where he stood, the world stilled,   25
the lit streaks of sunrise running off red
into the high bowl of morning.

She watched him, moving to touch, his hand out:
What is it, Daniel, do you like the duck?
He turned as though caught in the act,   30
saw the gentleness in her face and his body loosened.
I thought there was water on it —

he was finding the words, one by one,
holding them out, to see would they do us –
but there isn't.
He added this on, going small with relief
that his wing-drag of sounds was enough.

KERRY HARDIE • BORN 1951 IN SINGAPORE, GREW UP IN CO. DOWN, NORTHERN IRELAND • WORKED FOR THE BBC IN BELFAST • DEEPLY AFFECTED BY THE TROUBLES AND VIOLENCE IN NORTHERN IRELAND • WON THE NATIONAL POETRY PRIZE IN 1996 • JOINT WINNER OF THE HENNESSY AWARD FOR POETRY • LIVES IN KILKENNY WITH HUSBAND

●1stReading

1 Where does the poem take place?
2 Who is there?
3 What is the atmosphere in the room?
4 What effect does the dead duck have on the children?
5 What does Daniel do?

●●2ndReading

6 Describe the duck.
7 Make a list of all the colours that the poet uses in her description.
8 Describe the boy's movements.

●●●3rdReading

9 How does Daniel change during this experience, do you think?
10 From your reading of the poem, what type of boy do you think Daniel is?
11 What is the significance of his answer to the question that was put to him?

●●●●4thReading

12 What is the most effective image in the poem?
13 Did you like this poem? Explain your answer.

▼LinktoLanguage

14 Write a speech for a debate where you argue for or against blood sports.

When I set out for Lyonnesse
Thomas Hardy

*Prescribed for the **Ordinary Level** exam in **2012***

When I set out for Lyonnesse,
  A hundred miles away,
  The rime was on the spray,
And starlight lit my lonesomeness
When I set out for Lyonnesse   5
  A hundred miles away.

What would bechance at Lyonnesse
  While I should sojourn there
  No prophet durst declare,
Nor did the wisest wizard guess   10
What would bechance at Lyonnesse
  While I should sojourn there.

When I came back from Lyonnesse
  With magic in my eyes,
  All marked with mute surmise   15
My radiance rare and fathomless,
When I came back from Lyonnesse
  With magic in my eyes!

GLOSSARY

LYONNESSE: A mythical place between Cornwall and the Scilly Isles associated with the adventures of King Arthur and his wizard Merlin. 'Lyonnesse' is also the name of Hardy's wife's homeplace.
RIME: Frost formed from cloud or fog
SPRAY: Branches

BECHANCE: Experience
SOJOURN: Stay
DURST DECLARE: Dare to guess
SURMISE: Guess, conjecture
FATHOMLESS: Difficult to understand

THOMAS HARDY • BORN 1840 IN DORSETSHIRE, ENGLAND • STARTED WRITING POEMS AND ESSAYS IN HIS EARLY TEENS • HIS MOST SUCCESSFUL NOVEL, *FAR FROM THE MADDING CROWD*, PUBLISHED IN 1874 • HIS POETRY ADHERES TO TRADITIONAL RULES AND REGULATIONS • DIED IN 1928

●1stReading

1 This poem tells the story of a journey. What do you learn about the journey after your first reading?

●●2ndReading

2 How does the poet feel as he sets out on the journey to Lyonnesse?

3 Stanza 3 tells us about the poet on his return from Lyonnesse. What has changed? Compare the poet before and after his journey.

●●●3rdReading

4 Stanzas 1 and 3 deal with the going to and returning from Lyonnesse. What is the function of Stanza 2 in the poem?

5 The poet builds a sense of magic, mystery and fantasy by using archaic language and the image of a knight embarking on a quest. Discuss and pick out other words or phrases which also contribute.

6 Comment on the song-like qualities in the poem. What effect does this have on the overall poem?

▼LinktoLanguage

7 Imagine that you have gone on a life-changing journey. Write a letter home to family or friends detailing the journey and the personal transformation.

A Constable Calls *Seamus Heaney*

Prescribed for the **Ordinary Level** exams in *2012* and *2014*

His bicycle stood at the window-sill,
The rubber cowl of a mud-splasher
Skirting the front mudguard,
Its fat black handlegrips

Heating in sunlight, the 'spud'   5
Of the dynamo gleaming and cocked
  back,
The pedal treads hanging relieved
Of the boot of the law.

His cap was upside down
On the floor, next his chair.   10
The line of its pressure ran like a
  bevel
In his slightly sweating hair.

He had unstrapped
The heavy ledger, and my father
Was making tillage returns   15
In acres, roods, and perches.

Arithmetic and fear.
I sat staring at the polished holster

With its buttoned flap, the braid cord
Looped into the revolver butt.   20

'Any other root crops?
Mangolds? Marrowstems? Anything
  like that?'
'No.' But was there not a line
Of turnips where the seed ran out

In the potato field? I assumed   25
Small guilts and sat
Imagining the black hole in the
  barracks.
He stood up, shifted the baton-case

Further round on his belt,
Closed the domesday book,   30
Fitted his cap back with two hands,
And looked at me as he said goodbye.

A shadow bobbed in the window.
He was snapping the carrier spring
Over the ledger. His boot pushed off   35
And the bicycle ticked, ticked, ticked.

GLOSSARY

CONSTABLE: Policeman / member of the Royal Ulster Constabulary (RUC)
COWL: Hood-shaped covering
DYNAMO: Small generator producing an electric current propelled by the turning bicycle wheel

BEVEL: Line of a sloping edge
LEDGER: Book of accounts and records
TILLAGE: Crop-growing
DOMESDAY BOOK: Book referred to on Judgment Day. Also a book compiled by William the Conqueror in 1086 surveying ownership of the lands of England.

SEAMUS HEANEY • BORN 1939 IN MOSSBAWN, NEAR BELLAGHY, CO DERRY • SON OF A CATHOLIC FARMER • EDUCATED AT ST COLUMBA'S COLLEGE IN DERRY AND THEN AT QUEEN'S UNIVERSITY, BELFAST, WHERE HE WAS AWARDED A FIRST CLASS DEGREE IN ENGLISH LANGUAGE AND LITERATURE • GAINED A TEACHING DIPLOMA IN 1962 AND BECAME A LECTURER IN ENGLISH AT QUEEN'S UNIVERSITY, BELFAST • HIS FIRST VOLUME OF POETRY, *DEATH OF A NATURALIST*, IS AN OUTPOURING OF ALL HE KNEW FROM HIS HOMELIFE AND LOCAL COUNTRYSIDE • A PROLIFIC WRITER — HAS PUBLISHED MANY COLLECTIONS OF POETRY, CRITICISM AND TRANSLATIONS • IN 1988 HE WAS ELECTED PROFESSOR OF POETRY AT OXFORD • IN 1995 HE WON THE MUCH-ACCLAIMED NOBEL PRIZE FOR LITERATURE

■**Pre**Reading

1 Imagine a policeman calling to your home. How would your parents feel and react? How would you feel and react?

●**1st**Reading

2 Describe the Constable's visit. Is he welcome?

3 Describe the Constable's bicycle.

4 Are there any emotions evident in the poem?

●●**2nd**Reading

5 The Constable's appearance is described in detail — describe him. Do we learn anything about his personality?

6 The Constable appears in the Heaneys' home as a figure of authority. What words or images reinforce this?

7 Is the overall feeling towards the policeman one of fear, threat or respect? Where can this be seen in the poem?

8 A lie is told. What is the lie? Describe what you think the father's opinion of the lie is. What is the son's feeling about the lie?

9 In the final stanza the policeman becomes a 'shadow' and his bicycle 'ticked, ticked, ticked'. What images are conjured up in your mind when you hear this ticking sound?

●●●**3rd**Reading

10 'Tension mounts as the poem progresses.' Do you agree with this statement? Trace the mounting tension throughout the poem.

11 Write out the dialogue, as you imagine it would have been, between the Constable and the Heaneys throughout the visit. Include the silent thoughts of the child if you wish.

12 Is this poem a true reflection of a policeman's visit to a farmhouse, or do you feel that the tension is created because the Heaneys were part of the Catholic community in Northern Ireland during the conflicts?

▼**Link**to**Language**

13 'I knew as soon as the police car pulled up that the news was bad.' Write an essay based on or including this sentence.
Or
Write out the Constable's private diary entry for the day outlined in the poem.

A Call *Seamus Heaney*

*Prescribed for the **Ordinary Level** exams in **2012** and **2014***

'Hold on,' she said, 'I'll just run out and get him.
The weather here's so good he took the chance
To do a bit of weeding.'
       So I saw him
Down on his hands and knees beside the leek rig,   5
Touching, inspecting, separating one
Stalk from the other, gently pulling up
Everything not tapered, frail and leafless,
Pleased to feel each little weed-root break,
But rueful also ...   10

      Then found myself listening to
The amplified grave ticking of hall clocks
Where the phone lay unattended in a calm
Of mirror glass and sunstruck pendulums ...

And found myself then thinking: if it were nowadays,   15
This is how Death would summon Everyman.

Next thing he spoke and I nearly said I loved him.

GLOSSARY

RUEFUL: Showing or feeling good-humoured regret
EVERYMAN: Medieval morality play where God sends
Death, in person, to seek out Everyman and strip him of his
worldly goods, leaving him with only his good deeds by
which to judge him as he descends alone into the grave.

● 1st Reading

1 Who is speaking in the first three lines?
2 Who, do you think, the poet is waiting to speak to?
3 While the poet is waiting his mind wanders. Lines 4–10 describe his vision of his father weeding outside. Describe his father's actions and his feelings as Heaney imagines them.

●● 2nd Reading

4 In lines 11–14 the poet's attention is drawn to the sounds in the hallway of his parents' house. Describe them. What does he think about?
5 Lines 15–16 seem to step away from the personal and into a universal thought — what is that thought?

●●● 3rd Reading

6 When finally the poet hears his father's voice, why is he on the verge of telling him that he loves him?
7 Why, do you think, did the poet not tell his father that he loved him?
8 The tone of the poem changes as the poem progresses. Examine the poem and identify the changes in tone.

▼ Link to Language

9 'It was the most important phone call I would ever make in my life.'
Write a short story suggested by this statement.
Or
Write a letter to a newspaper highlighting the annoyance of mobile phones ringing constantly in public places.

The Underground *Seamus Heaney*

Prescribed for the **Ordinary Level** exams in **2012** and **2014**

There we were in the vaulted tunnel running,
You in your going-away coat speeding ahead
And me, me then like a fleet god gaining
Upon you before you turned to a reed

Or some new white flower japped with crimson   5
As the coat flapped wild and button after button
Sprang off and fell in a trail
Between the Underground and the Albert Hall.

Honeymooning, mooning around, late for the Proms,
Our echoes die in that corridor and now   10
I come as Hansel came on the moonlit stones
Retracing the path back, lifting the buttons

To end up in a draughty lamplit station
After the trains have gone, the wet track
Bared and tensed as I am, all attention   15
For your step following and damned if I look back.

GLOSSARY

THE UNDERGROUND: Underground rail system in London

VAULTED: Arched roof

GOING-AWAY COAT: Clothes worn by brides after they've changed out of their wedding gowns

HANSEL: 'Hansel and Gretel' is a children's story in which children find their way home by following a trail of pebbles.

FLEET GOD … TURNED TO A REED: Greek myth telling of a maiden who chooses to turn into a plant rather than succumb to the Greek god who is pursuing her

DAMNED IF I LOOK BACK: Refers to the ancient Greek story of Orpheus, a skilled musician and poet, whose wife, Eurydice, died following a fatal snake bite. He begs the gods to allow him enter their kingdom to rescue his beloved. He is allowed, but on the condition that he leads her from Tartarus, playing his lyre, without looking back at Eurydice. Almost at the end of their journey Orpheus looks back, and Eurydice is lost forever.

●1st Reading

1 What is the mood of the poet and his wife as they run through the Underground?

2 Explain the image of Hansel following a trail.

3 The wife is wearing her 'going-away coat'. Does that tell us anything about this visit to London?

●●2nd Reading

4 Throughout the poem Heaney is following his wife, but in the final stanza she is following him. Is he sure she is there? Does he look back? Why?

5 How would you describe the poet's mood in the final stanza?

6 Describe the Underground station.

●●●3rd Reading

7 This poem appears to be rich in imagery and elements of mythology. What images do you find most convincing? Describe them and comment on their effectiveness.

The Collar *George Herbert*

*Prescribed for the **Ordinary Level** exams in **2011** and **2014***

I struck the board, and cry'd, No more.
　　　　　I will abroad.
　　What ? shall I ever sigh and pine ?
My lines and life are free ; free as the rode,
　　Loose as the winde, as large as store.　　　　　5
　　　　　Shall I be still in suit ?
　　Have I no harvest but a thorn
　　To let me bloud, and not restore
　　What I have lost with cordiall fruit?
　　　　　Sure there was wine　　　　　10
Before my sighs did drie it : there was corn
　　　　Before my tears did drown it.
　　Is the yeare onely lost to me ?
　　　Have I no bayes to crown it ?
　　No flowers, no garlands gay ? all blasted ?　　　15
　　　　　All wasted ?
Not so, my heart : but there is fruit,
　　　　And thou hast hands.
　　Recover all thy sigh-blown age
On double pleasures : leave thy cold dispute　　　20
Of what is fit, and not. Forsake thy cage,
　　　　Thy rope of sands,
Which pettie thoughts have made, and made to thee
　　Good cable, to enforce and draw,
　　　　And be thy law,　　　　　25
While thou didst wink and wouldst not see.
　　　　Away ; take heed :
　　　　I will abroad.
Call in thy deaths head there : tie up thy fears.
　　　　He that forbears　　　　　30
　　To suit and serve his need,
　　　　Deserves his load.
But as I rav'd and grew more fierce and wilde
　　　　At every word,
Me thoughts I heard one calling, *Child* !　　　35
　　And I reply'd, *My Lord.*

GEORGE HERBERT • BORN 1593 IN MONTGOMERY, WALES, TO A WEALTHY FAMILY • EDUCATED AT CAMBRIDGE UNIVERSITY, WHERE HE BECAME PUBLIC ORATOR IN 1619 • IN 1624 HE BECAME MP FOR MONTGOMERY • HE GAVE UP HIS POLITICAL LIFE AND WAS ORDAINED A PRIEST IN 1630 • HIS POETRY EXAMINES RELIGIOUS THEMES, SUCH AS GOD'S LOVE, AS WELL AS HIS OWN RELATIONSHIP WITH GOD • HE DIED THREE YEARS AFTER HIS ORDINATION

■ **Pre**Reading

1 'The Collar' refers to the collar worn by priests and clergymen. Outline what you feel a collar represents.

● **1st**Reading

2 Is the speaker happy with his ministry?
3 What emotions are initially obvious?
4 Are these emotions that you would normally associate with priests and clergymen?

●● **2nd**Reading

5 Examine lines 1–16. What is the speaker complaining about?
6 What does the speaker wish he could do?
7 He admits that life did offer him some opportunities — 'wine' and 'corn'. What happened to these opportunities? Why did this happen?
8 What do you think the poet means in lines 14–16?
9 In lines 17–26 the speaker's soul contradicts the message of the first 16 lines. In what way?
10 What advice does the soul offer the speaker?

11 A plan of escape is formulated in lines 27–32. What does this plan entail?
12 The whole tone of the poem changes in lines 33–35. Why?

●●● **3rd**Reading

13 The speaker in this poem struggles as he tries to measure his success in life. In what ways does he feel he has failed?
14 Why, in your opinion, is this poem so irregular in structure, line length, rhyme, etc.?
15 This poem contains contrasting images of freedom and restraint / compliance. Highlight and explain each of these images.
16 Trace the speaker's train of thought in the poem.

▼ **Link**to**Language**

17 Write an essay based on the ideas of rebellion and defiance as suggested in Herbert's 'The Collar'.
Or
Write about a time you broke the rules and rebelled.

Spring *Gerard Manley Hopkins*

*Prescribed for the **Ordinary Level** exams in **2011** and **2013***

Nothing is so beautiful as Spring—
When weeds, in wheels, shoot long and lovely and lush;
Thrush's eggs look little low heavens, and thrush
Through the echoing timber does so rinse and wring
The ear, it strikes like lightnings to hear him sing;   5
The glassy peartree leaves and blooms, they brush
The descending blue; that blue is all in a rush
With richness; the racing lambs too have fair their fling.

What is all this juice and all this joy?
A strain of the earth's sweet being in the beginning   10
In Eden garden.—Have, get, before it cloy,

Before it cloud, Christ, lord, and sour with sinning,
Innocent mind and Mayday in girl and boy,
Most, O maid's child, thy choice and worthy the winning.

GLOSSARY

CLOY: Cause distaste by overindulgence

GERARD MANLEY HOPKINS • BORN 1844 IN STRATFORD, ENGLAND, INTO A FAMILY THAT ENCOURAGED HIS ARTISTIC ABILITY • A ROMAN CATHOLIC CONVERT AND JESUIT PRIEST • MOST OF HIS POETRY WAS PUBLISHED POSTHUMOUSLY • WIDELY ADMIRED AS A POETIC INNOVATOR • DIED 1889

■PreReading

1 Have somebody else in your class read this poem to you without discussing its meaning. Describe the sounds. What effect does it have on you?

●1stReading

2 Read the first line. Comment on its directness and simplicity.

3 What does the poet describe in the octet?

●●2ndReading

4 Which of the images has the strongest effect on you?

5 What is the significance of the question in line 9?

6 What power does the speaker ascribe to nature? Which is more important in this poem — nature or the perceiver of nature? Explain.

7 What prayer to Christ does the poem's sestet make?

●●●3rdReading

8 Comment on Hopkins' use of rhythm.

9 Comment on Hopkins' use of alliteration.

10 What effect does it have?

●●●●4thReading

11 What does the poem tell us about Hopkins' beliefs?

12 How would you compare this poem's emphasis on childhood innocence to other poems on the same theme?

13 Why does he associate spring with innocence?

Inversnaid *Gerard Manley Hopkins*

*Prescribed for the **Ordinary Level** exams in **2011** and **2013***

This darksome burn, horseback brown,
His rollrock highroad roaring down,
In coop and in comb the fleece of his foam
Flutes and low to the lake falls home.

A windpuff-bonnet of fáwn-fróth   5
Turns and twindles over the broth
Of a pool so pitchblack, féll-frówning,
It rounds and rounds Despair to drowning,

Degged with dew, dappled with dew
Are the groins of the braes that the brook treads through,   10
Wiry heathpacks, flitches of fern,
And the beadbonny ash that sits over the burn.

What would the world be, once bereft
Of wet and of wildness? Let them be left,
O let them be left, wildness and wet;   15
Long live the weeds and the wilderness yet.

GLOSSARY

BURN: Small river
DAPPLED: Speckled
BRAES: Hillside/slope

FLITCHES: Longitudinal cut
BEREFT: Deprived/lacking

■ **Pre**Reading

1 Where is Inversnaid?
2 What type of place do you imagine it would be?

● **1st**Reading

3 What is Hopkins describing in the first stanza?
4 What is 'fáwn-fróth'?
5 Do you think the phrase 'Despair to drowning' fits in with the rest of verse 2?

●● **2nd**Reading

6 Note all the wet imagery in the poem; how does it contribute to the atmosphere in the poem?
7 Make a list of all the made-up words Hopkins uses.
8 Why does he do this?
9 What effect do they have?
10 Which is your favourite word?

●●● **3rd**Reading

11 What does he have to say in the final verse?
12 Do you think that his final question needs an answer?
13 What do you think this poem tells us about nature?

▼ **Link**to**Language**

14 Write a travel guide for a scenic part of Ireland.

Shancoduff *Patrick Kavanagh*

*Prescribed for the **Ordinary Level** exams in **2011** and **2012***

My black hills have never seen the sun rising,
Eternally they look north towards Armagh.
Lot's wife would not be salt if she had been
Incurious as my black hills that are happy
When dawn whitens Glassdrummond chapel.   5

My hills hoard the bright shillings of March
While the sun searches in every pocket.
They are my Alps and I have climbed the Matterhorn
With a sheaf of hay for three perishing calves
In the field under the Big Forth of Rocksavage.   10

The sleety winds fondle the rushy beards of Shancoduff
While the cattle-drovers sheltering in the Featherna Bush
Look up and say: 'Who owns them hungry hills
That the water-hen and snipe must have forsaken?
A poet? Then by heavens he must be poor.'   15
I hear and is my heart not badly shaken?

GLOSSARY

ROCKSAVAGE, SHANCODUFF, FEATHERNA BUSH: Places in Co. Monaghan near the poet's father's farm

PATRICK KAVANAGH • BORN 1904 IN INNISKEEN, CO. MONAGHAN • MOVED TO DUBLIN IN THE 1930S • DIAGNOSED WITH LUNG CANCER IN 1955; RECOVERED • MARRIED KATHERINE MOLONEY IN 1967 • COLLECTION: *PLOUGHMAN*, 1936 • NOVEL: *TARRY FLYNN*, 1948 • DIED IN 1967

● 1st Reading

1 The title of the poem is taken from the name of the place where Kavanagh's family had a farm. It is derived from two Irish words: *sean* and *dubh*. Do you know what these words mean? If not, find out. What sort of a place would you expect from such a name?

●● 2nd Reading

2 How does Kavanagh describe this place? Draw a picture or find one that would represent what you would imagine this place to look like.

3 What is the cattle-drovers' attitude to the hills?

4 How does he feel about the cattle-drovers?

●●● 3rd Reading

5 The speaker personifies the place. How does he do this? What effect does it have?

6 The speaker names a lot of specific places in the poem, e.g. Glassdrummond, Featherna, Rocksavage. Why does he do this?

7 The speaker repeatedly uses the possessive 'my' when talking about the hills. Why does he do this? What does it tell us about the narrator?

8 What is the answer to the rhetorical question at the end?

9 How does the rest of nature relate to the hills?

10 What is the difference between the way the cattle-drovers speak and the way the narrator speaks?

●●●● 4th Reading

11 In an earlier version of the poem, Kavanagh used the word 'faith' instead of the word 'heart' in the last line of the poem. Why do you think he made that change? What effect does it have? Do you think that it was a good change to make?

12 In another poem Kavanagh says that 'Naming a thing is the love act and the pledge.' Relate that statement to 'Shancoduff'.

13 'Shancoduff' is a love poem. Do you agree?

▼ Link to Language

14 Think of a place you love. Describe it.

A Christmas Childhood *Patrick Kavanagh*

*Prescribed for the **Ordinary Level** exams in **2011** and **2012***

I

One side of the potato-pits was white with frost –
How wonderful that was, how wonderful!
And when we put our ears to the paling-post
The music that came out was magical.

The light between the ricks of hay and straw   5
Was a hole in Heaven's gable. An apple tree
With its December-glinting fruit we saw –
O you, Eve, were the world that tempted me

To eat the knowledge that grew in clay
And death the germ within it! Now and then   10
I can remember something of the gay
Garden that was childhood's. Again

The tracks of cattle to a drinking-place,
A green stone lying sideways in a ditch
Or any common sight the transfigured face   15
Of a beauty that the world did not touch.

II

My father played the melodeon
Outside at our gate;
There were stars in the morning east
And they danced to his music.   20

Across the wild bogs his melodeon called
To Lennons and Callans.
As I pulled on my trousers in a hurry
I knew some strange thing had happened.

Outside in the cow-house my mother   25
Made the music of milking;
The light of her stable-lamp was a star
And the frost of Bethlehem made it twinkle.

A water-hen screeched in the bog,
Mass-going feet   30
Crunched the wafer-ice on the pot-holes,
Somebody wistfully twisted the bellows wheel.

My child poet picked out the letters
On the grey stone,

In silver the wonder of a Christmas townland,   35
The winking glitter of a frosty dawn.

Cassiopeia was over
Cassidy's hanging hill,
I looked and three whin bushes rode across
The horizon – the Three Wise Kings.   40

An old man passing said:
'Can't he make it talk' –
The melodeon. I hid in the doorway
And tightened the belt of my box-pleated coat.

I nicked six nicks on the door-post   45
With my penknife's big blade –
There was a little one for cutting tobacco.
And I was six Christmases of age.

My father played the melodeon,
My mother milked the cows,   50
And I had a prayer like a white rose pinned
On the Virgin Mary's blouse.

GLOSSARY

MELODEON: A small accordion

CASSIOPEIA: A northern constellation

■ PreReading

1 The first part of the poem is an evocation of the poet's memories of his own childhood. What are your memories of Christmastime when you were young?

● 1stReading

2 What is the relationship between the narrator and nature?
3 Do you think that the narrator had a happy childhood?
4 Where in the poem does the narrator compare his village with Bethlehem? Why does he do this?

●● 2ndReading

5 Show how Kavanagh uses religious imagery throughout the poem. What effect does it have? Does the imagery change as the poem progresses?

6 What type of voice does the narrator use?
7 There is awe for the innocence of the past in this poem. Why is this? How is it conveyed?
8 Why is there full rhyme only in the last verse?

●●● 3rdReading

9 How does Kavanagh 'wallow in the habitual'?

●●●● 4thReading

10 What is the narrator's standing in relation to everybody else in the poem?
11 Do you think the narrator felt the same way about the subject of the poem when writing the poem as he did when he was young?

A Glimpse of Starlings Brendan Kennelly

*Prescribed for the **Ordinary Level** exams in **2011** and **2012***

I expect him any minute now although
He's dead. I know he has been talking
All night to his own dead and now
In the first heart-breaking light of morning
He is struggling into his clothes,   5
Sipping a cup of tea, fingering a bit of bread,
Eating a small photograph with his eyes.
The questions bang and rattle in his head
Like doors and cannisters the night of a storm.
He doesn't know why his days finished like this   10
Daylight is as hard to swallow as food
Love is a crumb all of him hungers for.
I can hear the drag of his feet on the concrete path
The close explosion of his smoker's cough
The slow turn of the Yale key in the lock   15
The door opening to let him in
To what looks like release from what feels like pain
And over his shoulder a glimpse of starlings
Suddenly lifted over field, road and river
Like a fist of black dust pitched in the wind.   20

BRENDAN KENNELLY • BORN 1936 IN KERRY • PROFESSOR OF ENGLISH AT TRINITY COLLEGE, DUBLIN • COLLECTIONS: *CROMWELL*, 1987; *THE BOOK OF JUDAS*, 1992; *FAMILIAR STRANGERS*, 2004

■PreReading

1 What type of birds are starlings? Find a picture of them, how they fly, etc.

●1stReading

2 Describe his father's daily ritual.
3 What are his questions?
4 What does he mean by the phrase 'Daylight is as hard to swallow as food'?
5 What does the poet see as he hears his father coming home?

●●2ndReading

6 How can one who's dead be expected?
7 What does this tell us about Kennelly's relationship with his father?

●●●3rdReading

8 What do the starlings represent?
9 What is the strongest image in the poem?
10 Comment on the sounds used in the poem.

●●●●4thReading

11 This poem describes the loneliness of two people. Do you agree with this statement?

▼LinktoLanguage

12 Write an obituary for somebody real or imagined.

Night Drive *Brendan Kennelly*

*Prescribed for the **Ordinary Level** exams in **2013** and **2014***

I

The rain hammered as we drove
Along the road to Limerick
'Jesus what a night' Alan breathed
And – 'I wonder how he is, the last account
Was poor.'   5
I couldn't speak.

The windscreen fumed and blurred, the rain's spit
Lashing the glass. Once or twice
The wind's fist seemed to lift the car
And pitch it hard against the ditch.   10
Alan straightened out in time,
Silent. Glimpses of the Shannon –
A boiling madhouse roaring for its life
Or any life too near its gaping maw,
White shreds flaring in the waste   15
Of insane murderous black;
Trees bending in grotesque humility,
Branches scattered on the road, smashed
Beneath the wheels.
Then, ghastly under headlights,   20
Frogs bellied everywhere, driven
From the swampy fields and meadows,
Bewildered refugees, gorged with terror.
We killed them because we had to,
Their fatness crunched and flattened in the dark.   25
'How is he now?' Alan whispered
To himself. Behind us,
Carnage of broken frogs.

II

His head
Sweated on the pillow of the white hospital bed.   30
He spoke a little, said
Outrageously, 'I think I'll make it.'
Another time, he'd rail against the weather,
(Such a night would make him eloquent)
But now, quiet, he gathered his fierce will   35
To live.

III
Coming home
Alan saw the frogs.
'Look at them, they're everywhere,
Dozens of the bastards dead.'   40

Minutes later –
'I think he might pull through now.'
Alan, thoughtful at the wheel, was picking out
The homeroad in the flailing rain
Nighthedges closed on either side.   45
In the suffocating darkness
I heard the heavy breathing
Of my father's pain.

● 1st Reading

1 What is the relationship between Alan and the narrator?
2 What is the purpose of their journey?
3 How do you think the two men feel as they go on their journey?
4 How do their reactions differ?

●● 2nd Reading

5 What is the relationship between the two men and nature?
6 How is the night described?
7 What is the significance of the frogs?
8 How does the tone change in the second verse?
9 Do you get any impression of what type of man the father was?
10 How is the journey home different?
11 Does the road seem different to the narrator?

●●● 3rd Reading

12 Why does the poet seem to put more emphasis on the journey than on his father's ill health?
13 How does the pace of the poem change throughout?
14 It is rare to see dialogue in poems; what effect does it have?
15 Compare Alan's attitude to the frogs and his attitude to the father.

●●●● 4th Reading

16 Kennelly succeeds in building tension expertly. Do you agree?
17 Kennelly has been criticised for being over-sentimental in his poems. Does this poem make you agree with those critics?

▼ Link to Language

18 Write a story entitled 'Night Drive'.

Thinking of Mr D. *Thomas Kinsella*

*Prescribed for the **Ordinary Level** exams in **2012**, **2013** and **2014***

A man still light of foot, but ageing, took
An hour to drink his glass, his quiet tongue
Danced to such cheerful slander.

He sipped and swallowed with a scathing smile,
Tapping a polished toe.   5
His sober nod withheld assent.

When he died I saw him twice.
Once as he used retire
On one last murmured stabbing little tale
From the right company, tucking in his scarf.   10

And once down by the river, under wharf-
Lamps that plunged him in and out of light,
A priestlike figure turning, wolfish-slim,
Quickly aside from pain, in a bodily plight,
To note the oiled reflections chime and swim.   15

THOMAS KINSELLA • BORN 1928 IN DUBLIN • EDUCATED AT UCD THEN JOINED THE CIVIL SERVICE WHERE HE WORKED FOR 19 YEARS • IN 1965 HE BECAME WRITER IN RESIDENCE AT THE UNIVERSITY OF SOUTHERN ILLINOIS BEFORE BECOMING A PROFESSOR OF ENGLISH AT TEMPLE UNIVERSITY, PHILADELPHIA • HE RETURNED TO LIVE IN IRELAND IN 1992

● 1st Reading

1 The speaker doesn't use the man's full name in the title. What does this tell us about their relationship?
2 Which physical features of Mr D. are shown to us in the poem?
3 Do we get any impression of his personality in the first two stanzas?
4 Do we see other people in the poem? Describe them. What do they do? How do they treat Mr D.?
5 How does Mr D. react to the other characters in the poem?

●● 2nd Reading

6 What part does the speaker play in the poem? Is he active or passive?
7 In the final two stanzas the poet remembers Mr D. twice. Describe each incident.

8 What does the image reflected from the water tell us?
9 What insights to Mr D.'s character do the adjectives 'priestlike' and 'wolfish' convey?

●●● 3rd Reading

10 What is your overall impression of Mr D.?
11 What is the atmosphere of the poem?
12 How do the sounds in the poem help set the atmosphere?
13 Do you think there is regret in the speaker's voice?
14 Do you think that the way Mr D. deals with his situation is to be admired?

▼ Link to Language

15 Write a short story based on the image below.

Mirror in February *Thomas Kinsella*

*Prescribed for the **Ordinary Level** exams in **2012**, **2013** and **2014***

The day dawns with scent of must and rain,
Of opened soil, dark trees, dry bedroom air.
Under the fading lamp, half dressed—my brain
Idling on some compulsive fantasy—
I towel my shaven jaw and stop, and stare,   5
Riveted by a dark exhausted eye,
A dry downturning mouth.

It seems again that it is time to learn,
In this untiring, crumbling place of growth
To which, for the time being, I return.   10
Now plainly in the mirror of my soul
I read that I have looked my last on youth
And little more; for they are not made whole
That reach the age of Christ.

Below my window the awakening trees,   15
Hacked clean for better bearing, stand defaced
Suffering their brute necessities,
And how should the flesh not quail that span for span
Is mutilated more? In slow distaste
I fold my towel with what grace I can,   20
Not young and not renewable, but man.

GLOSSARY

RIVETED: Entranced, spellbound
MADE WHOLE: Made complete, reached perfection
HACKED CLEAN FOR BETTER BEARING: Pruned, old
growth cut away to make way for new

DEFACED: Damaged, disfigured
QUAIL: Shrink back, shy away
SPAN: Period of time
DISTASTE: Dislike, disapproval

●1stReading

1 What does the speaker see when he looks in the mirror?

2 Why is this poem set in February? Do the seasons have any relevance here?

3 Why does the poet mention Christ in stanza 2?

4 Describe the mood of the poet.

●●2ndReading

5 In stanza 1, the poet dramatically sets the scene. Where is he? What is he doing? What is happening around him and in his own mind?

6 What evidence is there in the poem to indicate that the speaker is tired of life?

7 What is the tone of the poem? What words and images help to portray this tone?

8 Is there any evidence of optimism? Where?

●●●3rdReading

9 In stanza 3, the poet examines the pruned trees. Does he accept this to be a good or a bad thing? What relevance does it have for him and for the rest of mankind?

10 Having 'looked my last on youth', how does the speaker face the future? Use quotation from and reference to the whole poem to support your answer.

11 How does the poem end? Is the speaker bitter and depressed, optimistic and joyful or resigned and defeated?

●●●●4thReading

12 This poem is harsh and cruelly honest. Discuss.

13 Examine the parallels between nature and man. Is the cycle of life the same for both? Use evidence from the poem to support your answer.

14 Is this a deeply personal poem or is the poet commenting on a more universal theme of ageing and a 'lack of spring' for humans?

15 What does the speaker see when he looks at the mirror on the wall? What does he see when he looks deeper into the mirror of his soul?

▼LinktoLanguage

16 Write an essay entitled
'My hopes and dreams for the future'
Or
'I looked in the mirror and saw things clearly'
Or
Write a speech for or against the motion that 'A society can be judged by the way it treats its elderly'.

Ambulances *Philip Larkin*

*Prescribed for the **Ordinary Level** exams in **2012** and **2014***

Closed like confessionals, they thread
Loud noons of cities, giving back
None of the glances they absorb.
Light glossy grey, arms on a plaque,
They come to rest at any kerb: 5
All streets in time are visited.

Then children strewn on steps or road,
Or women coming from the shops
Past smells of different dinners, see
A wild white face that overtops   10
Red stretcher-blankets momently
As it is carried in and stowed,

And sense the solving emptiness
That lies just under all we do,
And for a second get it whole,   15
So permanent and blank and true.
The fastened doors recede. Poor soul,
They whisper at their own distress;

For borne away in deadened air
May go the sudden shut of loss   20
Round something nearly at an end,
And what cohered in it across
The years, the unique random blend
Of families and fashions, there

At last begin to loosen. Far   25
From the exchange of love to lie
Unreachable inside a room
The traffic parts to let go by
Brings closer what is left to come,
And dulls to distance all we are.   30

PHILIP LARKIN • BORN 1922 IN COVENTRY, ENGLAND • HIS FATHER WAS THE CITY TREASURER • EDUCATED AT OXFORD UNIVERSITY • WORKED AS A LIBRARIAN ALL HIS LIFE • WAS THE UNOFFICIAL POET LAUREATE OF HULL IN THE 1950S AND 1960S • REFUSED THE OFFER TO BECOME OFFICIAL POET LAUREATE OF THE UK IN 1984 • WAS A SHY, INTROVERTED PERSON WHO LOVED READING AND WRITING NOVELS, POETRY AND JAZZ REVIEWS • AWARDED THE QUEEN'S GOLD MEDAL FOR POETRY IN 1964 • DIED OF CANCER IN 1985

■**Pre**Reading

1 Have you ever been in an ambulance? What were the circumstances? How did you feel?

●**1st**Reading

2 How does the poet create an air of secrecy around the ambulances?
3 Where do they go?
4 How do they appear?
5 How do the patients appear to onlookers?
6 What do the onlookers do?
7 What do they say?
8 What do they realise?
9 How do people react to the inevitability of their own impending tragedies?

●●**2nd**Reading

10 What is the mood of the poem?
11 How many sentences are in the poem?
12 Comment on the structure of the poem.

●●●**3rd**Reading

13 What does the poem tell us about mortality?
14 Larkin has been accused of being too detached from his subjects. Do you agree?

▼**Link**to**Language**

15 Write a story with the title 'Accident'.

The Explosion *Philip Larkin*

*Prescribed for the **Ordinary Level** exams in **2012** and **2014***

On the day of the explosion
Shadows pointed towards the pithead:
In the sun the slagheap slept.

Down the lane came men in pitboots
Coughing oath-edged talk and pipe-smoke,   5
Shouldering off the freshened silence.

One chased after rabbits; lost them;
Came back with a nest of lark's eggs;
Showed them; lodged them in the grasses.

So they passed in beards and moleskins,   10
Fathers, brothers, nicknames, laughter,
Through the tall gates standing open.

At noon, there came a tremor; cows
Stopped chewing for a second; sun,
Scarfed as in a heat-haze, dimmed.   15

The dead go on before us, they
Are sitting in God's house in comfort,
We shall see them face to face –

Plain as lettering in the chapels
It was said, and for a second   20
Wives saw men of the explosion

Larger than in life they managed –
Gold as on a coin, or walking
Somehow from the sun towards them,

One showing the eggs unbroken.   25

GLOSSARY

SLAGHEAP: Pile of waste matter from coal mining

MOLESKIN: Soft leather-like fabric

● 1st Reading

1. What is the mood at the start of the poem?
2. What type of day are the miners having?
3. Describe the men who are walking to work.
4. What happened at noon?
5. How did it affect nature?
6. How did it affect the people?

●● 2nd Reading

7. What happens to the poem after stanza 5?
8. Who is talking in stanza 6?

●●● 3rd Reading

9. What is the mood in the poem?
10. How does the poet create this mood?
11. Do you think the poet brings the event to life?

●●●● 4th Reading

12. Do you think the poet believes that the dead can communicate with the living?
13. What do you think of Larkin's attitude to death?

▼ Link to Language

14. Write a newspaper report that would be written the day after the explosion.

What Were They Like? *Denise Levertov*

*Prescribed for the **Ordinary Level** exams in **2011** and **2012***

1. Did the people of Vietnam
   use lanterns of stone?
2. Did they hold ceremonies
   to reverence the opening of buds?
3. Were they inclined to laughter? 5
4. Did they use bone and ivory,
   jade and silver, for ornament?
5. Had they an epic poem?
6. Did they distinguish between speech and singing?

1. Sir, their light hearts turned to stone. 10
   It is not remembered whether in gardens
   stone lanterns illumined pleasant ways.
2. Perhaps they gathered once to delight in blossom,
   but after the children were killed
   there were no more buds. 15
3. Sir, laughter is bitter to the burned mouth.
4. A dream ago, perhaps. Ornament is for joy.
   All the bones were charred.
5. It is not remembered. Remember,
   most were peasants; their life 20
   was in rice and bamboo.
   When peaceful clouds were reflected in the paddies
   and the water buffalo stepped surely along terraces,
   maybe fathers told their sons old tales.
   When bombs smashed those mirrors 25
   there was time only to scream.
6. There is an echo yet
   of their speech which was like a song.
   It was reported their singing resembled
   the flight of moths in moonlight. 30
   Who can say? It is silent now.

GLOSSARY

REVERENCE: Respect

JADE: A green, semi-precious stone

ILLUMINED: Lit up

PADDIES: Fields where rice is grown

DENISE LEVERTOV • BORN 1923 IN ILFORD, ESSEX, ENGLAND • WORKED AS A NURSE DURING THE WAR • EMIGRATED TO THE USA • TAUGHT AT STANFORD UNIVERSITY • ANTI-VIETNAM WAR PROTESTOR • COLLECTION: *BREATHING THE WATER*, 1987 • DIED IN 1997

■PreReading

1   What do you know about the Vietnam War?

●1stReading

2   What sense of the Vietnamese do we get from the answers that are given?
3   Are there any signs of hope for the future in this poem?
4   How do the priorities of the Vietnamese and the priorities of the questioner differ?

●●2ndReading

5   What is the tone of the questions?
6   How does the tone of the answers differ from that of the questions?
7   What is your favourite image or phrase in the poem?
8   Examine each of the metaphors individually—the light, the bud, laughter, decoration, heritage and culture—and say how and why each one is used in the poem.

●●●3rdReading

9   Have you ever before read a poem that took the format of a question-and-answer sequence? What do you think of this format? What do you think is the purpose of this format?
10   What do you think the poet is trying to achieve? Does she achieve this successfully?
11   How important is the last line?

●●●●4thReading

12   Could this poem have been written in a more traditional way? Would it have been as effective?
13   While keeping the integral message and spirit of the poem, rewrite it in a more traditional way.
14   Rewrite this poem in your notebook by putting each answer beneath its question. Does this make the poem easier to follow?
15   Were you moved by this poem? What feelings did you have? Can you explain why?

▼LinktoLanguage

16   If you were to be put in the questioner's place and had to ask six specific questions to find out 'what they were like', what questions would you ask?

Kidspoem/Bairnsang *Liz Lochhead*

*Prescribed for the **Ordinary Level** exam in 2014*

it wis January
and a gey dreich day
the first day Ah went to the school
so my Mum happed me up in ma
good navy-blue napp coat wi the rid tartan hood   5
birled a scarf aroon ma neck
pu'ed oan ma pixie an' my pawkies
it wis that bitter
said *noo ye'll no starve*
gie'd me a wee kiss and a kid-oan skelp oan the bum   10
and sent me aff across the playground
tae the place Ah'd learn to say
it was January
and a really dismal day
the first day I went to school   15
so my mother wrapped me up in my
best navy-blue top coat with the red tartan hood,
twirled a scarf around my neck,
pulled on my bobble-hat and mittens
it was so bitterly cold   20
said *now you won't freeze to death*
gave me a little kiss and a pretend slap on the bottom
and sent me off across the playground
to the place I'd learn to forget to say
it wis January   25
and a gey dreich day
the first day Ah went to the school
so my Mum happed me up in ma
good navy-blue napp coat wi the rid tartan hood,
birled a scarf aroon ma neck,   30
pu'ed oan ma pixie an' my pawkies
it wis that bitter.

Oh saying it was one thing
but when it came to writing it
in black and white   35
the way it had to be said
was as if you were posh, grown-up, male, English and dead.

LIZ LOCHHEAD
• BORN 1947 IN MOTHERWELL, SCOTLAND • STUDIED AT GLASGOW SCHOOL OF ART • SUCCESSFUL PLAYWRIGHT • WELL KNOWN FOR HER PERFORMANCE OF HER POETRY • LOVE, POLITICS, COMEDY AND CHILDHOOD ARE HER REGULAR THEMES • COLLECTION: *BAGPIPE MUZAK*, 1991

●1stReading

1 Read the first 12 lines out loud. How much do you understand? Is it easy to assume a Scottish accent when reading the way the words are written? What words and phrases do you not understand? Make a guess at the meanings.

2 Start the poem again and read up to line 24. What has changed in your understanding of the poem?

3 Now read the whole poem from start to finish. What is the poet telling the reader? What is the message of this poem?

●●2ndReading

4 Describe the morning of the poet's first day at school.

5 What did the poet learn in school?

6 Does the poet prefer the Scottish way of saying things or the 'proper' way? Find evidence to support your answer.

7 How does the poet feel when she recites the poem 'the way it had to be said'?

●●●3rdReading

8 What features of this poem indicate that it is a 'kidspoem'? What part is written in an adult voice and what part in a child's voice?

9 Is the title 'Kidspoem/Bairnsang' a good indicator of the subject matter? Why does the poet not call it 'Bairnsang/Kidspoem'? Was this just incidental or premeditated?

10 Is the poet proud of her nationality? Is there evidence of this in the poem? Does the poet see herself as Scottish or has her education anglicised her?

11 Poetry appeals, above all else, to the ear. Do you agree with this statement in reference to 'Kidspoem/Bairnsang'?

12 A central theme of this poem is nostalgia. What is the poet nostalgic about?

13 What is the poet's opinion of 'proper' poetry as outlined in the last verse?

14 Describe the poet's style of writing. Is it traditional? Unconventional? Why is all punctuation omitted? Does the absence of punctuation help or hinder your comprehension of the poem?

Badger *Michael Longley*
for Raymond Piper

*Prescribed for the **Ordinary Level** exam in **2013***

I
Pushing the wedge of his body
Between cromlech and stone circle,
He excavates down mine shafts
And back into the depths of the hill.

His path straight and narrow   5
And not like the fox's zig-zags,
The arc of the hare who leaves
A silhouette on the sky line.

Night's silence around his shoulders,
His face lit by the moon, he   10
Manages the earth with his paws,
Returns underground to die.

II
An intestine taking in
patches of dog's-mercury,
brambles, the bluebell wood;   15
a heel revolving acorns;
a head with a price on it
brushing cuckoo-spit, goose-grass;
a name that parishes borrow.

III
For the digger, the earth-dog   20
It is a difficult delivery
Once the tongs take hold,

Vulnerable his pig's snout
That lifted cow-pats for beetles,
Hedgehogs for the soft meat,   25

His limbs dragging after them
so many stones turned over,
The trees they tilted.

MICHAEL LONGLEY
BORN 1939 IN BELFAST TO ENGLISH PARENTS • HIS FATHER FOUGHT IN BOTH WORLD WARS AND HIS EXPERIENCES OF THE HORRORS OF WAR FEATURE IN HIS POETRY • STUDIED THE CLASSICS AT TRINITY COLLEGE, DUBLIN • WORKED AS A SCHOOL TEACHER • JOINED THE ARTS COUNCIL OF NORTHERN IRELAND IN 1970

●1st Reading

1 Describe the badger as he is presented in the first section of the poem. What kind of life does he live?
2 In section II, what points does the poet make as he examines the badger's life in more detail and highlights its closeness to nature?
3 What evidence is there that the badger is a nocturnal animal?
4 What happens in section III?

●●2nd Reading

5 The poet has presented us with an image of an animal both skilful and significant to Irish history. Where in the poem can you find evidence of both of these?
6 Why has the badger a price on his head?
7 Do you think that the poet is happy with the treatment of the badger in section III? Explain your answer.
8 Does the poet portray the badger as a strong, independent animal, a threatening presence or a helpless victim? Discuss.

●●●3rd Reading

9 It is obvious from the poem that the poet is a great admirer of nature. Find evidence to support this claim.
10 'The trees they tilted.' Explain.

▼Link to Language

11 Write a debate for or against the motion that 'The Celtic Tiger has not been kind to Irish wildlife and nature'
Or
Write a letter to a newspaper for or against the sport of hunting in modern-day Ireland
Or
Write an article for your school magazine entitled, 'The value of the countryside'.

Meeting point _Louis MacNeice_

Prescribed for the **Ordinary Level** _exam in_ **2012**

Time was away and somewhere else,
There were two glasses and two chairs
And two people with the one pulse
(Somebody stopped the moving stairs):
Time was away and somewhere else.   5

And they were neither up nor down;
The stream's music did not stop
Flowing through heather, limpid brown,
Although they sat in a coffee shop
And they were neither up nor down.   10

The bell was silent in the air
Holding its inverted poise—
Between the clang and clang a flower,
A brazen calyx of no noise:
The bell was silent in the air.   15

The camels crossed the miles of sand
That stretched around the cups and plates;
The desert was their own, they planned
To portion out the stars and dates:
The camels crossed the miles of sand.   20

Time was away and somewhere else.
The waiter did not come, the clock
Forgot them and the radio waltz
Came out like water from a rock:
Time was away and somewhere else.   25

Her fingers flicked away the ash
That bloomed again in tropic trees:
Not caring if the markets crash
When they had forests such as these,
Her fingers flicked away the ash.   30

God or whatever means the Good
Be praised that time can stop like this,
That what the heart has understood
Can verify in the body's peace
God or whatever means the Good.   35

Time was away and she was here
And life no longer what it was,
The bell was silent in the air
And all the room one glow because
Time was away and she was here.

40

GLOSSARY

CALYX: Ring of sepals covering a flower bud

LOUIS MacNEICE • BORN 1907 IN BELFAST • PART OF THE GENERATION OF 'THIRTIES POETS', WHICH INCLUDED W. H. AUDEN, STEPHEN SPENDER AND C. DAY LEWIS • WORKED FOR THE BBC AND WROTE PLAYS, RADIO PLAYS AS WELL AS POETRY • BEST KNOWN WORK IS *AUTUMN JOURNAL* • DIED 1963

●1stReading

1 Describe the scene in the first verse.
2 What does he mean by 'two people with one pulse'?
3 How do the two people feel about each other?
4 What has happened to time for them?
5 How does the outside world impact on them?
6 What happens to the sounds around them?

●●2ndReading

7 Do you think that the image of the camels is incongruous?
8 What do they represent?
9 Which is your favourite image in the poem?

●●●3rdReading

10 How does the poet use repetition in the poem?
11 What effect does this have?
12 Do you think this is an effective love poem? Explain your answer.

▼LinktoLanguage

13 Write a love letter.

Grandfather *Derek Mahon*

*Prescribed for the **Ordinary Level** exams in **2013** and **2014***

They brought him in on a stretcher from the world,
Wounded but humorous; and he soon recovered.
Boiler-rooms, row upon row of gantries rolled
Away to reveal the landscape of a childhood
Only he can recapture. Even on cold   5
Mornings he is up at six with a block of wood
Or a box of nails, discreetly up to no good
Or banging round the house like a four-year-old –

Never there when you call. But after dark
You hear his great boots thumping in the hall   10
And in he comes, as cute as they come. Each night
His shrewd eyes bolt the door and set the clock
Against the future, then his light goes out.
Nothing escapes him; he escapes us all.

GLOSSARY

GANTRIES: Overhead structures with a platform supporting
a travelling crane; an essential tool of shipbuilding

DEREK MAHON • BORN 1941 IN BELFAST • STUDIED FRENCH AT TRINITY COLLEGE, DUBLIN • TRAVELLED THROUGH FRANCE, CANADA AND THE USA SUPPORTING HIMSELF THROUGH TEACHING AND ODD JOBS • WORKED AS A SCRIPTWRITER FOR THE BBC AND AS A FREELANCE WRITER FOR A NUMBER OF NEWSPAPERS • WRITES IN A SERIOUS TONE USING SPECIFIC OCCURRENCES TO EXPLORE WIDER UNIVERSAL THEMES

●1stReading

1 What do you think the poet means in the first line of the poem?
2 Can you picture the grandfather in your head? What do you see?
3 What is his daily life like?
4 What was his childhood like?
5 Why does he come in after dark so loudly?

●●2ndReading

6 What does the poet mean by the phrase 'Nothing escapes him'?
7 List the adjectives that are used to describe him. What do they tell us about him?
8 What does the poet mean by the phrase 'he escapes us all'?
9 What is the overall mood of the poem?
10 What sounds help create that mood?

●●●3rdReading

11 Do you think the poet wishes he were more like his grandfather?
12 How do you think the speaker in the poem felt about his grandfather?
13 How does the grandfather feel about the future?

▼LinktoLanguage

14 Write a personal essay about a family member who has had a major influence on your life.

After the **Titanic** *Derek Mahon*

Prescribed for the **Ordinary Level** *exams in* **2013** *and* **2014**

They said I got away in a boat
And humbled me at the inquiry. I tell you
I sank as far that night as any
Hero. As I sat shivering on the dark water
I turned to ice to hear my costly   5
Life go thundering down in a pandemonium of
Prams, pianos, sideboards, winches,
Boilers bursting and shredded ragtime. Now I hide
In a lonely house behind the sea
Where the tide leaves broken toys and hatboxes   10
Silently at my door. The showers of
April, flowers of May mean nothing to me, nor the
Late light of June, when my gardener
Describes to strangers how the old man stays in bed
On seaward mornings after nights of   15
Wind, takes his cocaine and will see no one. Then it is
I drown again with all those dim
Lost faces I never understood, my poor soul
Screams out in the starlight, heart
Breaks loose and rolls down like a stone.   20
Include me in your lamentations.

GLOSSARY

PANDEMONIUM: Chaos and confusion
WINCHES: The cranks of wheels

RAGTIME: A type of jazz music
LAMENTATIONS: Outpourings of grief

■PreReading

1 What do you know about the *Titanic*? Did you see the movie? Do some research on what happened.

●1stReading

2 What happened to the speaker in the poem?
3 What happened to the other people on the ship?
4 What does the speaker do now?
5 Why does he stay in bed at this time?
6 Who is the speaker talking to?
7 How is the speaker treated by his community?
8 What does he want the reader to do?

●●2ndReading

9 Does the speaker feel sorry for himself?
10 Should he feel sorry for himself?
11 How often does he say 'I' or 'me' in the poem? What does that make us think about him?

12 Which senses are described in the poem?
13 What happens to his senses?

●●●3rdReading

14 Why did the speaker not understand those 'lost faces'?
15 Do you feel sorry for the speaker?
16 Do you think he is a selfish person?
17 The personal tragedy is more difficult than the public. Do you agree?
18 Why do you think the poet gave voice to this man?

▼LinktoLanguage

19 Write a diary entry for a survivor on the *Titanic*, recalling the night of the tragedy.
20 Write a newspaper article about the sinking of the *Titanic* as it would have been written at the time.

Antarctica *Derek Mahon*
For Richard Ryan

*Prescribed for the **Ordinary Level** exams in **2013** and **2014***

'I am just going outside and may be some time.'
The others nod, pretending not to know.
At the heart of the ridiculous, the sublime.

He leaves them reading and begins to climb,
Goading his ghost into the howling snow;   5
He is just going outside and may be some time.

The tent recedes beneath its crust of rime
And frostbite is replaced by vertigo:
At the heart of the ridiculous, the sublime.

Need we consider it some sort of crime,   10
This numb self-sacrifice of the weakest? No,
He is just going outside and may be some time –

In fact, for ever. Solitary enzyme,
Though the night yield no glimmer there will glow,
At the heart of the ridiculous, the sublime.   15

He takes leave of the earthly pantomime
Quietly, knowing it is time to go.
'I am just going outside and may be some time.'
At the heart of the ridiculous, the sublime.

GLOSSARY

SUBLIME: Lofty, majestic
GOADING: Urging on
RIME: Frost formed from cloud or fog

VERTIGO: Dizziness causing loss of balance
ENZYME: An enzyme causes a living organism to change but is not changed itself.

■ **Pre**Reading

1 Where is Antarctica?
2 What images does it conjure up for you?
3 Do some research on Scott of the Antarctic and Lawrence Oates.

● **1st**Reading

4 Where is Oates going in the first line?
5 What will happen to him after he leaves?
6 Does the poet say how Oates should be judged?

●● **2nd**Reading

7 What does an enzyme do?
8 What is Oates trying to do?
9 What is the mood in the poem?
10 How does the repetition help this mood?
11 What effect does the rhyme have on the mood of the poem?

●●● **3rd**Reading

12 What does the poet mean by the phrase 'At the heart of the ridiculous, the sublime'?
13 What does the poet mean by the phrase 'earthly pantomime'?

●●●● **4th**Reading

14 Do you think that Oates was a hero or a fool? Why?
15 What does the poet think?
16 Do you think this is a powerful poem?

▼ **Link**to**Language**

17 Write Oates' diary entry for the night before he left the camp.

Bearhugs *Roger McGough*

*Prescribed for the **Ordinary Level** exam in 2012*

Whenever my sons call round we hug each other.
Bearhugs. Both bigger than me and stronger
They lift me off my feet, crushing the life out of me.

They smell of oil paint and aftershave, of beer
Sometimes and tobacco, and of women   5
Whose memory they seem reluctant to wash away.

They haven't lived with me for years,
Since they were tiny, and so each visit
Is an assessment, a reassurance of love unspoken.

I look for some resemblance to my family.   10
Seize on an expression, a lifted eyebrow,
A tilt of the head, but cannot see myself.

Though like each other, they are not like me.
But I can see in them something of my father.
Uncles, home on leave during the war.   15

At three or four, I loved those straightbacked men
Towering above me, smiling and confident.
The whole world before them. Or so it seemed.

I look at my boys, slouched in armchairs
They have outgrown. See Tom in army uniform   20
And Finn in air force blue. Time is up.

Bearhugs. They lift me off my feet
And fifty years fall away. One son
After another, crushing the life into me.

ROGER McGOUGH

• BORN 1937 IN LIVERPOOL, ENGLAND • EDUCATED AT HULL UNIVERSITY • ALONG WITH ADRIAN HENRI AND BRIAN PATTEN, KNOWN AS THE MERSEYBEAT POETS • WELL KNOWN FOR THE PERFORMANCE OF HIS POETRY • WRITES FUNNY, ACCESSIBLE POEMS ABOUT REAL CONCERNS • RECENTLY HE HAS USED HIS POETRY TO PROMOTE HUMAN RIGHTS

● 1st Reading

1   What is a bearhug?
2   Do you get an impression of the two sons? What do you think they look like? What are their personalities like?
3   Is the poet disappointed that they don't look like him?
4   What type of men were his father and uncles?
5   How do the boys remind the poet of his uncles and father?
6   In what ways are they different?

●● 2nd Reading

7   How do the 'fifty years fall away'?
8   How does the final verse mirror the first verse? What differences occur?

●●● 3rd Reading

9   How does the poet's time with the sons make him feel?
10 Do you think that there is a hint of regret in the poem? Where might this be?

▼ Link to Language

11 Write a story called 'Lost Memories' using the Aesthetic Use of Language.

When I Consider *John Milton*

*Prescribed for the **Ordinary Level** exam in **2013***

When I consider how my light is spent,
E're half my days, in this dark world and wide,
And that one Talent which is death to hide,
Lodg'd with me useless, though my Soul more bent
To serve therewith my Maker, and present   5
My true account, least he returning chide,
Doth God exact day-labour, light deny'd,
I fondly ask; But patience to prevent
That murmur, soon replies, God doth not need
Either man's work or his own gifts, who best   10
Bear his milde yoak, they serve him best, his State
Is Kingly. Thousands at his bidding speed
And post o're Land and Ocean without rest:
They also serve who only stand and waite.

GLOSSARY

CONSIDER: Think about, ponder
MY LIGHT IS SPENT: My eyesight is gone
ONE TALENT: His writing talent (referring to the Parable of Talents in the Bible: a servant buries the talent God gives him instead of using it and making the most of it. He is punished by God)
LODG'D: God lodged (invested) a talent in Milton

MORE BENT: Determined
MY MAKER: God
CHIDE: Scold, give out to
DAY-LABOUR: A full day's work
FONDLY: Foolishly
BEAR HIS MILDE YOAK: Put up with the little burdens
MURMUR: Quiet complaint
HIS BIDDING: Doing what he asks

JOHN MILTON • BORN 1608 IN LONDON • EDUCATED AT ST PAUL'S SCHOOL AND CHRIST CHURCH COLLEGE, CAMBRIDGE, RECEIVING A BA IN 1629 AND AN MA IN 1632 • RECEIVED THE NICKNAME 'THE LADY OF CHRIST'S' IN CHRIST CHURCH COLLEGE FOR HIS LONG FLOWING HAIR AND HIS GENTLE, MANNERLY AND POLITE WAYS • EARLY ATTEMPTS AT POETRY CONSISTED OF PARAPHRASING THE PSALMS • WROTE IN ENGLISH AND IN LATIN • PREDOMINANTLY RELIGIOUS THEMES • TRAVELLED TO FRANCE AND ITALY, WHERE HE MET GALILEO • BECAME POLITICALLY MOTIVATED ON HIS RETURN TO ENGLAND, COMMENTING ON THE RELIGIOUS AND POLITICAL UPHEAVAL AND THE CIVIL WAR • WROTE PAMPHLETS IN SUPPORT OF DIVORCE AFTER HIS HASTY MARRIAGE TO MARY POWELL IN 1642 • REJOINED HER IN 1645 • SUPPORTER OF OLIVER CROMWELL AND OF THE EXECUTION OF KING CHARLES IN 1649 • BECAME CROMWELL'S SECRETARY FOR FOREIGN TONGUES IN 1649 • BECAME BLIND IN 1652; MARY DIED HAVING BORNE HIM THREE DAUGHTERS • MARRIED KATHERINE WOODSTOCK IN 1655, BUT SHE DIED IN CHILDBIRTH IN 1658 • HIS POLITICAL CAREER ENDED IN 1660 WITH THE RETURN OF THE MONARCHY • RETURNED TO WRITING POETRY AND WROTE HIS TWO GREAT MASTERPIECES: *PARADISE LOST*, 1667 AND *PARADISE REGAINED*, 1671 • DIED IN 1674

■**Pre**Reading

1 Do you think God would be happy with how you have used the talents given to you?

2 What is your impression of God / a higher being? From where is this impression formed? What influences our view of God — parents? The Bible? Television?

●**1st**Reading

3 Milton is concerned that God will be angry with him for not making full use of his talent for writing. Why has he not fully used his talent? Where in the poem do you see this?

4 What is Milton's impression of the world?

5 Milton compares his relationship with God in banking terms: 'lodg'd' and 'my true account'. Explain these terms and Milton's use of them.

6 Where does Milton refer to his blindness?

7 What is the message of this poem?

●●**2nd**Reading

8 What are the main questions Milton is asking in the octet?

9 Trace the development of thought through the full poem. Where are there changes?

10 What is your impression of Milton? What words or images support your view?

11 What kind of picture does Milton present of God? Is this how you see God / a higher being?

12 Is the message of this poem a modern topic or is it a topic firmly rooted in the past?

●●●**3rd**Reading

13 What evidence is there in the poem of the poet's profound religious faith?

14 What is the meaning of the final line?

15 Light, banking and a divine king are three dominant images in this poem. Discuss each one using words and phrases to build your picture of each.

16 Outline the use Milton makes of the Petrarchan sonnet form in this poem.

All Day Long Noel Monahan

*Prescribed for the **Ordinary Level** exams in **2011** and **2012***

At school we see
Ink spilt on the floor.
Children get bored
Counting, conjugating verbs ....
All day long.   5

You never know
When some disappear
You never know
Where to find them.

Teachers are patient,   10
See with their eyes,
Children, not easily tamed,
See with their hearts,
And are made to sit in rows,
In blue and navy uniforms.   15

How can you know
When some disappear?
How can you know
Where to find them?

Principals, Deputy Principals,   20
Constantly counting the children,
Mornings and afternoons
Names and numbers put on files.

One never knows
When they go missing   25
One never knows
Where to find them.

NOEL MONAHAN · BORN 1948 · RETIRED AS A TEACHER IN SEPTEMBER 2008 · IN 2001 HE WON THE PRESTIGIOUS SEACAT NATIONAL POETRY AWARD, ORGANISED BY POETRY IRELAND · COLLECTIONS INCLUDE *THE FUNERAL GAME, OPPOSITE WALLS, SNOWFIRE, CURSE OF THE BIRDS* · HIS POETRY HAS BEEN TRANSLATED INTO A NUMBER OF LANGUAGES

●**1st**Reading

1 What impression do we get of children in the first verse?
2 What does the poet mean by the word 'disappear'?
3 Where do they go to?
4 How are they allowed to disappear?

●●**2nd**Reading

5 What are the differences between teachers and children?
6 How do young children feel about having to 'sit in rows/ in blue and navy uniforms.'?
7 What do principals and deputy principals spend their time doing?
8 Why do they do this?

●●●**3rd**Reading

9 What can they do about missing children?
10 What is the tone of this poem?
11 Do you think the poet is talking about himself?
12 Do you think he was a missing child or a teacher?

▼**Link**to**Language**

13 Write a piece of personal writing about your memories of primary school.

Strawberries *Edwin Morgan*

*Prescribed for the **Ordinary Level** exam in **2011***

There were never strawberries
like the ones we had
that sultry afternoon
sitting on the step
of the open french window   5
facing each other
your knees held in mine
the blue plates in our laps
the strawberries glistening
in the hot sunlight   10
we dipped them in sugar
looking at each other
not hurrying the feast
for one to come
the empty plates   15
laid on the stone together
with the two forks crossed
and I bent towards you
sweet in that air
in my arms   20
abandoned like a child
from your eager mouth
the taste of strawberries
in my memory
lean back again let me love you   25

let the sun beat
on our forgetfulness
one hour of all
the heat intense
and summer lightening   30
on the Kilpatrick hills

let the storm wash the plates

EDWIN MORGAN
• BORN 1920 IN GLASGOW, SCOTLAND • TAUGHT FOR MANY YEARS AT GLASGOW UNIVERSITY • HAS TRANSLATED POETRY FROM MANY LANGUAGES • HE WAS FIRST PUBLISHED IN 1952 • COLLECTION: *SELECTED POEMS*, 1985

● 1st Reading

1 Describe the scene of the poem in your own words.
2 What is the mood of the two people?
3 What type of relationship do they have?
4 Why were there never strawberries like the ones they had that day?
5 What happens as the poem develops?

●● 2nd Reading

6 How does the weather affect their mood?
7 What is your favourite image in the poem?
8 What are the dominant sounds in the poem?
9 How do they affect the mood?

●●● 3rd Reading

10 Why is the last line left on its own?
11 Why doesn't the poet use punctuation?
12 What effect does this have?

●●●● 4th Reading

13 In this poem the poet doesn't try to make a message as much as a mood. Do you agree?

▼ Link to Language

14 Write a story containing the line 'That sultry afternoon sitting on the step of the french window'.

Anseo *Paul Muldoon*

*Prescribed for the **Ordinary Level** exams in **2011**, **2012** and **2013***

When the Master was calling the roll
At the primary school in Collegelands,
You were meant to call back Anseo
And raise your hand
As your name occurred.   5
Anseo, meaning here, here and now,
All present and correct,
Was the first word of Irish I spoke.
The last name on the ledger
Belonged to Joseph Mary Plunkett Ward   10
And was followed, as often as not,
By silence, knowing looks,
A nod and a wink, the Master's droll
'And where's our little Ward-of-court?'

I remember the first time he came back   15
The Master had sent him out
Along the hedges
To weigh up for himself and cut
A stick with which he would be beaten.
After a while, nothing was spoken;   20
He would arrive as a matter of course
With an ash-plant, a salley-rod.
Or, finally, the hazel-wand
He had whittled down to a whip-lash,
Its twist of red and yellow lacquers   25
Sanded and polished,
And altogether so delicately wrought
That he had engraved his initials on it.

I last met Joseph Mary Plunkett Ward
In a pub just over the Irish border.   30
He was living in the open,
In a secret camp
On the other side of the mountain.
He was fighting for Ireland,
Making things happen.   35
And he told me, Joe Ward,
Of how he had risen through the ranks

To Quartermaster, Commandant:
How every morning at parade
His volunteers would call back Anseo
And raise their hands
As their names occurred.   40

PAUL MULDOON • BORN 1951 IN PORTADOWN, CO. ARMAGH • RAISED IN A SMALL VILLAGE CALLED THE MOY, WHICH FEATURED IN MANY OF HIS POEMS • EDUCATED AT QUEEN'S UNIVERSITY, BELFAST • WORKED FOR THE BBC • WORKS AS A UNIVERSITY LECTURER IN THE USA • COLLECTIONS: *QUOOF*, 1984; *MADOC*, 1990 • OPERA: *SHINING BROW*

■ PreReading

1 What are your own memories of primary school, your teachers, friends, characters in your own class, especially the ones that got into a lot of trouble?

● 1stReading

2 What does the word 'anseo' mean? When was it used in school?
3 Describe the master. What does his title say about him?
4 Why are Ward's forenames important?
5 What is Ward's life like at the end of the poem?
6 What do you imagine his soldiers' lives are like under his command?

●● 2ndReading

7 Why does Ward take such care with the stick?
8 The narrator of the poem and the master use puns. Isolate each pun and explain to what they are referring.

●●● 3rdReading

9 The tone in the first verse is very unemotional. What effect does this have on your reading of the poem? Does the tone change later on? If so, how?
10 What contradictions are there in the poem?
11 How do the first verse and last verse mirror each other? Why does the poet do this?

●●●● 4thReading

12 'What goes around comes around.' Do you think that this saying is relevant to this poem?
13 W. H. Auden said that 'Poetry makes nothing happen'. Compare that idea to Ward's statement that he was 'making things happen'.

Moonshine *Richard Murphy*

*Prescribed for the **Ordinary Level** exams in **2011** and **2012***

> To think
> I must be alone:
> To love
> We must be together.
>
> To think I love you   5
> When I'm alone
> More than I think of you
> When we're together.
>
> I cannot think
> Without loving   10
> Or love
> Without thinking.
>
> Alone I love
> To think of us together:
> Together I think   15
> I'd love to be alone.

RICHARD MURPHY • BORN 1927 IN CO. MAYO • LIVES IN CO. DUBLIN • COLLECTIONS: *THE BATTLE OF AUGHRIM*, 1968; *HIGH ISLAND*, 1974; *THE MIRROR WALL*, 1989 • AUTOBIOGRAPHY: *THE KICK*, 2001

■**Pre**Reading

1 What is moonshine?
2 Do you associate it with the theme of love?
3 What do you associate it with?

●**1st**Reading

4 Isolate the poet's alone moments from his together ones. Is there an obvious difference?
5 Do you think he prefers being alone or together?
6 Why do you think he needs to be alone to think?

●●**2nd**Reading

7 Explain the third verse.
8 How would the receiver of this poem feel?
9 How would you feel if your lover sent you this poem?

●●●**3rd**Reading

10 This poem has been described as being deceptively simple. Do you agree?

Wolves in the Zoo *Howard Nemerov*

*Prescribed for the **Ordinary Level** exam in 2014*

They look like big dogs badly drawn, drawn wrong.
A legend on their cage tells us there is
No evidence that any of their kind
Has ever attacked man, woman, or child.

Now it turns out there were no babies dropped   5
In sacrifice, delaying tactics, from
Siberian sleds; now it turns out, so late,
That Little Red Ridinghood and her Gran

Were the aggressors with the slavering fangs
And tell-tale tails; now it turns out at last   10
That grey wolf and timber wolf are near extinct,
Done out of being by the tales we tell

Told us by Nanny in the nursery;
Young sparks we were, to set such forest fires
As blazed from story into history   15
And put such bounty on their wolvish heads

As brought the few survivors to our terms,
Surrendered in happy Babylon among
The peacock dusting off the path of dust,
The tiger pacing in the stripéd shade.   20

HOWARD NEMEROV • BORN 1920 IN NEW YORK, USA • SERVED IN THE CANADIAN AND AMERICAN AIR FORCES IN THE SECOND WORLD WAR • WAS US POET LAUREATE FROM 1988 TO 1990 • HAS BEEN COMPARED TO ROBERT FROST • DIED IN 1991

● **1st**Reading

1 What does the first line tell us about the wolves?
2 Does the second sentence surprise you? Why?
3 What is the story that the poet refers to at the start of the second verse?
4 Why does he call Red Ridinghood and her Gran 'aggressors'?
5 Where are the wolves now?

●● **2nd**Reading

6 What has the overall effect of all the fairytales been on wolves?
7 What does the poet mean when he says 'brought the few survivors to our terms'?
8 Which sounds dominate the poem? What effect do they have?
9 How does the poet use alliteration in the poem?

●●● **3rd**Reading

10 Do you think that humans have given wolves a fair deal throughout history?

▼ **Link**to**Language**

11 Write an article for a tabloid newspaper about a celebrity who has been harmed by rumours.

Problems *Julie O'Callaghan*

*Prescribed for the **Ordinary Level** exam in **2013***

Take weeds for example.
Like how they will overrun
your garden and your life
if you don't obliterate them.
But forget about weeds   5
– what about leaves?
Snails use them as handy
bridges to your flowers
and hordes of thuggish slugs
will invade – ever thought about *that*?   10
We won't even go into
how leaves block up the gutters.
I sure hope you aren't neglecting
any puddles of water in your bathtub
– discoloration will set in.   15
There is the wasp problem,
the storms problem, the grass
growing-between-the-bricks-in-the-driveway problem.
Then there's the remembering to
lock-all-the-windows problem.   20
Hey, knuckleheads!
I guess you just don't appreciate
how many problems there are.

JULIE O'CALLAGHAN • BORN 1954 IN CHICAGO, ILLINOIS, USA • LIVES IN NAAS, CO. KILDARE • ALSO WRITES FOR YOUNG PEOPLE • COLLECTIONS: *EDIBLE ANECDOTES*, 1983; *WHAT'S WHAT*, 1992 • COLLECTION FOR YOUNG PEOPLE: *TAKING MY PEN FOR A WALK*, 1988

●1stReading

1 List the problems identified in the poem.
2 How would you rate these problems on a scale ranging from minor to serious?
3 Is the tone of the poem serious or tongue-in-cheek?

●●2ndReading

4 Is there evidence of exaggeration in the poem? Why does the poet do this?
5 Can weeds overrun 'your garden and your life'?
6 To whom is the poem addressed?
7 Comment on the poet's use of the term 'Knuckleheads'. What does this tell us about the speaker in the poem? What does it tell us about the person / people she is addressing?

●●●3rdReading

8 As the poem progresses the speaker seems to get increasingly frustrated. Comment on her state of mind from the start of the poem.
9 Is the speaker serious when she exclaims 'you just don't appreciate how many problems there are'? Explain your answer.
10 Do you think that this poem is the full story or just some of the 'rant'? Explain your answer.

11 What do you find humorous about the poem?

▼**Link**to**Language**

12 Write a rant about some of the problems you feel are impacting on your life.

The Net *Julie O'Callaghan*

*Prescribed for the **Ordinary Level** exams in **2011** and **2014***

I am the Lost Classmate
being hunted down the superhighways
and byways of infinite cyber-space.
How long can I evade the class committee
searching for my lost self?   5

I watch the list
of Found Classmates
grow by the month.
Corralled into a hotel ballroom
festooned with 70s paraphernalia,   10

bombarded with atmospheric
hit tunes, the Captured Classmates
from Sullivan High School
will celebrate thirty years
of freedom from each other.   15

I peek at the message board:
my locker partner,
out in California, looks forward
to being reunited with
her old school chums.   20

Wearing a disguise, I calculate
the numbers of months left
for me to do what I do best,
what I've always done:
slip through the net.   25

■PreReading

1 What are the different meanings of the word 'net'? What is the word short for?

●1stReading

2 Find out about the 'Lost Classmate' website. What does it do?

3 Describe the scene that she expects to find at her reunion?

4 Why does she call them 'Captured Classmates'?

5 What does her phrase 'thirty years of freedom from each other' tell us about her attitude to her old school friends?

6 What does her locker partner think of the event?

●●2ndReading

7 Why does she need to wear a disguise on the internet? How would she do this?

8 How does the writer play with language throughout the poem?

9 Do you think she had happy schooldays?

10 What type of person do you think the speaker in the poem is?

11 Do you think that this poem is sad or funny?

▼LinktoLanguage

12 Write a letter to a friend from primary school who you haven't seen in a few years.

The Sun *Mary Oliver*

*Prescribed for the **Ordinary Level** exams in **2012** and **2013***

Have you ever seen
anything
in your life
more wonderful

than the way the sun,   5
every evening,
relaxed and easy,
floats toward the horizon

and into the clouds or the hills,
or the rumpled sea,   10
and is gone –
and how it slides again

out of the blackness,
every morning,
on the other side of the world,   15
like a red flower

streaming upward on its heavenly oils,
say, on a morning in early summer,
at its perfect imperial distance –
and have you ever felt for anything   20

such wild love –
do you think there is anywhere, in any language,
a word billowing enough
for the pleasure

that fills you,   25
as the sun
reaches out,
as it warms you

as you stand there,
empty-handed –   30
or have you too
turned from this world –

MARY OLIVER • BORN 1935 IN MAPLE HEIGHTS, OHIO, USA • HER COLLECTION *NEW AND SELECTED POEMS* (1992) WON THE NATIONAL BOOK AWARD • KNOWN FOR BEING A NATURALIST POET

■ PreReading

1 Pay attention to the sun setting. How does it look to you?
2 Is the sun setting worthy of a poem?

● 1stReading

3 How is the sun described?
4 What is the most effective image in the poem?

●● 2ndReading

5 What are the rhetorical questions (if any) that she asks?
6 What do you think she means by the phrase 'wild love'?

7 Does the poem change in tone in the final six lines?

●●● 3rdReading

8 Do you think that this is a positive or a negative poem?
9 Why does the poet write the poem in only one sentence?
10 What effect does this have?

▼ LinktoLanguage

11 Write a story based on the image below.

Will We Work Together? *Marge Piercy*

*Prescribed for the **Ordinary Level** exams in **2013** and **2014***

You wake in the early grey
morning in bed alone and curse
me, that I am only
sometimes there. But when
I am with you, I light   5
up the corners, I am bright
as a fireplace roaring
with love, every bone in my back
and my fingers is singing
like a teakettle on the boil.   10
My heart wags me, a big dog
with a bigger tail. I am printed
With your face like
a new coin. My body wears
sore before I can express   15
on yours the smallest part
of what moves me. Words
shred. Poems
are refuse. I want to make
with you some bold new   20
thing to stand in the marketplace
like a statue of a goddess
laughing, armed and wearing
flowers and feathers.
Like sheep whose hair makes   25
blankets and coats, I want
to make from this fierce sturdy
rampant love some useful thing.

MARGE PIERCY • BORN 1936 IN DETROIT, MICHIGAN, USA • AUTHOR OF 17 NOVELS, INCLUDING *GONE TO SOLDIERS*, *BRAIDED LIVES*, *THE LONGINGS OF WOMEN* AND *WOMAN ON THE EDGE OF TIME* • PUBLISHED 17 VOLUMES OF POETRY • PROMINENT POLITICAL ACTIVIST

●1stReading

1 What is the mood in the first four lines?
2 What changes with the presence of the speaker?
3 How does this affect the person referred to as 'You'?
4 What type of person is the speaker?

●●2ndReading

5 Why does the poet use the image of the dog?
6 Is this an effective image?
7 What does the speaker try to express?
8 Why is language deemed obsolete by the speaker?
9 What does the speaker want?

●●●3rdReading

10 What does the poet intend with the image of the statue?
11 What does this represent to you?
12 Are the words 'fierce sturdy' a good description of love? What type of love?

●●●●4thReading

13 How many sentences are in the poem?
14 How does the flow of the poem change?
15 What effect do the two short sentences in the middle have?

▼LinktoLanguage

16 Write the lover's response to this poem.

Poppies in July *Sylvia Plath*

*Prescribed for the **Ordinary Level** exams in **2012**, **2013** and **2014***

Little poppies, little hell flames,
Do you do no harm?

You flicker. I cannot touch you.
I put my hands among the flames. Nothing burns.

And it exhausts me to watch you   5
Flickering like that, wrinkly and clear red, like the skin of a mouth.

A mouth just bloodied.
Little bloody skirts!

There are fumes that I cannot touch.
Where are your opiates, your nauseous capsules?   10

If I could bleed, or sleep! ——
If my mouth could marry a hurt like that!

Or your liquors seep to me, in this glass capsule,
Dulling and stilling.

But colorless. Colorless.   15

GLOSSARY

POPPIES: Summer flowers, often red in colour, associated with the drug opium, which is made from the seeds
OPIATES: Sedative drug containing opium

NAUSEOUS: Feeling of sickness
CAPSULES: Small soluble case containing medicine
MARRY: Join with

SYLVIA PLATH
• BORN 1932 IN BOSTON, USA • STUDIED AT SMITH COLLEGE AND THEN AT CAMBRIDGE • MARRIED THE POET TED HUGHES IN 1956 • SUFFERED FROM DEPRESSION AND HAD AN UNSTABLE LIFE • HUGHES LEFT HER AND HER TWO YOUNG CHILDREN IN 1962 • SHE KILLED HERSELF ON 11 FEBRUARY 1963

■PreReading

1 What do you expect a poem called 'Poppies in July' might be about? What images are conjured in the mind and what feelings do you associate with summer flowers?

●1stReading

2 What is the speaker's state of mind?

3 Does the speaker see the beauty in the flowers or does she see something else?

4 Describe the flowers.

5 Why does the poet put her hands among the flames? What does she expect to happen and how does she feel when 'Nothing burns'? Why can she not touch the flames? What can this mean?

6 What effect does the phrase 'little hell flames' have? Do you think this is accurate and apt?

●●2ndReading

7 Why is watching the flowers so exhausting?

8 Why is the poet talking directly to the flowers?

9 The poet wants to 'bleed, or sleep'. From what, do you think, is she trying to escape? Are there any hints in the poem? What is she yearning for?

10 The poem highlights the vivid colour of the poppies and of the blood. What happens when they lose their colour?

11 Why does she repeat the word 'colorless' in the last line?

●●●3rdReading

12 Why does she write in couplets?

13 Why is the last line on its own?

14 Identify what you believe to be the strongest image in the poem and explain your answer.

15 Did you like this poem? Discuss.

▼LinktoLanguage

16 'If only I could disappear.' Write a short story containing these words.

Child *Sylvia Plath*

*Prescribed for the **Ordinary Level** exams in 2012, 2013 and 2014*

Your clear eye is the one absolutely beautiful thing.
I want to fill it with color and ducks,
The zoo of the new

Whose names you meditate –
April snowdrop, Indian pipe,   5
Little

Stalk without wrinkle,
Pool in which images
Should be grand and classical

Not this troublous   10
Wringing of hands, this dark
Ceiling without a star.

●1stReading

1 What does the poet wish for her child?

●●2ndReading

2 Why does she want to 'fill it [his eye] with color and ducks'?

3 What do the ducks and the zoo represent to you?

4 April Snowdrop and Indian Pipe are flowers. Why does she include these in the poem?

5 What does she mean by 'grand and classical' images?

6 What do you think about the first line?

7 Think of all these images together. What do they represent now?

●●●3rdReading

8 How do you think the poet was feeling before the poem was written?

9 Do you think the poet's strategy would work?

●●●●4thReading

10 What is the atmosphere in the poem?

11 Do you think she is a good mother?

The Arrival of the Bee Box *Sylvia Plath*

*Prescribed for the **Ordinary Level** exams in **2013** and **2014***

I ordered this, this clean wood box
Square as a chair and almost too heavy to lift.
I would say it was the coffin of a midget
Or a square baby
Were there not such a din in it.   5

The box is locked, it is dangerous.
I have to live with it overnight
And I can't keep away from it.
There are no windows, so I can't see what is in there.
There is only a little grid, no exit.   10

I put my eye to the grid.
It is dark, dark,
With the swarmy feeling of African hands
Minute and shrunk for export,
Black on black, angrily clambering.   15

How can I let them out?
It is the noise that appals me most of all,
The unintelligible syllables.
It is like a Roman mob,
Small, taken one by one, but my god, together!   20

I lay my ear to furious Latin.
I am not a Caesar.
I have simply ordered a box of maniacs.
They can be sent back.
They can die, I need feed them nothing, I am the owner.   25

I wonder how hungry they are.
I wonder if they would forget me
If I just undid the locks and stood back and turned into a tree.
There is the laburnum, its blond colonnades,
And the petticoats of the cherry.   30

They might ignore me immediately
In my moon suit and funeral veil.
I am no source of honey
So why should they turn on me?
Tomorrow I will be sweet God, I will set them free.

35

The box is only temporary.

•1stReading

1 What opinion does the poet have of the box when she sees it first?
2 What is her initial impression of the bees themselves?
3 What does she see when she looks into the box?
4 How does she feel in the fifth verse?
5 Do her feelings change in the sixth verse?
6 If so, why?
7 What does she decide to do?

••2ndReading

8 Describe the sounds the bees make.
9 How do these sounds make her feel?
10 What is your favourite image in the poem?

•••3rdReading

11 What do you think would happen if she 'just undid the locks and stood back and turned into a tree'?
12 Why do you think the poet wrote this poem?
13 Why do you think that the last line is on its own?
14 What does the poet mean by the phrase 'I will be sweet God'?

Aunt Jennifer's Tigers *Adrienne Rich*

*Prescribed for the **Ordinary Level** exams in **2011**, **2012** and **2013***

Aunt Jennifer's tigers prance across a screen,
Bright topaz denizens of a world of green.
They do not fear the men beneath the tree;
They pace in sleek chivalric certainty.

Aunt Jennifer's fingers fluttering through her wool   5
Find even the ivory needle hard to pull.
The massive weight of Uncle's wedding band
Sits heavily upon Aunt Jennifer's hand.

When Aunt is dead, her terrified hands will lie
Still ringed with ordeals she was mastered by.   10
The tigers in the panel that she made
Will go on prancing, proud and unafraid.

GLOSSARY

TOPAZ: Yellow
DENIZENS: Those that frequent a particular place

CHIVALRIC: Noble, honourable

ADRIENNE RICH • BORN 1929 IN BALTIMORE, MARYLAND, USA • COLLECTIONS: *A CHANGE OF WORLD*, 1951; *THE FACT OF A DOORFRAME*, 1984 AND 2002; *AN ATLAS OF A DIFFICULT WORLD*, 1991; *MIDNIGHT SALVAGE*, 1999; *FOX*, 2001; AND *THE SCHOOL AMONG THE RUINS*, 2004

Questions on the poems of Adrienne Rich have not been included for copyright reasons.

The Uncle Speaks in the Drawing Room
Adrienne Rich

*Prescribed for the **Ordinary Level** exams in **2011**, **2012** and **2013***

I have seen the mob of late
Standing sullen in the square,
Gazing with a sullen stare
At window, balcony, and gate.
Some have talked in bitter tones,   5
Some have held and fingered stones.

These are follies that subside.
Let us consider, none the less,
Certain frailties of glass
Which, it cannot be denied,   10
Lead in times like these to fear
For crystal vase and chandelier.

Not that missiles will be cast;
None as yet dare lift an arm.
But the scene recalls a storm   15
When our grandsire stood aghast
To see his antique ruby bowl
Shivered on a thunder-roll.

Let us only bear in mind
How these treasures handed down   20
From a calmer age passed on
Are in the keeping of our kind.
We stand between the dead glass-blowers
And murmurings of missile-throwers.

Trying to Talk with a Man *Adrienne Rich*

*Prescribed for the **Ordinary Level** exams in **2011** and **2012***

Out in this desert we are testing bombs,

that's why we came here.

Sometimes I feel an underground river
forcing its way between deformed cliffs
an acute angle of understanding   5
moving itself like a locus of the sun
into this condemned scenery.

What we've had to give up to get here—
whole LP collections, films we starred in
playing in the neighborhoods, bakery windows   10
full of dry, chocolate-filled Jewish cookies,
the language of love-letters, of suicide notes,
afternoons on the riverbank
pretending to be children

Coming out to this desert   15
we meant to change the face of
driving among dull green succulents
walking at noon in the ghost town
surrounded by a silence

that sounds like the silence of the place   20
except that it came with us
and is familiar
and everything we were saying until now
was an effort to blot it out—
Coming out here we are up against it   25

Out here I feel more helpless
with you than without you
You mention the danger
and list the equipment
we talk of people caring for each other   30
in emergencies—laceration, thirst—
but you look at me like an emergency

Your dry heat feels like power
your eyes are stars of a different magnitude

116 SIGNS

they reflect lights that spell out: EXIT
when you get up and pace the floor

talking of the danger
as if it were not ourselves
as if we were testing anything else.

Sonnet 18 *William Shakespeare*

*Prescribed for the **Ordinary Level** exam in **2013***

Shall I compare thee to a summer's day?
Thou art more lovely and more temperate.
Rough winds do shake the darling buds of May,
And summer's lease hath all too short a date.
Sometime too hot the eye of heaven shines,   5
And often is his gold complexion dimmed;
And every fair from fair sometime declines,
By chance, or nature's changing course, untrimmed;
But thy eternal summer shall not fade,
Nor lose possession of that fair thou ow'st,   10
Nor shall Death brag thou wander'st in his shade,
When in eternal lines to time thou grow'st.
   So long as men can breathe or eyes can see,
   So long lives this, and this gives life to thee.

GLOSSARY

THEE: You
TEMPERATE: Even-tempered/self controlled
SUMMER'S LEASE … SHORT A DATE: The length of summer is too short
EYE OF HEAVEN: Sun

DIMMED: Clouded over
THY ETERNAL SUMMER: Your beauty is forever
THOU OW'ST: You own
ETERNAL LINES: The lines of the sonnet will last forever

WILLIAM SHAKESPEARE · BORN 1564 IN STRATFORD-UPON-AVON, ENGLAND · BACKGROUND NOT VERY CLEAR · FATHER WAS A LOCAL MAYOR AND JUSTICE OF THE PEACE · EDUCATED AT THE KING'S NEW SCHOOL · TRAINED IN FORMAL CLASSICAL ROMAN LITERATURE · JOINED A GROUP OF TRAVELLING ACTORS IN LONDON AND BECAME KNOWN BOTH AS A GOOD ACTOR AND PLAYWRIGHT · WAS PART OF THE MOST SUCCESSFUL THEATRICAL COMPANY OF HIS TIME · MARRIED ANNE HATHAWAY IN 1582; SHE REMAINED IN STRATFORD WHILE HE RETURNED TO LONDON · WROTE 37 PLAYS — COMEDIES, TRAGEDIES AND HISTORIES — AND 154 SONNETS · WAS PART-OWNER OF THE GLOBE THEATRE · DIED IN 1616

●1stReading

1 To whom do you think the sonnet is addressed?

2 What do you think the poet feels for this person?

3 What is the purpose of this sonnet?

●●2ndReading

4 In the first quatrain (lines 1–4) the poet compares his friend to a summer's day. What are the similarities and/or differences?

5 Comparing his friend to the sun (lines 5–8) is unsuccessful. Why?

6 Lines 9–12 explain why the poet's friend's beauty can never fade. Explain.

7 Discuss how the final rhyming couplet guarantees the beauty of the poet's friend forever.

●●●3rdReading

8 Are any of the images from nature permanent? Examine each individually.

9 Reflect on how the subject of the poem must have felt.

10 What do you think is the theme of the poem?

11 Is the poet more concerned about immortalising his friend or conquering time?

12 What is the answer to the question: 'shall I compare thee to a summer's day?'

Sonnet 60 *William Shakespeare*

*Prescribed for the **Ordinary Level** exam in **2013***

Like as the waves make towards the pebbled shore,
So do our minutes hasten to their end;
Each changing place with that which goes before,
In sequent toil all forwards do contend.
Nativity, once in the main of light,   5
Crawls to maturity, wherewith being crown'd,
Crooked eclipses 'gainst his glory fight,
And Time that gave doth now his gift confound.
Time doth transfix the flourish set on youth,
And delves the parallels in beauty's brow,   10
Feeds on the rarities of nature's truth,
And nothing stands but for his scythe to mow.
   And yet to times in hope my verse shall stand,
   Praising thy worth, despite his cruel hand.

GLOSSARY

OUR MINUTES: The minutes of our lives
HASTEN: Hurry
SEQUENT: Following one after the other
TOIL: Work
CROOKED ECLIPSES: Dangerous omens
CONTEND: Compete
NATIVITY: Birth (of all humans, not just Christ), birth of a new day

CONFOUND: Destroy
TRANSFIX: Freeze with fear
FLOURISH: Vigorous growth / thriving
FEEDS ON THE RARITIES OF NATURE'S TRUTH: Like a wild animal or monster devouring things that are truly beautiful and rare
HIS SCYTHE TO MOW: Image of death as the reaper with a scythe coming to claim his victims

▪ **Pre**Reading

1 This poem is a Shakespearean sonnet divided into three quatrains (lines of four) and a rhyming couplet. It is important to be aware of this as you examine the poem in detail.

2 This poem deals with the ageing process and the destruction of youth and beauty by the passage of time. What images do you expect to be presented with to convey this message?

● **1st**Reading

3 The poem opens with a simile making a statement about our time on Earth. What exactly is the poet saying in the first two lines?

4 Look now at the first quatrain. Is the speaker optimistic or pessimistic about the time we spend on Earth?

5 The next quatrain (lines 5–8) mentions the journey from birth to maturity. Describe that journey as outlined in the poem.

6 The third quatrain (lines 9–12) highlights the damage inflicted on youth by Time. Describe.

●● **2nd**Reading

7 How is Time or Death portrayed in the poem?

8 How does the tone change in the final two lines?

●●● **3rd**Reading

9 Time becomes more menacing and perilous as the poem progresses. Trace this development.

10 What images are most effective and vivid in your opinion? Explain your answer.

11 The final two lines pay tribute to an unnamed person. In what way does Shakespeare pay tribute to him?

12 Do you think that this poem deals with personal or universal issues? Explain your answer.

Ozymandias *Percy Bysshe Shelley*

*Prescribed for the **Ordinary Level** exam in **2012***

I met a traveller from an antique land
Who said: Two vast and trunkless legs of stone
Stand in the desert ... Near them, on the sand,
Half sunk, a shattered visage lies, whose frown,
And wrinkled lip, and sneer of cold command,   5
Tell that its sculptor well those passions read
Which yet survive, stamped on these lifeless things,
The hand that mocked them, and the heart that fed:
And on the pedestal these words appear:
'My name is Ozymandias, king of kings: 10
Look on my works, ye Mighty, and despair!'
Nothing beside remains. Round the decay
Of that colossal wreck, boundless and bare
The lone and level sands stretch far away.

GLOSSARY

OZYMANDIAS: Ramses II, Pharaoh of Egypt in the thirteenth century BC
ANTIQUE: Ancient
VAST: Huge
TRUNKLESS: Without a trunk (body)
VISAGE: Face
SNEER: Scornful expression, show of hatred and contempt
COLD COMMAND: Unfeeling, ruthless control and authority

PEDESTAL: Base
DESPAIR: Feeling of complete lack of hope
COLOSSAL: Gigantic, huge, immense
BOUNDLESS: Cannot see any borders or boundaries; nothing except sand for as far as the eye can see
A NARRATIVE: A poem telling a story or account of events
A SONNET: A 14-line poem, Petrarchan in form (divided into octet and sestet)

PERCY BYSSHE SHELLEY • BORN 1792 IN SUSSEX, ENGLAND •

SON OF AN ENGLISH WELL-TO-DO CONSERVATIVE GENTLEMAN • EDUCATED AT ETON COLLEGE AND OXFORD UNIVERSITY• EXPELLED FOR REFUSING TO RETRACT A PAMPHLET HE WROTE CALLED *'THE NECESSITY OF ATHEISM'* • HELD ANTI-RELIGIOUS AND ANTI-MONARCHY VIEWS • SPOKE OUT ABOUT THE NEED FOR REFORMS IN SOCIETY AND IN POLITICAL SPHERES • SAW THE ROLE OF POET AS IMPORTANT IN SOCIETY • MARRIED A YOUNG SCHOOLGIRL IN 1811, BUT ELOPED TO EUROPE WITH MARY WOLLSTONECRAFT GODWIN, AUTHOR OF *FRANKENSTEIN* • HAD FEW ADMIRERS IN HIS LIFETIME BUT IS MUCH RESPECTED NOW • DROWNED AGE 30 IN A BOATING ACCIDENT • A ROMANTIC — NOT A WRITER OF LOVE POETRY BUT INSTEAD SOMEONE WHO REACTED AGAINST FORMALITY AND RESTRAINT. ROMANTICS BELIEVED THAT THE INDIVIDUAL'S FEELINGS AND IMAGINATION WERE IMPORTANT AND THAT SOCIETY WAS A CORRUPTING INFLUENCE. ROMANTICS CELEBRATED ART AND NATURE OVER CITY LIFE AND CIVILISATION

■PreReading

1 Say the word 'Ozymandias' aloud or in your head. What does the word conjure up for you? If a person were called Ozymandias, in what period of history do you think they would have lived? What would they have been like?

●1stReading

2 After you read this poem for the first time divide it into sentences, writing out each one. Now re-read it and see if the poem becomes easier to read and understand.
3 Describe the statue the traveller saw in the desert.
4 What state was it in?
5 How did it come to be in that state?
6 Describe the Pharaoh and say what kind of person you imagine Ozymandias was.
7 How did the Pharaoh want to be remembered? What does his epitaph on the pedestal tell us about him?
8 Why was the statue of Ozymandias originally constructed?

●●2ndReading

9 What do we learn about the sculptor? Was he good at his job?
10 What does the poet mean in the line 'The hand that mocked them, and the heart that fed:'?
11 Why does the poet talk about the sand?
12 How important to the poem is the image of the desert?

●●●3rdReading

13 Nature is more powerful than any one man. Do you think that this is one of the messages of the poem?
14 What does this poem tell the reader about power?
15 What do you think was Shelley's attitude to the statue as it lay wrecked in the sand?
16 There are three voices in the poem; name them and state what does each have to say? Which voice is the most powerful? Why?

Jungian Cows *Penelope Shuttle*

*Prescribed for the **Ordinary Level** exams in **2011**, **2012** and **2013***

In Switzerland, the people call their cows
Venus, Eve, Salome, or Fraulein Alberta,
beautiful names
to yodel across the pastures at Bollingen.

If the woman is busy with child or book,   5
the farmer wears his wife's skirt
to milk the most sensitive cows.

When the electric milking-machine arrives,
the stalled cows rebel and sulk
for the woman's impatient skilful fingers   10
on their blowzy tough rosy udders,
will not give their milk;

so the man who works the machine
dons cotton skirt, all floral delicate flounces
to hide his denim overalls and big old muddy boots,   15
he fastens the cool soft folds carefully,
wraps his head in his sweetheart's sunday-best fringed scarf,
and walks smelling feminine and shy among the cows,

till the milk spurts, hot, slippery and steamy
into the churns,   20
Venus, Salome, Eve, and Fraulein Alberta,
lowing, half-asleep,
accepting the disguised man as an echo of the woman,
their breath smelling of green, of milk's sweet traditional climax.

PENELOPE SHUTTLE • LIVES IN FALMOUTH ON THE SOUTH COAST OF CORNWALL, NOT FAR FROM LAND'S END • WAS MARRIED TO THE POET PETER REDGROVE, WHO DIED IN 2003, AND HAS AN ADULT DAUGHTER, ZOE • HAS PUBLISHED SEVEN VOLUMES OF POETRY

■ PreReading

1 Do some research on Carl Jung.
2 What did he have to say about mothers and fathers and the roles of women and men?

● 1stReading

3 What do the names tell us about the people?
4 Who usually does the milking?
5 Who is the substitute?
6 What do the cows do when the milking machine is used?
7 Do you think that the cows are over-sensitive?
8 Describe the udders.
9 What does the man have to do?
10 Describe his actions.
11 Does it work?

●● 2ndReading

12 How do the cows react?
13 What does the poet mean by the phrase 'an echo of the woman'?
14 What does the poet imply in the final line?

●●● 3rdReading

15 What is the mood of the poem?
16 Did you find this poem funny? Explain your answer.
17 What does the poem tell us about men and women?

▼ LinktoLanguage

18 Write the dialogue between the cows.

Zoo Morning *Penelope Shuttle*

*Prescribed for the **Ordinary Level** exam in 2014*

Elephants prepare to look solemn and move slowly
though all night they drank and danced, partied
and gambled, didn't act their age.

Night-scholar monkeys take off their glasses,
pack away their tomes and theses,   5
sighing as they get ready for yet another long day
of gibbering and gesticulating, shocking
and scandalizing the punters.

Bears stop shouting their political slogans
and adopt their cute-but-not-really teddies' stance   10
in the concrete bear-pit.

Big cats hide their flower presses, embroidery-frames
and watercolours;
grumbling, they try a few practise roars.
Their job is to rend the air, to devour carcasses,   15
to sleep-lounge at their vicious carnivorous ease.

What a life.
But none of them would give up show-business.

The snakes who are always changing,
skin after skin,   20
open their aged eyes and hinged jaws in welcome.

Between paddock and enclosure
we drag our unfurred young.
Our speech is over-complex, deceitful.
Our day is not all it should be.   25
The kids howl, baffled.

All the animals are very good at being animals.
As usual, we are not up to being us.
Our human smells prison us.

In the insect house   30
the red-kneed spider dances on her eight light fantastics;
on her shelf of silence she waltzes and twirls;
joy in her hairy joints, her ruby-red eyes.

● 1st Reading

1 What do the elephants do in the morning time?
2 What did they do the night before when no one could see them?
3 What do the monkeys do in the morning time?
4 What did they do the night before when no one could see them?
5 What do the bears do in the morning time?
6 What did they do the night before when no one could see them?
7 What do the lions and tigers do in the morning time?
8 What did they do the night before when no one could see them?
9 Describe the spider's actions.
10 How does it compare to the humans' actions?

●● 2nd Reading

11 Why would they not give up show-business?
12 Describe the human reaction to the zoo.
13 How do the children react?
14 What does she mean by the phrase 'we are not very good at being us'?
15 Why is the image of the snake important?

●●● 3rd Reading

16 What is the mood of the poem?
17 What is the theme of the poem?
18 What is your favourite image in the poem?

Madly Singing in the City *Peter Sirr*
after Po Chü-i

*Prescribed for the **Ordinary Level** exams in **2013** and **2014***

And often, when I have finished a new poem,
I climb to the dark roof garden
and lean on a rail over an ocean of streets.
What news I have for the sleeping citizens
and these restless ones, still shouting their tune   5
in the small hours. Fumes rise from the chip-shop
and I am back at the counter, waiting my turn.
Cod, haddock, plaice, whiting.
The long queue moves closer;
men in white coats paint fish with batter,   10
chips leap in the drying tray.
There's a table reserved for salt and vinegar
where the hot package is unswaddled,
salted, drenched, wrapped again
and borne out into the darkness.   15
In darkness I lean out, the new words ready,
the spires attentive. St Werburgh's, St Patrick's, Nicholas
of Myra. Nearby, the Myra Glass Company
from where we carried the glass table-top.
In a second I will sing, it will be as if   20
a god has leaned with me, having strolled over
from either of the two cathedrals, or from the green
and godly domes of Iveagh Buildings.
Ever since I was banished from the mountains
I have lived here in the roar of the streets.   25
Each year more of it enters me, I am grown
populous and tangled. The thousand ties of life
I thought I had escaped have multiplied.
I stand in the dark roof garden, my lungs swelling
with the new poem, my eyes filled with buildings   30
and people. I let them fill, then,
without saying a word, I go back down.

PETER SIRR • BORN IN WATERFORD IN 1960 • WON THE PATRICK KAVANAGH AWARD • COLLECTIONS OF POETRY ARE *MARGINAL ZONES*, *TALK, TALK*, *WAYS OF FALLING*, *THE LEDGER OF FRUITFUL EXCHANGE*, *BRING EVERYTHING*, *NONETHELESS* • FORMER DIRECTOR OF THE IRISH WRITERS' CENTRE • FORMER EDITOR OF *POETRY IRELAND REVIEW* • A MEMBER OF AOSDÁNA • LIVES IN DUBLIN

■PreReading

1 This poem is 'after Po Chü-i'. This means that it is a version of an older poem by this poet rather than a direct translation. Find out what you can about Po Chü-i.

●1stReading

2 The poem begins in celebration. What is the speaker celebrating?
3 At what time of the day does the poem happen?
4 What does he smell?
5 How does he describe the chip shop?
6 Does he do it justice?
7 What do the churches represent?

●●2ndReading

8 What has changed in his life?
9 In what ways has he adapted?
10 In what ways has he not?
11 How has he changed as a person?

●●●3rdReading

12 Is the ending of the poem an anti-climax?
13 What is your favourite image in the poem?
14 Why do you think that the poet wrote this poem?

▼LinktoLanguage

15 Write a short piece of personal writing with the title 'A Moment of Madness'.

Traveling through the Dark
William Stafford

*Prescribed for the **Ordinary Level** exams in **2012** and **2013***

Traveling through the dark I found a deer
dead on the edge of the Wilson River road.
It is usually best to roll them into the canyon:
that road is narrow; to swerve might make more dead.

By glow of the tail-light I stumbled back of the car   5
and stood by the heap, a doe, a recent killing;
she had stiffened already, almost cold.
I dragged her off; she was large in the belly.

My fingers touching her side brought me the reason —
her side was warm; her fawn lay there waiting,   10
alive, still, never to be born.
Beside that mountain road I hesitated.

The car aimed its lowered parking lights;
under the hood purred the steady engine.
I stood in the glare of the warm exhaust turning red;   15
around our group I could hear the wilderness listen.

I thought hard for us all — my only swerving —
then pushed her over the edge into the river.

WILLIAM STAFFORD
• BORN 1914 IN HUTCHINSON, KANSAS, USA • CONSCIENTIOUS OBJECTOR DURING THE SECOND WORLD WAR • BEST-KNOWN BOOKS ARE *THE RESCUED YEAR* (1966), *STORIES THAT COULD BE TRUE: NEW AND COLLECTED POEMS* (1977), *WRITING THE AUSTRALIAN CRAWL AND AN OREGON MESSAGE* (1987) • DIED 1993

●1stReading

1 Where is the poem set?
2 What does the speaker meet on the road?
3 What is the usual practice?
4 Why is this?
5 What does he mean by the phrase 'make more dead'?
6 What does he find when he examines the doe?
7 Why does he hesitate?
8 How does he interact with the rest of the surrounding wilderness?

●●2ndReading

9 What is his final decision?
10 How does he come to it?
11 Do you think it was the right one?
12 What would you have done?

●●●3rdReading

13 Compare this poem to 'The Road Not Taken' by Robert Frost.
14 Which one do you prefer?
15 What type of person do you think the speaker in the poem is?

▼LinktoLanguage

16 Write a piece of personal writing with the title 'A difficult decision'.

Do Not Go Gentle into That Good Night
Dylan Thomas

*Prescribed for the **Ordinary Level** exams in **2013** and **2014***

Do not go gentle into that good night,
Old age should burn and rave at close of day;
Rage, rage against the dying of the light.

Though wise men at their end know dark is right,
Because their words had forked no lightning they   5
Do not go gentle into that good night.

Good men, the last wave by, crying how bright
Their frail deeds might have danced in a green bay,
Rage, rage against the dying of the light.

Wild men who caught and sang the sun in flight,   10
And learn, too late, they grieved it on its way,
Do not go gentle into that good night.

Grave men, near death, who see with blinding sight
Blind eyes could blaze like meteors and be gay,
Rage, rage against the dying of the light.   15

And you, my father, there on the sad height,
Curse, bless, me now with your fierce tears, I pray.
Do not go gentle into that good night.
Rage, rage against the dying of the light.

DYLAN THOMAS • BORN 1914 IN THE WELSH SEAPORT OF SWANSEA • NO FORMAL THIRD-LEVEL EDUCATION • WORKED IN THE LOCAL NEWSPAPER OFFICES AND HEADED FOR LONDON IN 1934 • WORKED AS A BROADCASTER, PROSE WRITER, POET AND LECTURER • DRANK EXCESSIVELY AND LIVED A TUMULTUOUS LIFE • HIS POETRY OFTEN REFLECTS HIS LIFE AND IS FULL OF ENERGY AND BURNING INTENSITY • SAID: 'MY POETRY IS THE RECORD OF MY INDIVIDUAL STRUGGLE FROM DARKNESS TOWARDS SOME MEASURE OF LIGHT.' • DIED IN 1953 IN NEW YORK, USA, DURING A POETRY-READING TOUR

■ **Pre**Reading

1 What do you think the poet means by the phrase 'that good night'?

● **1st**Reading

2 To whom is the poem addressed?

3 How does he think that 'old age' should react?

4 What do wise men do when they near death?

5 Why?

6 What do good men do?

7 Why?

8 What do wild men do?

9 Why?

10 What do grave men do?

11 How do they do it?

●● **2nd**Reading

12 What does the poet wish for his father to do in the last verse?

13 What is the poet's tone of voice throughout the poem?

14 How do you think the poet lived his own life?

15 Do you think the poet and his father are close?

●●● **3rd**Reading

16 How does the poet use the image of light, darkness and blindness throughout the poem?

17 What type of man do you think the poet's father is?

▼ **Link**to**Language**

18 Write a eulogy.

Chronicle David Wheatley

*Prescribed for the **Ordinary Level** exams in **2013** and **2014***

My grandfather is chugging along the back roads
between Kilcoole and Newtown in his van,
the first wood-panelled Morris Minor in Wicklow.
Evening is draped lazily over the mountains;
one hapless midnight, mistaking the garage door   5
for open, he drove right through it, waking my father.

The old man never did get to farm like his father,
Preferring to trundle his taxi along the back roads.
Visiting, I stand in his workshop door
and try to engage him in small talk, always in vain,   10
then climb the uncarpeted stairs to look at the mountains
hulking over soggy, up-and-down Wicklow.

Cattle, accents and muck: I don't have a clue,
I need everything explained to me by my father.
Clannish great-uncles somewhere nearer the mountains   15
are vaguer still, farming their few poor roods,
encountered at Christmas with wives who serve me oven-
baked bread and come to wave us off at the door.

My grandfather pacing the garden, benignly dour,
a whiskey or a Woodbine stuck in his claw,   20
a compost of newsprint in the back of his van.
You're mad to go live in Bray, he told my father,
somewhere he'd visit on rare and timorous raids,
too close to 'town' to be properly *Cill Mhantáin*.

All this coming back to me in the mountains   25
early one morning, crossing the windy corridor
to the Glen of Imaal, where schoolchildren read
acrostics to me of 'wet and wonderful Wicklow',
and driving on down to Hacketstown with my father
we find grandfather's grandfather under an even   30

gravestone gone to his Church of Ireland heaven,
and his grandfather too, my father maintains,
all turned, long since turned to graveyard fodder
just over the county line from their own dear Wicklow,

the dirt tracks, twisting lanes and third-class roads
they would have hauled themselves round while they endured,

before my father and I ever followed the roads
or my mountainy cousins first picked up a loy
or my grandfather's van ever hit that garage door.

DAVID WHEATLEY • BORN 1970 IN DUBLIN • COLLECTIONS ARE *THIRST, MISERY HILL, MOCKER STREAM* AND *I AM THE CROCUS*, A VOLUME OF CHILDREN'S POETRY • IS A LECTURER AT THE UNIVERSITY OF HULL, ENGLAND

■ **Pre**Reading

1 What is a chronicle?

● **1st**Reading

2 Describe the speaker's grandfather.
3 Describe the setting of the poem.
4 What does the grandfather do?
5 What is the relationship between the speaker and his father like?
6 Do they have much in common?
7 How do they communicate?
8 Describe the speaker's wider family.
9 What was the relationship between the father and grandfather?
10 How does the grandfather feel about town life?

●● **2nd**Reading

11 What do they find at the graveyard?
12 How have times changed?
13 Would you agree that the countryside becomes a character in the poem?

●●● **3rd**Reading

14 What is the speaker's attitude to his relatives?
15 What is the tone of the poem?
16 Why does the poet finish with a half verse?
17 Comment on the structure of the poem.

▼ **Link**to**Language**

18 Write a pen-portrait of a family member.

The Writer Richard Wilbur

*Prescribed for the **Ordinary Level** exam in 2011*

In her room at the prow of the house
Where light breaks, and the windows are tossed with linden,
My daughter is writing a story.

I pause in the stairwell, hearing
From her shut door a commotion of typewriter-keys   5
Like a chain hauled over a gunwale.

Young as she is, the stuff
Of her life is a great cargo, and some of it heavy:
I wish her a lucky passage.

But now it is she who pauses,   10
As if to reject my thought and its easy figure.
A stillness greatens, in which

The whole house seems to be thinking,
And then she is at it again with a bunched clamor
Of strokes, and again is silent.   15

I remember the dazed starling
Which was trapped in that very room, two years ago;
How we stole in, lifted a sash

And retreated, not to affright it;
And how for a helpless hour, through the crack of the door,   20
We watched the sleek, wild, dark

And iridescent creature
Batter against the brilliance, drop like a glove
To the hard floor, or the desk-top,

And wait then, humped and bloody,   25
For the wits to try it again; and how our spirits
Rose when, suddenly sure,

It lifted off from a chair-back,
Beating a smooth course for the right window
And clearing the sill of the world.   30

It is always a matter, my darling,
Of life or death, as I had forgotten. I wish
What I wished you before, but harder.

RICHARD WILBUR • BORN 1921 IN NEW YORK CITY, USA • RAISED IN NEW JERSEY, USA • ENLISTED IN THE ARMY IN 1942 AND WORKED AS A CRYPTOGRAPHER • STARTED WRITING IN THE ARMY IN AN EFFORT TO RATIONALISE HIS FEELINGS DURING WARTIME • RETURNED HOME AND TAUGHT IN MANY UNIVERSITIES • HAS WRITTEN POETRY, LITERARY ESSAYS, CHILDREN'S BOOKS AND TRANSLATIONS OF CLASSIC WORKS • HIS POETRY SHOWS A LOVE OF THE WORLD AROUND HIM • WON THE PULITZER PRIZE IN 1956 • BECAME US POET LAUREATE IN 1987

●1stReading

1 Who are the characters in the poem?
2 What is each doing?
3 List the nautical references.

●●2ndReading

4 Explain why the poet often refers to a boat on a journey.
5 What does the poet wish for his daughter?
6 Describe the plight of the starling.
7 What is the relevance of the bird's story to the poem?
8 Is the speaker sympathetic towards the bird and towards his daughter? Describe the similarities.

●●●3rdReading

9 What does the poet feel when the bird finally finds its way out of the room? How does this relate to his daughter?
10 This poem is rich in imagery. Pick out the images that appear to you the most effective. Describe them and comment on their effectiveness.

A Summer Morning Richard Wilbur

*Prescribed for the **Ordinary Level** exams in **2012** and **2013***

Her young employers, having got in late
From seeing friends in town
And scraped the right front fender on the gate,
Will not, the cook expects, be coming down.

She makes a quiet breakfast for herself.　　　　　　　5
The coffee-pot is bright,
The jelly where it should be on the shelf.
She breaks an egg into the morning light,

Then, with the bread-knife lifted, stands and hears
The sweet efficient sounds　　　　　　　10
Of thrush and catbird, and the snip of shears
Where, in the terraced backward of the grounds,

A gardener works before the heat of day.
He straightens for a view
Of the big house ascending to stony-gray　　　　　　　15
Out of his beds mosaic with the dew.

His young employers having got in late,
He and the cook alone
Receive the morning on their old estate,
Possessing what the owners can but own.　　　　　　　20

● 1st Reading

1 What impression do we get of the cook?
2 Describe her young employers.
3 What does the cook do for the morning?
4 What does she listen to?
5 What is the gardener doing?

●● 2nd Reading

6 Do you think the young employers appreciate what they have?
7 Do you think the cook and the gardener appreciate their lives?
8 What, according to the poet, is the difference between ownership and possession?
9 What does the poem tell us about the life of the upper classes?

●●● 3rd Reading

10 Comment on the verse structure of the poem.
11 Comment on the rhyming scheme.
12 What is the theme of the poem?

▼ Link to Language

13 Write a diary entry for either the cook or the gardener.

This Is Just To Say
William Carlos Williams

Prescribed for the **Ordinary Level** *exam in* **2014**

I have eaten
the plums
that were in
the icebox

and which   5
you were probably
saving
for breakfast

Forgive me
they were delicious   10
so sweet
and so cold

WILLIAM CARLOS WILLIAMS • BORN 1883 IN NEW JERSEY, USA • STUDIED MEDICINE • LIVED AND PRACTISED IN RUTHERFORD, NEW JERSEY • ALSO WROTE FICTION, DRAMA AND ESSAYS • WAS CONCERNED WITH CREATING A DISTINCTLY AMERICAN FORM OF ART • HIS PHILOSOPHY OF WRITING WAS SUMMED UP BY HIS PHRASE 'NO IDEAS BUT IN THINGS' • DIED IN 1963

● 1st Reading

1 Is this a poem or a note?
2 What did the speaker do?
3 Did he enjoy doing it?

●● 2nd Reading

4 Does he really feel guilty?
5 What is the mood of the poem?
6 How do the sounds of the words contribute to the mood of the poem?
7 Why is there no punctuation in the poem?
8 What is the theme of this poem?

▼ Link to Language

9 Write a poem about your favourite food.

She dwelt among the untrodden ways
William Wordsworth

*Prescribed for the **Ordinary Level** exams in **2011** and **2013***

She dwelt among the untrodden ways
Beside the springs of Dove,
A Maid whom there were none to praise
And very few to love:

A violet by a mossy stone   5
Half hidden from the eye!
—Fair as a star, when only one
Is shining in the sky.

She lived unknown, and few could know
When Lucy ceased to be;   10
But she is in her grave, and, oh,
The difference to me!

GLOSSARY

DWELT: Lived
UNTRODDEN: Isolated/unknown

DOVE: Name of a river
CEASED TO BE: Died

WILLIAM WORDSWORTH • BORN 1770 IN COCKERMOUTH, CUMBERLAND, NORTH OF THE LAKE DISTRICT, ENGLAND • EDUCATED AT ST JOHN'S COLLEGE, CAMBRIDGE UNIVERSITY • LIVED WITH HIS SISTER, DOROTHY, IN THE LAKE DISTRICT • PUBLISHED LYRICAL BALLADS (ONE OF THE MOST IMPORTANT WORKS IN THE HISTORY OF ENGLISH LITERATURE) WITH SAMUEL TAYLOR COLERIDGE IN 1798 • BELIEVED THAT POETRY SHOULD BE 'LANGUAGE REALLY USED BY MEN' • HE WANTED POETRY TO BE REAL AND EVERYDAY, NOT JUST FOR THE ELITE • HE BECAME A REPUBLICAN AND SUPPORTER OF THE FRENCH REVOLUTION • CHALLENGED EPICS AND OTHER TRADITIONAL FORMS OF POETRY • BECAME POET LAUREATE IN 1843, BUT DIED SEVEN YEARS LATER

•1stReading

1 Describe Lucy. Do we learn much about her or about the life she led?
2 What happened to Lucy?
3 Is this a typical lament or elegy? Explain your answer.

••2ndReading

4 Is Lucy conveyed as a real person or does she possess a mystical and magical feel about her?
5 How does the speaker feel about Lucy?
6 How does her death affect the poet?
7 The poet uses a simile and a metaphor to describe Lucy in stanza 2. Examine both and discuss their effectiveness.
8 Examine the rhyming scheme employed by Wordsworth in this poem. Comment on its effect in the poem as a whole.

•••3rdReading

9 In this poem Wordsworth tells us more about how knowing and losing Lucy affected him than telling us anything about her in detail. Do you agree with this statement? Discuss.
10 Why does the poet admire Lucy so much?

From The Prelude: *Skating [ll 425–463]*
William Wordsworth

*Prescribed for the **Ordinary Level** exams in **2011** and **2013***

And in the frosty season, when the sun
Was set, and visible for many a mile
The cottage windows blazed through twilight gloom,
I heeded not their summons: happy time
It was indeed for all of us—for me   5
It was a time of rapture! Clear and loud
The village clock tolled six,—I wheeled about,
Proud and exulting like an untired horse
That cares not for his home. All shod with steel,
We hissed along the polished ice in games   10
Confederate, imitative of the chase
And woodland pleasures,—the resounding horn,
The pack loud chiming, and the hunted hare.
So through the darkness and the cold we flew,
And not a voice was idle; with the din   15
Smitten, the precipices rang aloud;
The leafless trees and every icy crag
Tinkled like iron; while far distant hills
Into the tumult sent an alien sound
Of melancholy not unnoticed, while the stars   20
Eastward were sparkling clear, and in the west
The orange sky of evening died away.
Not seldom from the uproar I retired
Into a silent bay, or sportively
Glanced sideway, leaving the tumultuous throng,   25
To cut across the reflex of a star
That fled, and, flying still before me, gleamed
Upon the glassy plain; and oftentimes,
When we had given our bodies to the wind,
And all the shadowy banks on either side   30
Came sweeping through the darkness, spinning still
The rapid line of motion, then at once
Have I, reclining back upon my heels,
Stopped short; yet still the solitary cliffs
Wheeled by me—even as if the earth had rolled   35
With visible motion her diurnal round!
Behind me did they stretch in solemn train,
Feebler and feebler, and I stood and watched

PRELUDE: Introduction
I HEEDED NOT THEIR SUMMONS: I ignored the calls to come in
RAPTURE: Intense delight
EXULTING: Rejoicing
SHOD: Wearing (especially footwear)
CONFEDERATE: Allied together
IMITATIVE: Imitating, copying

RESOUNDING: Booming, echoing sound
DIN: Long-lasting, loud noise
SMITTEN: Hit hard
PRECIPICES: Sheer cliff edges
CRAG: Steep, rugged rock
TUMULT: Uproar
THRONG: Crowd
DIURNAL: Daily

■PreReading

1 Describe an occasion when you and a group of others had unbridled or unrestrained fun, skating, playing sports, etc. How did it feel? Is it something that can be planned or must it be spontaneous?

●1stReading

2 Describe the setting — what words or images stand out to help set the scene?

3 Who is involved in the scene?

4 Even though the poet is summonsed to go inside, he ignores the calls: why?

5 What words help create the sense of togetherness felt by the poet and his friends in the poem?

●●2ndReading

6 The activity described in the poem is portrayed both visually and through sounds. Discuss.

7 How is the sense of speed and furious activity portrayed in the poem?

8 The poet compares himself to an 'untried horse' and to part of a hunting 'pack'. What is the effect of these images on the scene?

9 Describe the poet's mood in lines 1–22.

●●●3rdReading

10 The poet moves from the horseplay of a group of boys to a more personal reflective experience. Where in the poem does this change happen?

11 What insights does the poet discover as he meditates alone?

12 When is the poet happier — with the group of friends or alone?

13 What does this change signify?

It is a beauteous evening, calm and free
William Wordsworth

*Prescribed for the **Ordinary Level** exams in **2011** and **2013***

It is a beauteous evening, calm and free,
The holy time is quiet as a Nun
Breathless with adoration; the broad sun
Is sinking down in its tranquility;
The gentleness of heaven broods o'er the Sea: 5
Listen! the mighty Being is awake,
And doth with his eternal motion make
A sound like thunder—everlastingly.
Dear Child! dear Girl! that walkest with me here,
If thou appear untouched by solemn thought,   10
Thy nature is not therefore less divine:
Thou liest in Abraham's bosom all the year;
And worshipp'st at the Temple's inner shrine,
God being with thee when we know it not.

GLOSSARY

BEAUTEOUS: Beautiful
BROODS: Ponders, meditates
MIGHTY BEING: God
DEAR CHILD: He is addressing his daughter, Caroline, by Annette Vallon. She was ten years old when the sonnet was written, and it was Wordsworth's first meeting with her

APPEAR UNTOUCHED BY SOLEMN THOUGHT: Seems unaware of God's greatness around her
ABRAHAM'S BOSOM: Final resting place, close to God
THE TEMPLE'S INNER SHRINE: Place reserved only for the most holy, sacred priests

●1stReading

1 List the words used to describe the 'beauteous evening, calm and free'.
2 Who is present to witness the scene?
3 Does the beautiful evening impact upon the child?

●●2ndReading

4 Is God present in the poem? Where is his presence noticeable?
5 How does the presence of God affect 1) the poet, 2) the child?
6 The poet concludes that while the child is not overwhelmed by the moment of beauty and calmness, she is still closer to God than he is. Explain.

●●●3rdReading

7 This is a Petrarchan sonnet divided into two sections: lines 1–8 and lines 9–14. Is there a difference in theme and tone between the two sections? Explain.
8 Describe the mood of the sonnet.
9 Do you think that the title of the sonnet is a good one? Discuss.
10 This poem is a symbol of the poet's respect and adoration of God. Do you agree? Discuss.

▼LinktoLanguage

11 Write a letter home from your holidays describing a beautiful scene that had a calming effect on you
Or
Write an essay based on the idea that children see the world very differently from adults.

Poems for Breakfast *Enda Wyley*

*Prescribed for the **Ordinary Level** exam in **2014***

Another morning shaking us.
The young potted willow
is creased with thirst,
the cat is its purring roots.
Under our chipped window   5
the frail orange flowers grow.
Now the garden gate clicks.
Now footsteps on the path.
Letters fall like weather reports.
Our dog barks, his collar clinks,   10
he scrambles, and we follow,
stumble over Catullus, MacUser,
Ancient Greek for Beginners,
cold half-finished mugs of tea,
last week's clothes at the bed's edge.   15
Then the old stairs begin to creak.
And there are the poems for breakfast –
favourites left out on the long glass table.
We take turns to place them there
bent open with the pepper pot,   20
marmalade jar, a sugar bowl –
the weight of kitchen things.
Secret gifts to wake up with,
rhythms to last the whole day long,
surprises that net the cat, the dog,   25
these days that we wake together in –
our door forever opening.

ENDA WYLEY • BORN 1966 IN DUBLIN • COLLECTIONS: *EATING BABY JESUS, IN THE GARDEN* AND *POEMS FOR BREAKFAST* • WAS POET IN RESIDENCE IN MELBOURNE UNIVERSITY, AUSTRALIA, IN 1996, HAVING RECEIVED THE VINCENT BUCKLEY MEMORIAL AWARD THAT YEAR • HER BOOKS FOR CHILDREN ARE *BOO AND BEAR* AND *THE SILVER NOTEBOOK* • SHE LIVES IN DUBLIN

■ Pre Reading

1 What does the title imply? Can a poem be eaten?

● 1st Reading

2 Describe the house that the speaker is in.
3 Is it an unusual place?
4 Is there anticipation for the post?
5 Make a list of the domestic items in the poem.
6 How do these items help create the mood of the poem?

●● 2nd Reading

7 Do you think there is love in the house?
8 Is it a comfortable place for the people in the poem?
9 How do they treat their poems?

●●● 3rd Reading

10 Why would someone want to wake up to poetry?
11 How do the poems make them feel?
12 What impression does the final line leave on you?
13 Did you like this poem? Explain your answer.
14 What was your favourite image in the poem? Explain your answer.

▼ Link to Language

15 Write the dialogue between a typical Irish family at breakfast time.

The Wild Swans at Coole *W. B. Yeats*

*Prescribed for the **Ordinary Level** exams in **2011** and **2014***

The trees are in their autumn beauty,
The woodland paths are dry,
Under the October twilight the water
Mirrors a still sky;
Upon the brimming water among the stones   5
Are nine-and-fifty swans.

The nineteenth autumn has come upon me
Since I first made my count;
I saw, before I had well finished,
All suddenly mount   10
And scatter wheeling in great broken rings
Upon their clamorous wings.

I have looked upon those brilliant creatures,
And now my heart is sore.
All's changed since I, hearing at twilight,   15
The first time on this shore,
The bell-beat of their wings above my head,
Trod with a lighter tread.

Unwearied still, lover by lover,
They paddle in the cold   20
Companionable streams or climb the air;
Their hearts have not grown old;
Passion or conquest, wander where they will,
Attend upon them still.

But now they drift on the still water,   25
Mysterious, beautiful;
Among what rushes will they build,
By what lake's edge or pool
Delight men's eyes when I awake some day
To find they have flown away?   30

W. B. YEATS • WILLIAM BUTLER YEATS, BORN 1865 IN DUBLIN OF A CO. SLIGO FAMILY • MOVED TO LONDON AT THE AGE OF TWO AND BACK TO DUBLIN IN HIS TEENS • HIS POETRY SHOWS AN INTEREST IN IRISH MYSTICISM, MYTHOLOGY, HISTORY, FOLKLORE AND SUPERSTITIONS • WAS ONE OF THE FOUNDERS OF THE ABBEY THEATRE, DUBLIN, IN 1904 • WROTE PLAYS AS WELL AS POETRY • HIS BROTHER, JACK B. YEATS, WAS A WELL-KNOWN IRISH ARTIST • HAD A FIXATION AND GREAT LOVE FOR MAUD GONNE, WHO REFUSED TO MARRY HIM ON MANY OCCASIONS BUT HE REMAINED OBSESSED WITH HER ALL THROUGH HIS LIFE • BECAME A SENATOR IN 1922 AND HAD AN ACTIVE PUBLIC LIFE • AWARDED THE NOBEL PRIZE FOR LITERATURE IN 1923 • DIED IN 1939 IN ROME AND HIS BODY COULD NOT BE RETURNED TO IRELAND UNTIL AFTER THE WAR

■**Pre**Reading

1 Where is Coole?

●**1st**Reading

2 Describe the scene painted by Yeats with his words in the first six lines.
3 What has he seen there every year for the last nineteen years?
4 What has happened to him since the first time he went there?
5 What has happened to the swans since the first time he saw them?
6 What question does he ask in the final verse?

●●**2nd**Reading

7 Do you think that the poet is jealous of the swans?
8 Which images in the poem are your favourites?
9 Make a list of the verbs that Yeats uses. What mood do they help create in the poem?
10 What sounds dominate the poem?

●●●**3rd**Reading

11 How are the swans presented throughout the poem?
12 What does the poet tell us about himself in the poem?

●●●●**4th**Reading

13 Do you think the poet has a lot of regrets about his life?
14 Do you think the poet spends too much time looking backwards to the past?

An Irish Airman Foresees His Death
W. B. Yeats

*Prescribed for the **Ordinary Level** exams in **2011** and **2014***

I know that I shall meet my fate
Somewhere among the clouds above;
Those that I fight I do not hate,
Those that I guard I do not love;
My country is Kiltartan Cross,   5
My countrymen Kiltartan's poor,
No likely end could bring them loss
Or leave them happier than before.
Nor law, nor duty bade me fight,
Nor public men, nor cheering crowds,   10
A lonely impulse of delight
Drove to this tumult in the clouds;
I balanced all, brought all to mind,
The years to come seemed waste of breath,
A waste of breath the years behind   15
In balance with this life, this death.

■ **Pre**Reading

1 After reading the title, what did you expect from this poem?

● **1st**Reading

2 Why do you think the speaker is so definite in the first two lines?

3 What is the speaker saying in lines three and four?

4 What do you expect him to tell us later on?

5 What is his relationship with the people of Kiltartan Cross?

6 How was the war affecting them?

●● **2nd**Reading

7 Why was war not an attractive option for the speaker in the poem?

8 What were his reasons for going to fight?

●●● **3rd**Reading

9 What do you think the speaker's frame of mind was when he decided to go to war?

10 How does the poet use rhyme in the poem?

11 How does the poet use repetition in the poem?

12 What effect does this have?

▼ **Link**to**Language**

13 Write the diary entries of the airman in the days before his death.

Fleur Adcock *For Heidi with Blue Hair*

THIS IS A POEM about teenage rebellion, refusal to conform and what happens when there is a clash with adults. The poet is addressing this poem directly to Heidi, her niece. She speaks to her: 'When you dyed your hair . . . you were sent home from school.' The story is told in a straightforward and clear way. Heidi, in an act of freedom of expression, dyes her hair blue. There is a vivid description of the hair: ultramarine on the short, clipped sides and jet black on the spiky top. Heidi is then sent home from school. The headmistress is not impressed, and we can almost hear her tone as she chastises 'apart from anything else'. She cannot send Heidi home just because she dyed her hair, as this is not against the school rules. Instead, Heidi is sent home because her hair is not dyed in the school colours. Heidi takes this punishment badly; there are tears and we can imagine quite a scene.

In complete contrast to the strict and rigid headmistress, Heidi's father is 'freedom-loving'. He rings the school and supports his daughter, explaining that Heidi and he discussed the hair-dying before she did it, and they also checked the school rules. He may be freedom-loving, but he still encourages Heidi to stay within the boundaries. He continues to defend his daughter, saying that her image may be punk, but it is only an image, and her behaviour does not match the image. We see she has a clean record and has never been in trouble before: 'The school had nothing else against you.'

Heidi is adamant that she will not change back her hair for a number of reasons. She says it cost $25, and also, it is a permanent colour and will not wash out. She refuses to conform. The poem then reveals something significant about Heidi's past. In verse 5 we learn that Heidi's mother has died and this shimmers like a ghost behind all the arguments. It is not discussed in great detail, but it is very much an issue and wins our sympathy for Heidi. We see her as young and vulnerable and dealing with the huge issue of her mother's death, and this shows just how ridiculous the hair issue is in the bigger scheme of things. The teachers are portrayed as silly and frivolous as they 'twitter' and finally give in to the argument.

In the final verse we learn that Heidi's black friend continues to challenge the school authorities and dyes her hair in the school colours. This is a show of support for Heidi and adds to the feeling of victory; it is unnecessary, as Heidi has already won the battle to display her individuality.

Maya Angelou *Phenomenal Woman*

REVIEWER MONICA STARK described this poem as 'an anthem of women's strength in their own womanhood'. It is indeed a poem full of confidence, self-love and pride. The title, 'Phenomenal Woman', encapsulates everything the poet is attempting to say in the poem — that she is a 'phenomenal woman.'

The poem opens with a straightforward statement that pretty women, obviously intimidated yet intrigued by the speaker, question her about her secret, i.e. how she became, and is, so phenomenal. She tells us that she is not the traditional female icon, being neither cute nor thin. The answer the speaker gives is unsatisfactory to the 'pretty women'. They cannot believe that her phenomenal status is based simply on her arms, hips, walk and the curl of her lip. Of course the message here is simple. The speaker is phenomenal because she is herself. Lines 14–20 tell us the effect she has on men: they find her irresistible, they stand or fall and swarm around her like bees around honey. Women question her, but men adore her.

The short, simple sentences and childish rhyming scheme make the speaker's message very clear and matter-of-fact. There are no hidden meanings. One element is essential in promoting yourself to the heights of being a Phenomenal Woman, and that is self-belief. The speaker repeats her claim — each verse ends with the refrain 'I'm a woman / Phenomenally. / Phenomenal Woman, / That's me' — to emphasise her point, to repeat and reiterate her message. She is extraordinary, exceptional and sensational because she is herself — 'That's me'. The poem exudes confidence and self-assurance. Here is a woman who knows herself well, is at peace with herself and knows the effect she has on those around her.

This poem is a celebration of what it means to be a woman, not a stick-thin model or a manufactured 'nipped and tucked' airbrushed woman, but an ordinary, simple woman. It is a poem about being comfortable with your own self-image and sexuality. It is a poem about accepting and rejoicing. She exposes her inner strength, which is her femininity. She does not brag or boast, she hopes that others will see her and that they too will celebrate — 'It ought to make you proud'. Every move she makes, every step she takes shows that she is in full control, she knows what she is doing and everything is intentional. She is brimming over with confidence and happiness because she is a 'phenomenal woman'.

Simon Armitage *It Ain't What You Do, It's What It Does to You*

THE TITLE OF this poem outlines the whole message of the poem. The poet's message is clear and simple; he promotes the belief that it is not what you do, it is the feeling you get when doing it that matters. He gives us a number of examples of exotic, extraordinary things people do and he contrasts them with ordinary, banal, everyday things that he has done. His conclusion is that the outcome — the feeling — is just the same.

In verse 1 he shows that he did not need to bum across America with just a dollar and a knife to get a feeling of adventure and excitement. Instead he 'lived with thieves in Manchester'. In verse 2 he admits that he has not walked through the Taj Mahal in India, so focused and meditative that he could hear the soft padding every time his foot hit the marble floor. Instead he has experienced the intense serenity of skimming stones across a lake in Lancashire. He was so at one with nature at that moment that he could feel the stone losing power, slowing down and finally sinking.

Finally, in verse 3 Armitage tells us that he has not felt the rush of adrenalin from sitting on the edge of a small plane playing with the parachute cord that could ultimately save his life. He declares that he has felt this adrenalin rush, this heightened sense of excitement and fulfilment, from helping a physically handicapped child. He has experienced these feelings by holding the child's 'wobbly head' and by rubbing his 'fat hands'.

In conclusion, the last four lines reveal just what these emotions feel like. He describes a tightness in his throat and an overwhelming, flowing sensation deep inside. This feeling is 'something else', not usual, not ordinary and can be achieved without doing the very adventurous and exotic things.

W. H. Auden **Funeral Blues**

THIS POEM IS most recognisable as it was recited in the movie *Four Weddings and a Funeral* by a character mourning the death of a loved one. The speaker calls for the world to stop because he feels he cannot continue due to the overwhelming grief he feels at the loss of his beloved.

This poem can be read as an elegy as the poet is rendered completely helpless by the death of his loved one. He wants time to stop, he wants to sever all communication with the outside world, he wants to quieten the dog by giving him a juicy bone. No music is to be played; the only sound acceptable to the speaker is the 'muffled drum' heralding the arrival of the coffin and the mourners. All of these feelings can be accepted as those of someone recently bereaved. Verse 2, however, takes the mourning process a step further. The speaker calls for aeroplanes to circle in the sky transmitting the message 'He Is Dead'. He would like to put ribbons on the public

doves and replace the traffic policemen's white gloves with black ones as a mark of respect. Verse 2 shows how irrational the speaker feels with loss, how exaggerated he makes his expression of sorrow in an attempt to communicate how deeply he feels the grief, pain and loss.

Verse 3 tells us what the deceased meant to the speaker. He was his direction in life, he filled his thoughts always during work and rest — he was his everything. He believed that love was forever and is now completely devastated to find that there is no forever; love has ended.

Verse 4 shows the raw grief felt at the death of his partner as he faces the world alone. He no longer needs things of beauty (the stars, sun, moon, ocean, wood) as alone he cannot appreciate beauty. The future is bleak: 'For nothing now can ever come to any good.'

This poem can also be read as a satire as the poet is ridiculing the public for their exaggerated outpourings of grief at the death of a public figure. The images are outlandish and lavish; the speaker's requests are over-the-top and at times ridiculous.

Whichever way the reader chooses to interpret it, this poem reflects feelings of grief, desolation and heartbreak, whether deeply felt at the loss of a soulmate or felt by an ordinary member of the public at the loss of a much-loved popular figure.

Patricia Beer **The Voice**

THIS SENTIMENTAL LYRIC is written in memory of a sad, eccentric aunt who suffers the tragedy of losing a son. When this happens a kind neighbour gives her a gift of a parrot. The aunt takes to the parrot immediately and buys a beautiful cage to keep it in. She behaves just like an eager mother who rushes out to buy a cot for a new baby.

When he first arrives, the parrot doesn't seem to fit in. He takes adjusting to. His colours make him stand out for a while. He doesn't make any noises at all and this is disconcerting. Parrots are usually associated with lots of noise, but this one has to be taught what to say. **'He came from silence but was ready to become noise.'**

The aunt gradually teaches him to talk using nursery rhymes, just like she would with a child. The parrot becomes part of her, takes on all her idiosyncrasies and adds some of his own for good measure. He even takes on the aunt's Devon accent. In the end, **'He fitted in.'**

He also gets old. Eventually, just before he dies, he loses his memory and descends into parrot senility. He starts to get his nursery rhymes mixed up. This is distressing for the aunt. Eventually, just like Jill in the nursery rhyme, he **'tumbled after'.**

Much humour is used throughout the poem especially in the way the poet uses colour, and in the way she uses nursery rhymes to illustrate the bird's speech, but the poem is dominated by the sadness and regret in the final verse. The poet tells us that her aunt died soon after her pet, with little left to hang on to. She has lost her husband, her son, her companion and her pride. The poet tells us that she can no longer hear her aunt's voice, but she can still recall the parrot's. The poet ends on a slightly more positive note by reminding us of the thing that gave her aunt purpose in her last years.

Elizabeth Bishop The Fish

THIS IS A very long but straightforward poem telling of the poet's experience while out fishing. Immediately she tells us she catches a **'tremendous'** fish. He isn't just big, he is amazing and fascinating. She does not bring the fish into the boat immediately, she holds him half out of the water and sees that her hook is firmly fixed in the side of his mouth. The fish does not battle to go free. On first sight she sees that the fish is very battered and worthy of her respect, but also plain and ordinary. His skin reminds the poet of old wallpaper in pattern, but in texture the poet tells us the fish is speckled with barnacles, growths of lime and sea lice and that strips of green weed trail under him. The poet pays particular attention to the fish's gills that gulp in oxygen — dangerous to the fish. The gills appear frightening as they are very sharp and look **'fresh and crisp with blood'.**

The poet looks beyond the fish's external appearance; she imagines the meat — **'white flesh'** inside the fish's body packed piece on top of piece like tightly packed feathers. She thinks of the fish's intestines — red and black and pink. In his eyes she can see a blankness; he does not return her stare. She admiringly examines his face and the structure of his jaw. She notices five pieces of fishing line and describes each in detail. They remind her of medals worn proudly after a war, or of a wise old man's beard trailing from his sore and aching jaw.

A sense of victory fills the boat as she examines the fish, like the rainbow colours of spilt engine oil. Everything is then transformed. Overwhelmed by this feeling the poet releases the fish to fight another battle. She feels she should not be the one to end the life of such a worthy soldier who has fought so many battles and always won. She respects the fish's courage and rewards him with another chance of freedom and it is the poet who then feels a great sense of achievement. The victory and exultation spreads from the warrior fish through the boat and into the poet. The victory is not the usual victory of a fisherman who catches a big fish, instead it is the feeling of releasing your great catch back into the wild.

Elizabeth Bishop *The Filling Station*

BISHOP RECREATES IN minute detail a visit to a petrol-filling station. What is a routine, everyday experience is transformed as she looks into the situation and dissects it to see the human side of a dirty, greasy petrol station.

The poem opens unexpectedly with an exclamation: 'Oh, but it is dirty!' She was not expecting the extent of the filth and is surprised when she sees it up close. The title of the poem places us firmly in the scene and the rest of the poem is spent delving beneath the dirty surface. The poet investigates who lives there, imagines what goes on, sees that somebody cares and slaves away to make the petrol station somewhere special to live. There is a hint of danger (or is it humour?) in line 6 — 'Be careful with that match!'.

The filling station, usually a male-dominated location, seems to have evidence of a woman's touch. There are many indications that it is more than a place of work, that it is a home. The dirt has character; there is something endearing in

it; we see that it belongs to somebody and that makes it special — maybe it is the father's or the son's or even the dog's. The only deviations from the blackness and dirt are the presence of comic books and a doily. Someone, it seems, is aiming at something higher than grease and dirt; someone is making an effort to improve the surroundings. This 'somebody' makes little changes so that the ever-present dirt is forgotten, as there is an effort to enhance and refine the filling station.

There is a beautiful softness in the lines

> . . . *Somebody*
> *arranges the rows of cans*
> *so that they softly say:*
> *ESSO-SO-SO-SO*

This sibilant 's' sound is calming and soothing and creates a sense of tranquillity and peacefulness in a place of 'high-strung automobiles'.

Elizabeth Bishop *The Prodigal*

THIS POEM IS semi-autobiographical as Bishop struggled with alcoholism and feelings of exile for most of her life. In this poem, the poet concentrates not on the good times experienced by the Prodigal as he spends his money, nor does she concentrate on the great reunion with his father. Instead, it focuses on the hardships and squalor he endured in self-imposed exile. He is immersed, in filth, living with pigs. He does not seem to judge or condemn or even question his position; he just survives.

He observes his surroundings long enough to know that the dung is 'glass-smooth' on the walls and that the pigs have personalities and characteristics of their own: 'Light-lashed, self-righteous ... a cheerful stare'. He does not judge or take sides, but instead displays affection, 'leaned to scratch' the head of a sow who 'always ate her young'. He has done things of which he is ashamed and so seems to refuse to pass judgment even on the most horrific deeds, like those committed by the sow.

Sometimes, the prodigal gets a glimpse beyond the muck and the dung. Mornings after a drinking bout the sunrise seems special as it casts a red haze on the barnyard. The Prodigal finds this reassuring, and it helps him to struggle on for another year or more. But in spite of these glimpses of hope, the evening brings a warning in the shape of the first star.

This is followed by the arrival of the farmer coming to close up the cows and the horses in the relative comfort of the barn. It is very different from the living conditions of the pigs and the Prodigal. All appears to be as 'safe and companionable as in the Ark'. But the Prodigal is dragged back to the reality of his situation by the sights and sounds of the snoring pigs.

Once again the Prodigal sees something special and beautiful. The farmer's lantern casts a shining halo-like light. Around the ugliness of the dirty farmyard the Prodigal sees flashes of beauty and hope and possibly redemption. His soul has been awakened, 'his shuddering insights beyond his control, touching him.' These insights then set him on a path homeward. It is not a decision he makes lightly, but his mind is made up 'to go home'.

Eavan Boland Child of Our Time

This poem was written after the poet saw a press photograph of a fire-fighter carrying a child from the wreckage of the Dublin bombings in 1974. The poem is an elegy written to the child, and is an apology from the poet for the behaviour of adults who have cost the child his life.

Immediately the poet tells us that she has been made to change her way of thinking by the events that she has witnessed in the photograph. She has had to look within herself to force out a poem that could justifiably reflect what she has seen. She says the tone of the poem will be set by 'your final cry'. The poet recognises the contradiction in what she attempts to do when she cries out for the child's 'unreasoned end', and she says that this will inspire her. In fact, she says that this poem must be written because of what happened. She says that she does not have a choice in the matter. The death of the child is pushing the very rhythm, and driving her motives for writing the poem.

> *Its rhythm from the discord of your murder*
> *Its motive from the fact you cannot listen.*

In the second verse she tells the child that adults have a duty to teach children peaceful things about animals and nursery rhymes; that adults should protect children. Children should learn from adults. In this case, however, the adults have to learn from the death of this young child. She insists that they must 'for your sake' find 'a new language'.

Eavan Boland **Love**

THIS POEM IS obviously a love poem. It is set in two different periods of time. In the past, the poet and her husband are in a time of personal difficulty. One of their children is near death. This brings the couple closer together and makes their love for each other more intense. It is a situation that neither of them wants to be in, but it brings out the best in their love. There is an air of simplicity about their lives. They are living in a mid-western town, and seem to have their priorities straight. They are completely focussed on what they have to do to help their child through the ordeal.

Her placing of the poem at dusk suggests a world that is neither here nor there. The dark of night is coming, but the brightness of morning is not that long gone. The image of Aeneas also appears in the first verse. He was an ancient Greek hero who had to cross between worlds to save his people. He gave enormous self-sacrifice to save others. Perhaps this represents the couple's plight to save their child and sacrifice their own happiness.

In the second half of the poem, her tone changes. She speaks in short, staccato sentences. They are clipped and to the point.

> *I am your wife.*
> *It was Years ago.*
> *Our child was healed.*

Everything is matter-of-fact. Importantly, she says that they 'love each other still'. However, love is now 'plain' and 'clear'. She wishes to return to when the passion was more intense, when they had something to care about, when every minute counted, and when their lives seemed 'epic'. She wants the intensity that came to them during their time of crisis.

Unfortunately, her parting lines suggest that this is not about to happen:
'You walk away and I cannot follow.'

Eavan Boland **This Moment**

THIS BRIEF LYRIC creates an immediate atmosphere within its own brevity. The poet creates a scene and allows us to view it in much the same way that we would view a picture or a painting. The poet is sparing with her detail, yet because of this every detail that she does give gains more importance. There is nothing extra in this lyric. In some of the sentences she does not even bother with verbs.

The poet begins with the place and time. However, they are both vague at best. They are delivered staccato-like, as if they were secrets that were not to be uncovered except to a select few.

She follows with more mystery. Something is about to 'happen / out of sight'. She is not telling us what. There is anticipation everywhere, even in nature itself. Things are coming to life and having their moment while everybody else goes to sleep and stops. There is always something happening whether we are aware of it or not.

Then she introduces two people: a mother and a child. They perform a simple act. The child runs into the mother's arms. She continues mothering no matter what time it is nor what place it is, no matter what is or isn't going on outside. The poet reminds us that nature goes on too:

> *Stars rise.*
> *Moths flutter.*
> *Apples sweeten in the dark.*

This is a simple poem about the simplicity of life, the continuing circle of nature and of motherhood and the idea that what may seem banal has its own importance.

Emily Dickinson *I felt a Funeral, in my Brain*

THIS POEM IS clearly about death, but there is disagreement as to whether or not the speaker is imagining her own death or the death of her sanity. Is she lying in a coffin listening to the funeral activity going on outside, or is she cataloguing her descent into mental breakdown? The images of the mourners 'treading — treading', the funeral service, the drum 'beating — beating', the coffin being lifted, the heavy footsteps and the funeral bell are all pressures building towards the climax, which seems to be the breakdown of and subsequent loss of consciousness. The tone of the service is solemn and serious. The treading of stanza 1 and the beating of stanza 2 create a numbness of mind. Death and the funeral service are felt in the speaker's brain. All reason is abandoned and links with reality are severed as the speaker becomes fixated on the sounds surrounding her. She becomes totally obsessed, and the only part of her that seems alert and alive is her sense of hearing.

The poem reaches its climax in stanza 5 and the speaker loses her grip on her sanity as the plank snaps under tremendous pressure. The collapse of the speaker's sanity replaces any sense of epiphany. Instead of insight and clarity, we are left with obscurity. The poem ends before the speaker can share her thoughts: 'And finished knowing — then —'

Emily Dickinson *I heard a Fly buzz — when I died*

This poem, written in the first person, describes the moments leading up to the speaker's death. The room is still and silent, the mood is solemn. It is like the calm before a storm. The people at the bedside have dried their tears and are holding their breath for the inevitable arrival of Christ into the room at the moment of death. The speaker appears to be ready to die. She has tidied up her affairs, written her will and given out keepsakes to help people remember her. She doesn't appear to be sad or reluctant to die and leave these people. In fact, she refers to them as 'eyes' and 'breaths'.

All is going to plan when the buzzing fly disrupts the solemnity of the moment. This small common housefly distracts the dying speaker and breaks the spell of death. It is an intrusion unsuited to the occasion, which was calm and controlled before its arrival. The fly removes the focus away from the seriousness of death as it stumbles along aimlessly. It is hard to see how such a tiny insect could come 'Between the light and me'. We learn that the speaker's focus drifted from what was important. What was solemn and spiritual is downgraded to the second-most important thing happening in the room as the fly dominates the scene.

Carol Ann Duffy *Valentine*

THIS IS A love poem, but it is not a typical, slushy, romantic love poem. Indeed, in the first line we see that the poet is putting great emphasis on the fact that her love (the emotion and the person) is not ordinary and therefore the poet is not going to give a traditional gift for Valentine's day, such as a 'red rose or a satin heart'. Instead, the poet is going to give her lover an onion.

The rest of the poem explains why she feels she should give an onion to her lover. The onion becomes an extended metaphor.

She points out that the onion can give light in a time of darkness, just like the moon. She examines the erotic nature of an onion. She compares the onion to a lover who brings out the truth regardless of the price. She says that a love affair, like an onion, can make the protagonists see sides of themselves that they'd rather not see.

She talks about how its taste is difficult to shift, but like the taste of an onion, a love affair can eventually end as well. Then she compares the ringed inside of an onion to a wedding ring, but says that this is lethal.

All of these images are harsh, and in a way they are cold. The poet seems to be bringing a 'wake-up call' to her lover. The implication could be that they do not have a traditional romantic relationship and therefore to give a traditional romantic present would be the wrong thing to do, and would be dishonest.

At the end she adds her own caution: getting too close is dangerous, and love can be 'lethal'.

She uses a forceful, matter-of-fact tone. There is little ambiguity. Note her use of the definite 'It will' and 'I give' instead of 'It could' or 'I offer'. There is a sense that these are the facts; if you don't like them, 'tough', although there is a little hint of teasing in the poem as well.

She uses very few formal, traditional poetic devices although she is careful

with her use of sound, especially in lines such as 'Its fierce kiss will stay on your lips'.

The metre in the poem seems to be purpose-built. She varies her line lengths a lot, even including one-word lines. What do you think is the significance of these short lines?

Paul Durcan *Going Home to Mayo, Winter, 1949*

IN THIS CONVERSATIONAL narrative Durcan uses an event from his childhood in the winter of 1949 to outline the main differences between city life and life in the countryside, and expresses his feelings on both. The poem opens with father and son escaping the 'alien, foreign city of Dublin'. We are left in no doubt but that young Durcan feels he does not fit in in Dublin. This is a special, magical occasion and Durcan remembers it in great detail. He remembers driving 'through the night in an old Ford Anglia' with a 'rexine seat of red leatherette'. Durcan absorbs every little detail of this memorable journey. He enjoys the trip and the game he plays with his father. As the moonlight shines through the windscreen his childish exuberance explodes, and he cries out 'Daddy, Daddy . . . pass out the moon'. There is a sense of closeness between father and son as they share the journey westwards. They speed onwards towards their destination and the young Durcan remembers in wonderment the place — names of all the towns they pass through; each one a marker telling them they are getting closer to 'home'.

Although they cannot pass out the

moon, he is not disappointed. A bigger and better prize awaits him when they arrive in Turlough, 'in the heartland of Mayo'. Durcan now feels at home, in the heart of his family. This is a homely place dominated by women. His bedroom is over the pub, and in the morning his ears are filled with the sounds of country animals waking up — 'cattle-cries and cock-crows'. Movement and comfort, noise and life surround him. Life here is like an endless, expansive piece of material that has no beginning and no end. Durcan and his father are close and enjoy a relaxed relationship in Mayo. They go walking and talking 'in the high grass down by the river'. They connect in a way that would never happen if they were in Dublin.

From line 21 onwards the picture becomes bleak and desolate. Durcan is disillusioned as he tells us that 'home was not home' and although Mayo was where the heart was, it was not where they lived. The image of Dublin is stark and glaring in the daylight. It is like a waking 'nightmare', and he attempts to deal with his return to Dublin in the same way he dealt with not being able to outrun the moon. He cannot fight it so he grudgingly accepts it.

The return journey is in stark contrast to the journey west. There is no fun, no games, no closeness, no communication and no connection. The journey is slow and impersonal and they reluctantly 'chug' down by the canal into the city. As they pass every lock gate on the canal it seems to be a bell tolling a death march as they return to the drabness and dullness of Dublin. Durcan registers and despises every detail of this journey:

> And railings and palings and asphalt and traffic lights,
> And blocks after blocks of so-called 'new' tenements.

These images are heavy with misery and gloom. He feels imprisoned by the railings and palings. The final three lines are dark and depressing as they point to death. Every step of the journey seems to indicate a cross, marking out loneliness and despair for his father. This all culminates in the expansive image of a 'wide, wide cemetery'. Like life in Mayo, life in Dublin is seamless; it seems to have no beginning and no end, but in a negative, deathly manner.

Robert Frost The Tuft of Flowers

THIS IS A typical Robert Frost poem, based on nature. It is deceptively simple. It uses a normal situation to illustrate a deeply human point about life and culture and, most importantly, what it means to be human.

The poem begins with a simple statement, defining time, place and action:

> I went to turn the grass once after one
> Who mowed it in the dew before the sun.

The speaker then looks around for his predecessor, who had started the work that he was there to complete. Frost controls the pace of the poem with tight rhyming couplets, bringing a sense of serenity to the poem.

The speaker seems to hope for an encounter with his colleague, for a bit of human contact to make the task go quicker. He accepts his solitude with the couplet:

> 'As all must be,' I said within my heart.
> 'Whether they work together or apart.'

He is awoken from his contemplation by the sight of a butterfly from the corner of his eye. He follows the flight of the butterfly as it floats to a single 'tall tuft of flowers beside a brook'. The speaker is fascinated by the scene and finds a commonality between his colleague and himself.

When he sees that the previous worker has avoided the flowers and deliberately worked around them, he feels a tremendous empathy towards him. He sees someone who is like-minded, someone who reacts to things in the same way as himself. He appreciates beauty and decides to preserve things that are worth preserving.

The speaker comes to the conclusion that there is always somebody out there who will appreciate the fine, natural things in life. He feels it is important that people find a soulmate, someone whose thoughts mirror one's own. He comes to his uplifting conclusion that:

> 'Men work together,' I told him from
>   the heart,
> 'Whether they work together or apart.'

Robert Frost Out, Out–

THIS SAD NARRATIVE tells of a horrific accident that leads to the death of a young boy. The title of the poem comes from Shakespeare's tragedy, *Macbeth*. When Macbeth is told that his wife is dead he cries:

> Out, out, brief candle!
> Life's but a walking shadow, a poor
>   player
> That struts and frets his hour upon the
>   stage,
> And then is heard no more.

The title emphasises how short life is, and how it can be ended as easily as blowing out a candle. This poem is based on a real event that occurred in New Hampshire, in America, in 1910. A young boy was cutting wood with a chainsaw when it hit a loose pulley and severed his hand. The boy died of shock, blood-loss and heart failure. The incident made a tremendous impression on Frost.

The poem opens with vivid images comparing the saw to vicious creatures. It buzzes threateningly like a swarm of bees, snarls like a savage animal and rattles like a venomous rattlesnake. There is a sense of unease, and the scene is set for disaster as the saw fiercely reduces the wood to dust. There is a sense of foreboding and dread.

The tone changes and the scene becomes tranquil and homely. The wood is fragrant and a light breeze blows. The scenery is picturesque as the sun sets behind the mountains. Although the setting sun is a romantic and beautiful image, we cannot forget that darkness then follows. Line 7 reminds us of the menacing saw as it 'snarled and rattled, snarled and rattled'. The danger and threat is emphasised. It was a day when 'nothing happened' and the poet wishes it had remained like that: 'Call it a day, I wish they might have said'. In retrospect, had the boy been released from work a half-hour early, he would have been delighted and the disaster would have been avoided.

We are reminded that this is a domestic scene by the arrival of the boy's sister wearing an apron and announcing supper. Line 16 begins the tragedy. The saw leaps from the boy's hand and the hand is severed. The poet is shocked and exclaims 'But the hand!' This short, simple phrase reflects the shock and fright felt by all present. The boy's reaction is at first a regretful laugh, but as the reality of the situation becomes clear he swings around helplessly, appealing for help as he tries to keep the blood and the life from spilling from his wound. The boy is old enough to grasp the severity of the situation, but childish enough to beg his sister not to allow the doctor to remove his hand completely.

The word 'So' followed by a fullstop has a daunting sense of finality about it. The shortening lines and quickening pace of the poem mirror the rising tension and the feeling that everything is happening very quickly. The line 'But the hand was gone already' is purely factual and reserved. It seems the poet cannot reveal any emotion for fear of breaking down. He purely relays the story from here on, as he has removed himself from the scene. The doctor in this story does not symbolise hope; he can do nothing except drug the boy in an attempt to dull the pain and the reality.

Then the unexpected happens — 'No one believed' — the boy's heart stops, and he dies. Again the sentences are short and informative, hiding all emotion. Everyone turns 'to their affairs'; the boy is dead. The last line is vague. Does everyone continue with their daily chores because they are dazed with shock or because they realise there is nothing now to be done except survive and carry on as best they can?

The frozen soil, the high winds and rampaging hunters have all knocked rocks and stones and boulders from the boundary. Frost and his neighbour meet and walk the length of the wall, each one at his own side, and they replace or pick up where there has been damage done. They walk side-by-side but are separated by the wall running between them.

Frost sees the wall as more than a physical barrier. He sees it as something that is coming between them. His neighbour is more conservative. He says that 'Good fences make good neighbours.'

The speaker then starts thinking up counter-arguments to this thesis. He points out that there are no cows that might wander to the other side. The pine cones and apples will fall directly to the ground; neither will cross sides. He says that there is a force out there that keeps knocking down their wall. Maybe it is not meant to be. Eventually the speaker gives up because he believes there is no changing this 'old-stone savage'.

The poem seems to be about the confluence of an old-fashioned world that refuses to change against a modern, liberal ethos of sharing. This poem represents many things, especially where the old meets the new.

Robert Frost Mending Wall

THIS POEM TELLS a simple story about a simple ritual. Frost and his neighbour had a habit of going out every spring after the boundary wall between their respective farms had been ravaged by the forces of winter.

Tess Gallagher The Hug

THIS IS A quirky poem that recalls a single moment and the effect it had on the poet. It is told in a very forthright, matter-of-fact manner. It begins with a scene in which the poet and her husband happen upon a woman 'reading a poem on the street'.

They become part of the audience, and the emotion of the moment overcomes her and she hugs her husband, deeply at first and then subsiding. A man approaches her and asks to be hugged just like that. He asks the husband, who gives his assent. The woman is disappointed that her husband does not want to keep her hugs for himself. She sees it as symbolic of their love: 'for me only'.

When she does begin the hug, she starts to question herself about how deep the hug should be. She finds the size of the man overwhelming. He starts to reciprocate and she knows

> he's
> getting it. This hug. So truly, so
>   tenderly
> we stop having arms

The surrounding world, her husband, the poet and the poem have all disappeared, and they have surrendered to the moment of the hug. She concludes by contemplating the hug and saying that a hug can't be a half-hearted thing. It must 'be a masterpiece of connection'.

Kerry Hardie Daniel's Duck

THIS POEM USES exact and careful detail to show the innocence of a child and his reaction to a dead duck. The poem begins with a calm yet dramatic action. The speaker brings the duck into the family home and hands it over. Time stops in the kitchen, but only momentarily, and everybody returns to what they were doing. The poet cleverly shows how the duck becomes part of what was already there.

> Then the kitchen life — warm, lit,
>   glowing —
> moved forward, taking in the dead bird

Slowly, one of the children drifts towards the duck, taking in its colours and the 'downward-dragginess of death'. Daniel takes in the scene and has a realisation about death and mortality. A duck is no longer just something to feed in the park but a real, dead thing in front of him. He starts to understand what death means.

When the adult reappears in the poem, she is there as a guide who tries to make things easier for him. Daniel can still not articulate what he sees:

> I thought there was water on it —

He retracts back into himself, 'going small with relief', and the adult sees the pressure leave him, the pressure of coming face to face with death. It's the pressure of growing up.

Thomas Hardy When I set out for Lyonnesse

THIS SHORT BALLAD has all the ingredients of a medieval romance. It is a love poem about an extraordinary, life-changing journey. It fails, however, to tell us what actually happened at the traveller's destination to bring about the transformation.

Stanza 1 begins with the poet embarking on a journey. He is lonesome and nature reflects his mood — 'the rime was on the spray'. There is a sense of mystery, as we do not know why the speaker is lonesome or indeed why he is setting out on this journey.

Stanza 2 further develops the sense of mystery by introducing enchantment and archaic language. He does not detail what happened in Lyonnesse, but he tells us that no prophet would dare to tell nor could any wizard ever guess.

Stanza 3 describes the speaker after his strange and mysterious journey. He is a changed man and this is obvious to those around him who look on in silent surprise — 'All marked with mute surmise'. He has found love and there is magic in his eyes, glowing and full of joy. In true medieval romantic style, the hero has returned having battled his demons and is now invigorated by having found true love.

The tone of the poem is one of optimism and joy as the speaker has undergone a metamorphosis from lonesomeness to fulfilment.

Seamus Heaney *A Constable Calls*

THIS POEM IS the second in a sequence called 'Singing School' from Heaney's collection *North*. In this collection he outlines some of his formative moments growing up in Northern Ireland in the 1950s and 1960s. Heaney is remembering an incident from his childhood when a Constable called to his parents' house to record tillage returns in his ledger. Before we even see the Constable, we sense his authority from the description of his bicycle. The pedals are relieved that the Constable is giving them a break:

'The pedal treads hanging relieved / Of the boot of the law.'

When we are introduced to the Constable we see he is out of place in the Heaneys' farmhouse kitchen. There is no mention of a welcome or small talk or even an offer of a cold drink to revive him and his 'slightly sweating hair'. His job at the farmhouse appears to be two-fold — 'Arithmetic and fear.' He is recording in detail, 'acres, roods and perches', the tillage activities of the farmer, but he is also casting threat and fear over the proceedings. We do not know if it is felt by all present, but certainly the young boy feels a powerful sense of menace and risk. He examines in detail the Constable's gun:

the polished holster
With its buttoned flap, the braid cord
Looped into the revolver butt.

The father tells a lie, omitting a line of turnips. The boy is consumed by fear as he assumes 'small guilts' and imagines the consequences — a trip to the 'black hole in the barracks.' The ledger is referred to as 'the domesday book', perhaps recalling the survey made by William the Conqueror in 1068, or perhaps, more frighteningly, referring to 'The Doomsday Book,' which lists all good and bad deeds when Judgment Day comes.

When the Constable leaves there is no sense of relief. Instead, his presence remains on as a shadowy figure. As his bicycle moves away the ticking sound of the wheels is intense. We are left thinking of a clock ticking towards Judgment Day or, more menacingly, a time bomb ticking closer to an explosion.

Seamus Heaney *A Call*

SEAMUS HEANEY'S FATHER died in 1986. This poem remembers one particular phone call. At first glimpse it does not seem to have been a very important phone call as nothing extraordinary happens. On further examination of the poem, however, we see that the importance of the phone call lies in the thoughts that occupy Heaney's mind as he waits for his father to come to the phone.

The poem starts off very normally, with someone, probably the poet's mother, answering the phone and going to get the father to speak to their son. While Heaney waits, he imagines his father, weeding his leek rig, in minute detail. He examines each stalk carefully, and happily removes each weed one by one.

Heaney's attention is then drawn to the hallway of his parents' home, where the phone sits waiting to be picked up by his father. He hears the amplified ticking of the hall clock and the sound suggested is 'grave' and solemn and perhaps even causing a little anxiety. His mind wanders further and he thinks of the *Everyman* play, where God sends Death, in person, to summon Everyman to Judgment Day. Heaney thinks that if this medieval play were set in modern times, Death would just phone Everyman to send for him.

When finally Heaney's father answers the phone, the poet feels the urge to tell his father that he loves him. The thoughts of death and time ticking away evoked while he waited have made him think of how his father may not always be just a phone call away. However, Heaney does not say the words, and the conversation commences as normal.

- -

Seamus Heaney The Underground

THE SCENE IS immediately set as the poet describes the Underground tunnel through which he and his new wife are rushing. Although the poem is set in the London Underground railway station

Heaney refers to Greek mythology and we are transported to a mythical underground. His wife is 'speeding ahead' and he pursues her like in a scene of a hero's quest from a Greek myth. He is like a 'fleet god' so in love with his intended that he refuses to accept her refusal to submit to his charms. Like the maiden Syrinx who turned into a reed to escape the half-man / half-goat god Pan or indeed the nymph Daphne who called upon her father to turn her into a plant to escape the great warrior Apollo, Heaney fears his wife may metamorphose into 'some new flower japped with crimson' before he catches her.

In the rush of the chase the buttons of her coat fall to the ground leaving a trail on the floor of the underground station. Does she leave the trail intentionally so he can find her as Hansel and Gretel followed the trail of pebbles to find their way home? They may appear to be carefree honeymooners rushing to the Proms but there are hints of uncertainty and doubt.

There is an unusual change of tone as we examine the final stanza. The poem concludes where it began 'in draughty lamplit station'. The trains have gone, the track is wet and the poet feels 'tensed'. The station once again becomes a mythical place. He is concentrating hard listening to hear his wife's footstep behind him. He is 'bared and tense' and fights the urge to look back to reassure himself of her presence. He feels like a modern day Orpheus, the Greek god who lost his wife forever when, despite warnings from the gods, he looked behind him to see if she, Eurydice, was still there.

George Herbert **The Collar**

IN THIS POEM the speaker yearns for freedom from the constraints of his ministry. In lines 1–16 he outlines how he pines for a release. He opens on a note of defiance and rebellion: 'I struck the board'. He feels he is working for nothing; there are no rewards for his hard work and self-sacrifice. In lines 17–26 he examines in detail the state of his life and discovers that there were rewards and opportunities, but that he was blind to them as he was so focused on his vocation. His soul suggests that he should indulge in 'double pleasures' to make up for lost time. He is urged to walk away from 'thy cage' — the life that has imprisoned him — and to grasp life and all the opportunities it has to offer.

In lines 27–32, a plan is formulated. The speaker is going to break free; he will take 'thy deaths head' (the symbol of death) and cast it aside. He tells himself that he has no one to blame except himself for his confined situation, as anyone who tolerates such a life without trying to improve it deserves their suffering.

The whole direction of the poem alters in the final four lines. The chaos and disorder, rebellion and conflict are halted. The speaker has spun out of control — 'I rav'd and grew more fierce and wilde' — as he considers the freedom, choices and pleasures available to him if he casts off the collar. Order is restored in the form of an authoritative voice calling 'Child!' The speaker accepts this call submissively, and answers, 'My Lord.' Chaos becomes order and rebellion becomes compliance as the paternal voice of God calls.

This poem is wildly dramatic in its imagery, form and structure as the poet strives to reflect the speaker's disordered, chaotic state of mind spiralling out of control, searching for things he feels he should desire and need in an effort to feel a measure of success and achievement.

Gerald Manley Hopkins **Inversnaid**

THE FIRST STANZA describes a burn, or stream, which is brown, perhaps because it is shaded 'darksome', and perhaps because it is so turbulent that there is silt in it — until it goes over a waterfall 'roaring down' the 'rollrock highroad' and falling 'home' to the lake below.

In the second stanza Hopkins notes the contrast of the delicate froth over the seething water 'broth' of a dark whirlpool — as if light and airy things can survive in a place that would be fatal to man. And the third stanza describes the dew sprinkled on the hillsides through which the burn passes, where one can see tufts of heather and fern and the berries on the ash tree.

In the final stanza Hopkins asks the question: What would the world be without the wild places? In place of an answer, he makes a repeated plea for them to be left, leading to the triumphant wish for them to live long — a statement we are used to hearing made about a person, but perhaps not about 'weeds' and 'wilderness'.

The poem is consistent in that the poet refers only to natural things or features of the Highland landscape, and he does not introduce himself into the scene, other than in the direct appeal to the reader in the questions of the last stanza.

The argument of the poem is simply shown in its structure: three stanzas of description, followed by one in which the poet reflects on the value of natural beauty.

But the most obvious technical feature that marks Hopkins' verse is his vocabulary, and his readiness to play with words and invent new ones, relying on the sound to suggest the meaning. For example, we do not need to know what 'twindles' means (in a dictionary sense) to imagine the froth on the pool that Hopkins describes in the second stanza. This is just as well, because we will not find 'twindles' in most dictionaries. Other inventions include 'rollrock', 'fáwn-fróth', 'heathpacks' and 'beadbonny'.

The poem contains many striking images, most of which we can read literally. But Hopkins is a devout Catholic, who finds heaven (and maybe hell) all around him, so the image of the fáwn-fróth falling over the waterfall's edge and into the pitchblack pool may well be intended as a metaphor for the human soul. The froth is almost nothing, yet it can survive the destructive torrent and the pool of Despair.

At the end of the poem Hopkins praises 'wildness and wet'. The whole poem celebrates the life-giving properties of water, which is often a symbol of life in the poetry of the Bible. It may seem a dangerous and destructive force as it plunges over the waterfall, but in reality all natural life depends on the rivers and streams and pools.

Gerard Manley Hopkins Spring

HOPKINS' POEMS DEPEND on sound and association as much as on a literal reading. Therefore, it is important that his work be read aloud and that the reader try to hear what Hopkins is saying before going for a literal understanding of his poetry.

In 'Spring', Hopkins tries to show the wonder of God by showing an appreciation for His creation of spring. His first sentence is a statement of fact: 'Nothing is so beautiful as spring'. He presents this clearly, allowing no equivocation. He then goes on to give a series of examples to prove his point. He takes parts of nature that dominate the springtime to flesh out his statement. With a rush of words and sounds, he lists off the flowers, the birds, the trees, the sky and the lambs as all testament to the fact that 'Nothing is so beautiful as spring'.

In the sestet, he makes a plea that we should appreciate what we have before it is gone from us. He makes reference to the Virgin Mary and a sense of freshness that needs to be cherished.

Patrick Kavanagh Shancoduff

ACCORDING TO THE critic Antoinette Quinn, 'Shancoduff is a north-facing hill farm depicted at its wintry worst, frostbound, starved of grass, swept by sleety winds.' Yet this is a love poem to it. Kavanagh had a love–hate relationship with the countryside of his youth. One of his most famous poems is 'Stony Grey Soil'. In that poem the poet accused the area where he was reared of burgling 'his bank of youth'. He describes the area as being one that is lifeless and soulless, and he questions how he managed to survive in a place where even plantlife struggled to maintain an existence.

Yet in this poem his attitude is different. He is more interested in finding the good in his **'black hills'**. He turns any notion of something negative into something positive. He transforms the faults of Shancoduff in the same way that a lover transforms his partner's faults into something to be loved. The immediate question that must be asked is why would anybody write a love poem to Shancoduff?

The answer must be because it is his. He claims ownership four times. He calls them **'My black hills'** twice in the first verse and then **'My hills'** and **'my Alps'**. Possession of this land is obviously very important to Kavanagh. After all, the hills are eternal. Shancoduff will last long after he has gone and, more importantly, it will still be there after the people who sneer at it are gone. He also personifies the hills. They are given a personality like a lover would have. The hills can **'look'**, they are **'incurious'**, they are **'happy'**, they **'hoard'**.

Kavanagh relishes their drabness. Anything that might be confused as being negative can be construed as a positive. For example, the fact that the hills are so incurious or inactive that they can't even be bothered to look at the sun is seen as a good thing when Kavanagh compares it with the fate of Lot's wife in the Bible, who was turned to salt for looking back as she left Sodom and Gomorrah.

Kavanagh places a lot of emphasis on the local placenames. He lists them with pride: **Glassdrummond, Rocksavage, Featherna Bush**; these are as important as the Alps. The names themselves have mythic qualities. They sound tough and treacherous. They have the resonance of something from an action movie where a hero stands proud above the hills. They all have a grandness granted to them by being multi-syllabic.

Kavanagh's own importance in the poem is also highlighted here as the person who has

. . . climbed the Matterhorn
With a sheaf of hay for three perishing
* calves*

This act itself seems heroic, as if he had climbed the most dangerous mountain-face in the world, whereas all he has done is walk up a hill to feed the cows. This use of hyperbole shows the love that Kavanagh has for this place.

The rebellious nature of the hills is also shown as the hills refuse to conform to the usual structures of nature. They are oblivious to the changes in the seasons and the weather. Their immortality is stressed by the fact that they are unchanged by the travails of time. Springtime cannot catch up with them as his

. . . hills hoard the bright shillings of
* March*
While the sun searches in every
* pocket.*

The poem turns at this point; the poet has come to the realisation, albeit after being told so, that his mountains are not the glorious thing of beauty that he may have thought they were. The farmers who are in a more sheltered, wealthier place sneer at him. Even though his hills are personified with their **'rushy beards'**, nobody else declares them worth looking after. When he is acknowledged as a poet, it is almost done as a form of derision. A poet may be someone who is seen as poor.

Kavanagh departs with a rhetorical question that is forced on him by the comments of the other men. This affects him deeply, just as if his wife or lover were to be described as ugly or disgusting. He asks himself **'is my heart not badly shaken?'**. The love that he felt for the hills is broken by the reality forced on him.

Patrick Kavanagh A Christmas Childhood

IN THIS POEM, Kavanagh seems to be very conscious of his voice and the voice that he is using in the poem. Kavanagh adopts an innocent, naive attitude in this poem and this seems to be central to both the style and the substance. It is this merging of what he is saying and how he is saying it that gives this poem real quality. It uses simple, direct language and this simplicity is also important in what the poet is attempting to say. This is, however, in this reader's eyes a poem of two halves, to use the football cliché. Indeed this poem was originally published as two separate pieces; the first part was published in 1943, the second part was published a full three years earlier.

PART I

The poem begins with a simple description of a potato field where one side was in the sun and was beginning to thaw out. The other side was still frozen over and 'white with frost'. Nature dominates everything; it takes over and liberates inanimate objects. The paling-post that was once merely supporting a fence now sends music out through it:

> And when we put our ears to the paling-post
> The music that came out was magical.

The way that nature attacks all the senses is important to Kavanagh. He goes through sight, taste and hearing in order to give us a holistic vision of how the Christmas spirit invades everything.

He then inserts an over-the-top repetition of his emotions. Hyperbole pervades through this part with even the fence providing 'magical' music. He continues with this mixture of the simple and the marvellous when comparing a gap of light with 'a hole in Heaven's gable'. Even an apple tree reminds him of the temptation of Adam. The death of innocence and a longing to return to innocence is a familiar theme in Kavanagh's poetry, and this reinforces it. The world has taken him, like Eve took Adam, from what he supposed was a better life.

> O you, Eve, were the world that tempted me
> To eat the knowledge that grew in clay
> And death the germ within it!

He then sets up the second part of the poem by leaving us tranquil symbols of the 'gay / Garden that was childhood's', the most important being the final image 'Of a beauty that the world did not touch.'

There is a longing here to return to a better time for himself. In that time people were more dependent on nature. This closer interaction with nature is epitomised and made clearer by the amount of religious imagery that runs through the first section. There is an abundance of religious imagery present, such as 'Heaven's gable' and Eve and the apple. The time was more sacred to Kavanagh; he saw it as a time that was also good and holy.

PART II

The second part of the poem continues with the religious imagery, and makes striking comparisons between an Irish town and Bethlehem with its 'stars in the morning east'. There is a genuine excitement pervading this part, and it is less diluted by an adult knowingness than the first part. There are simple descriptions of what was going on in his childhood, and this allows him to retain an attitude of childlike wonder. The voice in the second half of the poem is certainly clearer.

The setting for the second half of the poem is almost completely outdoors, and this natural, open setting allows him to go from the local to the universal, or even biblical, with ease. There is a seamless intertwining of the personal and the public. Again, the significance of the fact that the father was playing his music outdoors cannot be underplayed. He finds harmony with nature and allows it to influence his playing. The stars manage to recognise his father's music, and are so captivated that they decide to dance to it.

Rapidly, Kavanagh brings us back to his own townland and remarks on the unspoken signs between the families. Whereas in 'Epic' he describes local rivalries, here the unspoken language of music is a uniting force as 'his melodeon called / To Lennons and Callans'. Kavanagh remarks that he 'knew some strange thing had happened'. The harmonising power of his father's music is highly significant when one reflects on the first verse, where the music from the paling-post is described as magical.

His mother's daily ritual of milking the cows becomes inspired by 'the frost of Bethlehem'. The religious imagery continues here. Bethlehem brought new hope to people, and this time of year, with its sense of a new start, also suggests rebirth. Nature in the form of ice and wind and the water-hen is recalled. It is the sense of 'wonder of a Christmas townland' where even the dawn is personified and winks. Yet again Kavanagh tries to show how all of the senses are affected. Sight with the 'child-poet [who] picked out letters', the sound of the melodeon and when the 'water-hen screeched in the bog' and the

Mass-going feet
Crunched the wafer-ice on the pot-
holes

In the sixth verse, Kavanagh shows exquisite skill at mixing the northern constellation Cassiopeia with 'Cassidy's hanging hill', using run-through lines with clever use of alliteration to expose the child's sense of awe at Christmas. This also introduces the religious notion again, and suggests the northern star that guided the three wise men towards the birth of Christ; instead the stars guide people towards his father's house.

There is one wise man who proves his intelligence by commenting on the poet's father's melodeon playing. His father is working just like nature when the inanimate is brought to life as the man says, 'Can't he make it talk'.

Pleasant childhood memories of Christmas are exposed graciously throughout the poem; his father's way of making the melodeon talk, his mother's commitment to the daily work on the farm, his presents and an overall satisfaction that nature has provided all of these things.

Brendan Kennelly A Glimpse of Starlings

THIS POEM IS about the poet's father. It is a heartfelt portrait of his father as the poet revisits the last painful days before his death. The poem starts with a paradox:

I expect him any minute now although
He's dead.

The poet then goes on to describe his father's morning rituals. He prays 'to his own dead', gets dressed, eats his breakfast and stares at a photograph that raises a lot of questions for him. This image of the photograph is very strong; the father eats it with his eyes. This points to an idea that he may be trying to reconcile the present with the past.

This idea recurs when we see the father struggle with the question of how he came into this position where 'Daylight is as hard to swallow as food.' Kennelly switches senses, from taste to hearing. He starts remembering sounds from his past, the feet, the cough and the turn of the key in the door all bring back memories of his father's death.

The open door symbolises his father's release from his painful end: 'to what looks like release from what feels like pain'.

He re-emphasises this point with the image of the starlings, as he sees his father's soul lifting up to heaven. He also sees the release of pressure on his father's life. This image can also be seen to represent the leaving behind of one life, the migration of the soul, and the beginning of another.

Brendan Kennelly
Night Drive

THIS IS A narrative poem. It tells of three separate scenes; firstly the journey from Dublin to Limerick taken by the poet and Alan, his brother perhaps. The second part tells us what they find when they get there. The third part describes the journey home.

Their journey to Limerick is done in a night when the weather is madness. Alan does all the talking on the journey while the poet is unable to say a word. Most of this section describes the weather. He describes the weather as being like a mad, rabid animal. He shows the wind trying to lift the car and move it. He shows the river breaking its banks and grabbing the car. He shows the trees reaching out from the side of the road and breaking their journey. Then the strangest thing happens: the frogs are forced out of the marshland by the weather and onto the road.

Section two is set in the hospital where the poet's father is lying still, yet sweating. There is serenity in this part of the poem compared to the madness and wildness in the first section. The colours are white; the pillow and the 'white hospital bed'. The contrast is striking. Their father tries to fight back the inevitable and succeeds temporarily at least. He has been reduced by his battle however; he is no longer able to 'rail against the weather'.

The third section allows time for reflection. Darkness returns in this last piece. The brothers have been made sombre by their experience and death is the first thing to greet them as they make their journey home. Alan is distracted by having to focus on his driving and does not have as much room to contemplate as his brother does. He shows his optimism when he suggests 'I think he might pull through now'.

On the other hand, nature has left the poet in a more pessimistic mode as he is haunted:

In the suffocating darkness
I heard the heavy breathing
Of my father's pain.

Nature has become overwhelming.

Thomas Kinsella
Thinking of Mr D.

THIS DECEPTIVELY SIMPLE portrait is filled with nuance and depth. It paints a picture of a man referred to only as Mr D. He is a character who is observed from a distance. We get a hint of what he looks like, but the descriptions tell us more about his personality than his looks.

He seems quiet and reserved. There is talk surrounding him, and he takes it in without comment or retaliation. Instead his 'quiet tongue /Danced' in silence and he is seen 'Tapping a polished toe'. He does not acquiesce to the 'cheerful slander' that comes from less reserved mouths all around him. His 'scathing smile' reveals more than a thousand words ever could.

Twice, since he has died, the speaker has visualised him in different situations. One occasion brought to mind the man's dignity as he left the seemingly 'right company', removing himself from the telling of 'one last murmured little tale'.

He also remembers Mr D. 'down by the river' in the shadowy light. He moves quickly away from the source of his hurt, and concentrates instead on the murky reflection that he sees in the river.

Throughout the poem, Kinsella uses rhyme and assonance to heighten the atmosphere in the poem as he describes the plight of a man isolated from those around him.

Thomas Kinsella
Mirror in February

THE FIRST STANZA dramatically sets the scene. It is morning time in February. The room is half dark; the speaker is half dressed and half awake when he is suddenly riveted by the image looking back at him from the mirror. The heavy alliteration and repetition of the 'd' sound, long vowel sounds and the use of dashes reflect the sense of lifelessness and weariness felt by the poet.

The room is musty and damp — the soil opened outside his window. On the one hand, this represents ploughing and preparing the soil for planting seeds and crops, but the open soil can also present us with the image of an open grave. The air is stale, as is the poet's mood, and his exhausted eyes and down-turned mouth suggests cynicism and disdain. The image he sees in the mirror captivates him, and he looks deeper, beyond the image in the mirror, and tries to see into his soul. This is an important moment of reflection and realisation for the poet.

In stanza 2 the poet accepts that he must, once again, open his mind to learning in an effort to accept the harsh reality that has eluded him up to this moment. He has to accept that youth is gone and that, unlike Christ, at the age of 33 he has achieved little and is not complete or fulfilled. He still has to take up his cross and face his future.

Outside his window he notices the severely pruned trees awakening with buds and signs of renewed life. It is a harsh necessity that trees must be cut back if they are to improve their fruitfulness. They may be defaced, but it is to their advantage in the long run. The poet reflects that life defaces humans but it is not to their advantage, and it is not for renewal. Ageing only adds to the suffering of man. There is nothing to be benefited from it. There is no second springtime for man. The poet does not like this fact — 'In slow distaste' he pulls himself together and with some degree of dignity and grace he folds the towel in a gesture of resignation. He is forced to accept that he is getting older and, unlike the trees, he will have no opportunity for renewal. He must learn to tolerate what the future has in store for him.

Philip Larkin
Ambulances

IMAGES OF MALADY and death are the main concerns of this poem. The vehicle represents death itself, which can take anybody away at any time.

Inside the ambulance the ill are confined and cannot do anything against this. In 'Ambulances', the people inside are described as immobile subjects 'that overtop / Red stretcher-blankets', while outside are 'women coming from the shops / Past smells of different dinners', smells which are pleasant.

Death and life are dreams in this poem. Life is a dream of unreachable happiness while death is an unconscious dream that nobody alive knows about. The ill of 'Ambulances' are unconscious, while the ambulance men, like death itself, 'come to rest at any kerb'. From the personal tragedy the spell of death becomes communal, even if it is described as a 'personal fate'. The simile of 'confessional' provides a religious interpretation for the poem, where the people get into the confessional to experience rebirth and get back to a new life. This interpretation involves the real function of ambulances, i.e. to help to heal the body, just as confessionals help to heal the soul.

Voyage is an important notion in the poem: an ambulance travels all day. Perhaps Larkin is referring to the idea that the ambulance is on a constant circuit of death, picking up and moving on. It is a continuous circle, only broken temporarily to deliver the dead or nearly dead.

It is also interesting to see that life outside the ambulance continues for those whom death has not touched. It 'dulls to distance all we are.'

Philip Larkin **The Explosion**

THIS LYRIC TELLS the story of an accident at a mine in England where many people were killed. It is said to be based on real events. It describes two groups of people: miners and their wives. The first five verses describe a group of miners on their way to work on the day of the explosion. The rest of the poem looks at the wives they leave behind, their reaction to the catastrophe and the choices that they face for the future.

The first part of the poem is told in a passive, objective voice. It is very matter-of-fact. The poet is not a part of this community. He talks about 'men' and 'they'. The first sign gives nature an ominous role as the 'shadows pointed' at the scene of the impending doom, giving a feeling of inevitability. The men are shown without too much emotion. They are simple men making their way to work without any awareness of what is coming for them:

> . . . men in pitboots /
> Coughing oath-edged talk and
> pipe-smoke.

There is innocence in the men. They chase rabbits and examine birds' eggs like children might. This innocence is soon to be lost. They are part of a community — 'Fathers, brothers, nicknames' — a community soon to be torn apart.

When the explosion happens, Larkin gives it only a brief mention:

> At noon, there came a tremor; cows
> Stopped chewing for a second . . .

He begins the second section of the poem with a quote that is full of hope and redemption. He tells us of the closeness of the men to their families as their wives see their husbands in a vision. The poet urges that this redemption and hope be shown to the women. He wishes them faith, and that they would take heart in their love for their lost men. He hopes that the men will be seen by those they leave behind as having gone to a better place, as pure as they were when they left.

This poem is positive at the end where it shows the innocence of the men hasn't had a chance to be broken. Even though they have met a horrible fate, the poet shows hope for their souls in the image of the 'eggs unbroken'.

Denise Levertov What Were They Like?

THIS IS A direct, angry, political poem about the Vietnam War. The poet sets up a question-and-answer session. Six questions are asked and then later they are answered. The tension is felt all through the poem. There is a boiling anger, yet the speaker in the poem is trying her best to be reserved and cautious.

The questions come first. They seem to be coming from an anthropologist who is trying to find information about a lost society. The questions seem to be harmless, but when they are balanced by the answers their significance becomes obvious. The questions refer to innocuous items like 'lanterns of stone', 'opening of buds', 'laughter', 'ornament', poetry and 'speech and singing'. But when we hear the tenor of the responses we know these things are very important indeed.

In the first answer the speaker takes the metaphor of stone used in referring to their lanterns and uses it to refer to their hearts. In fact, the thought of even asking about lanterns seems anathema to the speaker. She implies that it cannot matter about light when you have no heart.

Next she explains that without life or the beginnings of life there was no place for flowering beauty, never mind celebrations of that. The third answer is perhaps the most terrifying and bleak, yet also the plainest:

Sir, laughter is bitter to the burned mouth.

It is obvious from the fourth answer that ornament is only an afterthought when you consider that they barely had bodies to put the ornament on.

In the fifth answer she explains that the victors often write history. There is nothing in these people's immediate history that they would want to celebrate. Even nature was destroyed for these people. They could not look in pools of water and see themselves any longer. Their language had been reduced to the language of the panic-stricken:

When bombs smashed those mirrors there was time only to scream.

Again, the speaker tells us that singing can no longer be heard from these people, who have been frightened into silence. She gives us the most beautiful image in the poem when she tells us that when they did sing, 'their singing resembled / the flight of moths in moonlight'. This encapsulates the great, unified beauty that they were once capable of. She then reminds us of the fact that all that beauty is now irrelevant, for there is nothing left to see or hear.

This is a hauntingly powerful poem that tells the story of a forgotten people.

Liz Lochhead
Kidspoem/Bairnsang

THIS POEM WAS originally written to teach schoolchildren the difference between dialect (local forms of language) and the conventional English language.

The poem can be divided into three sections. Section 1 (lines 1–12), in the distinctly Scottish dialect, recalls a child's first day at school. Section 2 (lines 13–24) translates the first 12 lines into understandable 'proper' English. The only change made to the text is that Section 2 is introduced in line 12 by saying that school was where she learned to forget her Scottish way of speaking. Section 3 (lines 25–37) repeats the start of the story all over again in the Scottish dialect, proving that she hasn't forgotten it after all. But the final five lines bring about a bitter twist to the childish manner in which the rest of the poem is written:

> *Oh saying it was one thing*
> *but when it came to writing it*
> *in black and white*
> *the way it had to be said*
> *was as if you were posh, grown-up,*
> *   male, English and dead.*

These lines are a direct attack on the bland, homogenised, stuffy and lifeless English language often referred to as 'Proper English'. Liz Lochhead is very proud of her Scottish accent and way of speaking; she refuses to conform as that would mean losing her identity. She is unwilling to see her Scottishness as an obstacle to her aims as a writer. She once said that for a woman to excel in Scotland she had to have a very good relationship with her male side.

Lochhead rejects all the demands on her to conform to the preconceived notions of what a good poet should be. The message in this poem is direct and crystal clear. Lochhead's poetry is the poetry of the everyday person, no airs or graces, it appeals to the child in everyone, it rejects the traditional view of the English poet and most importantly it is alive. She considers that a poem is a voice and insists that it is spoken out loud.

Michael Longley
Badger

THIS POEM IS divided into three sections. Section I, three stanzas long, admires the badger in his natural habitat. He is easily placed in nature but also in history. He is not out of place as he moves 'Between cromlech and stone circle'. He is skilful, not just digging indiscriminately but 'excavating' like miners 'down mine shafts'. The poet compares him to the fox and the hare and it is obvious that he feels that the badger is superior in his movements to both. As a nocturnal animal the badger does not interrupt the silence of the night, instead he becomes one with the darkness, wearing it 'around his shoulders'. This is an image of a strong, skilful, independent animal posing no threat to anyone or anything. Even in death he does not impinge on others, he just 'Returns underground to die.'

Section II concentrates on the detailed workings of the badger's body. The badger's stomach digests 'dog's mercury', 'brambles, the bluebell wood;', while his foot turns acorns and his head, a head sought by others, brushes easily through the undergrowth. This animal is an integral part of Ireland and has lent his name to many placenames.

Section III highlights the hunt for the badger. No reason is offered as to why this inoffensive animal — 'earth dog' — is being hunted. He is dragged from the earth by a tongs. It is referred to as 'a difficult delivery', but it is not a birth being described here but rather a death, possibly a murder. The once skilful, agile animal is now described as vulnerable. No respect is shown as he is dragged over stones towards a cruel end. 'The trees they tilted' in sorrow at such a cruel, violent end for this strong, independent animal.

Louis MacNeice
Meeting point

THIS IS A well-known love poem with an even better known first line: 'Time was away and somewhere else'. The setting is romantic and intimate. Interestingly, the poet is an observer not a participant. He seems to be looking back yet at the same time intimately involved. Time is an esoteric entity that means nothing to two people in love. The world that goes on around them means nothing to them. They are so caught up in each other that they ignore everything. The escalator is stopped in mid-flow and the couple themselves are similarly suspended, 'neither up nor down.'

The furnishings in the coffee shop where they sit seem to come to life around them. All of nature changes for their love. The stream makes music just for them. The coffee in their cups becomes stagnant like the stream, 'limpid brown'. The sounds that are made by the bells and the pictures presented by the flowers seem to be for them alone. Then, camels seem to arrive from nowhere to carry out a mystical task across the desert, again just for them. The world seems to be centred around their table in the restaurant. The waiter ignores them, time stands still and they are allowed to live within each other's eyes. Time stands still so much that the poet repeats his first line.

The real world has no effect on them, the stock market, nature, all are trivial compared to their love for each other. Finally he makes a prayer of thanks to 'God or whatever means the Good' for understanding the importance of their love.

MacNeice uses a lot of repetition in this poem to reinforce his idea that time is standing still for the lovers. However, he finishes the poem with a half repeat of his first line but changing it to include the woman: 'Time was away and she was here.'

This is a clever, well-constructed poem about being so in love that the rest of the world seems a world away.

Derek Mahon
Grandfather

THIS SONNET PRESENTS a portrait of the poet's grandfather in old age. He used to work as a boilermaker, and later as a foreman in the Harland and Wolfe shipyard in Belfast. His work would have been intensive and tough at the time and would have required physicality. The grandfather is now retired, and Mahon writes about his life after he has no further use for his energy.

The first line is a curious one: 'They brought him in on a stretcher from the world'. There is a sense of a strange journey here. This is a man who has had to be forced to get, where he ended up. His previous life is ended and he is at the beginning of a new one. However, despite his reluctance he is 'wounded but humorous'.

His working life has given way to a simpler one. He is eager and ready to take on the world again now that he has been freed from the burdens of employment. This journey has brought him back to his childhood, where he could play away to his heart's content. He is up at six in the morning, ready to take on the world 'with a block of wood / Or a box of nails'. He is clearly enjoying this journey of self-discovery. His enigma is clear in the second verse where he is hard to track down: 'Never there when you call'. He is only found 'after dark'.

The poet describes his grandfather as 'cute', which could refer to his childlike attitude or his shrewdness. When night-time comes, he is careful to protect himself from the world. The final line of the poem tells us that the grandfather does not need to be pitied or patronised. He is living life as free and aware as ever. He is someone to be admired: 'Nothing escapes him; he escapes us all.'

Derek Mahon *After the* Titanic

THIS LAMENT IS written in the voice of Bruce Ismay, who was the manager of the White Star Line, owners of the *Titanic*. Ismay survived the *Titanic*'s sinking and was one of very few men who escaped alive. He was vilified later in his life as a coward. The *Titanic* itself was built in Belfast, where Derek Mahon is from, and was, as the name suggests, a colossus of a ship. On its maiden voyage to America it struck an iceberg and sank, leading to the death of 1,500 of its passengers and crew. The name is synonymous with disaster. This poem tells the story of what became of Ismay. It is presented in his own voice and is full of self-pity.

There is denial in the very first line: 'They said I got away in a boat' as if it were not true. There is also the accusing 'They'. Ismay sees himself as a victim. He gives out about being 'humbled' and having sunk 'as far that night as any / Hero'. The truth is that he didn't. He lived and many others died. He talks about the sinking of various things:

> . . . in a pandemonium of
> Prams, pianos, sideboards, winches,
> Boilers bursting and shredded
> ragtime.

But he does not talk about people sinking to their deaths. It sounds as if he cares more about what happened to these material things than about all the people who died.

He brings us forward to his life in the present, and describes himself as a pathetic creature hiding in his big house, hiding from nature and the world. He maintains that he is doing his suffering now just like the people who died on the *Titanic*. He tells us that he is locked away as if he were in prison. He tells us of his drugged-out nightmares:

> I drown again with all those dim
> Lost faces I never understood, my poor
> soul
> Screams out in the starlight . . .

He ends the poem wishing to be treated like the rest of the dead. He wishes the people to allow his living soul to be pitied. The question is whether he deserves this: 'Include me in your lamentations.'

Derek Mahon
Antarctica

CAPTAIN LAURENCE OATES is the subject of this poem. Oates was one of the explorers who travelled to Antarctica in 1911–12. Scott wanted to be the first person to reach the South Pole. Eventually when they reached their destination they discovered that they had been beaten by an expedition led by a Norwegian, Roald Admunsen. They had been beaten to the Pole by just three weeks. A catalogue of awful luck covered their return journey. The temperature plunged as low as –50 degrees. Another member of the team, Edgar Evans, died after a fall, having struggled on for two more weeks. They started to run out of food and their animals died.

Oates' feet became gangrenous. He asked the other surviving members to leave him behind and to save themselves. He was slowing them down. They refused to abandon him. Eventually he got up himself and walked out of the tent to his certain death. His last words were the ones quoted in this poem: 'I am just going outside and may be some time.'

Tragically, the rest of the explorers nearly made it to their base; they were only 11 miles away. A blizzard struck. Their bodies were not found for a further eight months. It would be easy to suggest that Oates' death was in vain, but Mahon suggests that it was not.

The poem itself is quite simple. It is very tightly structured with two chorus lines. The first, 'I am just going outside and may be some time', is the quote from Oates as he goes to die. The second, 'At the heart of the ridiculous, the sublime', is Mahon's comment on the act. Even though the statement is a ridiculous one for someone who is about to die, the poet, through his use of the word 'sublime', also sees it as a massively heroic act.

In the first verse he refers to the complicity of the others in this act. They are passive. He goes on to describe how Oates forces himself out to his death, 'Goading his ghost', and shows Oates looking back at the tent, going through the processes of his forthcoming death.

The fourth verse introduces the question of judgment of the act. Mahon is clear that this should not be seen as something weak or even 'some sort of crime'. He says that Oates can be seen as a catalyst for good, for not being selfish and for self-sacrifice. See how much Oates contrasts with the other man from his own times, Bruce Ismay in 'After the *Titanic*'.

The final verse repeats the two choruses together after first telling us that Oates should be admired for 'Quietly, knowing it is time to go.'

Roger McGough
Bearhugs

THIS LYRIC IS a portrait of the poet's two sons, who have grown up, and his relationship with them. It is a warm, loving picture that we get and is written in simple colloquial language.

From the start, the relationship is clear. The poet tells us about the hugs, but he points out that 'we hug each other'. The relationship is clearly two-way. The boys are growing up, but the poet has no regrets about this as you might expect him to have. He is proud of their growth into manhood. He does not condemn them for their smell of 'beer', 'tobacco' or 'women / Whose memory they seem reluctant to wash away'. His affection for them is still fatherly though, in the way that they are described when they were small — 'tiny'. He takes their visits as a sign of love.

When he examines them, he cannot see any resemblance to himself, but he can to his father and his uncles. When he was very young he looked up to these men who were fighting in the Second World War. He admired their confidence and self-assurance at the time and he sees the same traits in his sons now. Their confidence can be seen in the way they slouch back in their chairs, and he imagines them in the uniforms of their grandfather and grand-uncle.

The poet finishes the poem beautifully. He repeats much of the first verse with one crucial difference. He recognises the life, love and energy that he gets from his two sons.

John Milton *When I Consider*

In this sonnet, the poet meditates how half his life has been spent in darkness due to his blindness ('light deny'd'). He wonders if God will be angry with him for not making full use of his writing talent. He makes reference to the Parable of Talents in line 3. In this parable it is believed that God will punish ('is death to hide') those who do not make full use of the gifts (talents) he has bestowed upon them. Milton feels that his talent, writing, is now of little use to him as he can no longer see ('Lodg'd with me useless'). He is, however, still determined to serve God to the best of his ability and on Judgment Day he hopes to present to God a true and honest account of how he has made the most of his talent, and the condition of blindness in which he finds himself. He fears God may 'chide' him, and he questions whether or not God will expect his day's work to be equal to that of a fully sighted person. God is seen as an investor who has invested in Milton. Milton is deeply concerned about the repayment of dividends to God on Judgment Day.

In the octet the poet is full of anxiety and apprehension, but the tone changes dramatically in the sestet. In the sestet Milton receives a whispered reply from God, putting his mind at ease. God does not need the talents he has provided to be returned to him. If man bears the burden and makes the most of his situation, he is serving God to the best of his ability. God is like a king; there are thousands of servants speeding over land and sea without rest, doing his bidding. Milton concludes that one can be loyal to God by standing and waiting to openly receive his word and message. Not all of God's servants must be active 'doers'. Both active and passive service to God is cherished and valued.

Noel Monahan *All Day Long*

THIS POEM EXAMINES how school-children can get lost within the school system. The school curriculum seems to be devised in a way that is out of sync with the way children behave naturally. The poet points out how easily 'children get bored' with the mundane rituals of daily school work 'All day long.'

He then points out how some children 'disappear' within the school system. They are ignored and fall through the cracks in a system that functions on appearances rather than emotional needs.

The poet points out that we shouldn't try to make children fit in neat little boxes and grow up in unison. He points out that when they are pigeonholed in such a uniform way, the system notices that one of them has started to drift away.

He tells us that the people who are supposed to be looking after them have so much of their time consumed by paperwork that it becomes impossible to do their primary work: helping children to grow up and to learn.

He also points out that once they have become 'lost', it then becomes very difficult to bring them back on track again.

One never knows
When they go missing
One never knows
Where to find them

This is a heartfelt poem that points out the dangers of a society that allows a system to take precedence over the people it is designed to protect. It is well constructed with short lines that flow evenly towards the poem becoming questioning rather than polemical.

Edwin Morgan
Strawberries

THIS LOVE POEM does not have any punctuation, which helps it to set in motion a beautiful reminiscence. The poet tells how the taste of strawberries brings him back to a particular moment. This moment was obviously very precious to him and as he recounts it, he wishes to return to it. The lack of punctuation adds a wistful, dreamlike atmosphere to the story. There are also very strong 's' sounds scattered throughout the poem, which add to a feeling of sensuality.

The memory is simple: the poet and his lover sit on a window eating strawberries on a humid afternoon. They face each other eating their strawberries, and even dipping the strawberries in sugar takes on a sensuality for them. When they cross their forks together it symbolises a coming together for the pair. They are completely at one with each other. As the poet kisses his lover he takes back the taste of strawberries from her mouth, and holds her with all the care given to an abandoned child.

He uses this memory to suggest that he would like to repeat that afternoon. To finish he recites an incantation that it should all happen again. He introduces images from nature to suggest the authenticity and naturalness of the scene.

This is a beautifully simple love poem.

Paul Muldoon **Anseo**

CYCLES OF POWER are described in this poem, as is how the abused can often become the abuser.

The initial scene is set in a typical Irish primary school. The poet describes the roll-call system where everybody would answer *'anseo'* as their name was called out. This word **'Was the first word of Irish I spoke'**, as was the case, and possibly still is, for many Irish schoolchildren.

The poet remembers what would happen at the start of every class, when the teacher would call out the last name on the roll, which belonged to Joseph Mary Plunkett Ward. This name is significant for a number reasons. Joseph Mary Plunkett was one of the leaders of the Easter Rising in 1916. The 'Mary' part of it is also significant insofar as it is a name usually associated with girls rather than boys, and certainly not with a military leader of 1916, or the leader that this boy would become. Finally, the name is also important because it gives the teacher a chance to make a pun on the boy's name. Every day he would ask the same question: **'And where's our little Ward-of-court?'** There was a sense of expectancy around this question; the other students would look at each other to see their reaction to it. The teacher was obviously having fun at Ward's expense.

In the second verse we see the twisted nature of the teacher, as he would send Ward out to find his own stick to be beaten with. The teacher would refuse different options until he got the right one to beat him with. This sort of ritual made an impression on Ward, and we see later on that he learned from it as well. The poet gives us fine detail as he describes exactly the effort that Ward would go to in preparing his own tormentor. We can almost imagine Ward being given a lecture about it from the teacher, or taking pride in his work. We can see the engraving almost like a commemoration on a gift:

> *Its twist of red and yellow lacquers*
> *Sanded and polished,*
> *And altogether so delicately wrought*
> *That he had engraved his initials on it.*

The poet then brings us further along in time. Joseph Mary Plunkett Ward is now doing what his namesake had also done. He is leading a secret IRA battalion, and has risen through the ranks. There are many contradictions in his life when we see that

> *He was living in the open,*
> *In a secret camp*

He is no longer the boy who is being bullied and victimised. Instead he is **'Making things happen'**. He has become an important person in a vicious world. He has also learned from his old school teacher. He calls a roll, just like in primary school. One feels the punishment for not answering the roll call this time could be much more severe than getting beaten by a hazel-wand.

He is now the one in the position of authority. He is able to put people in their place and tell them what to do. People are now afraid of him.

Muldoon makes a simple point in a clever way and uses the simple Irish word *'Anseo'* to illustrate it. He says that power must be used carefully. He also says that if not cared for properly, the bullied can become the bully.

Richard Murphy
Moonshine

A CLEVER, PITHY little lyric, this poem highlights the contradiction of wanting to be with someone yet also needing one's own space. It is extremely compact. It spells out its message over four, one-sentence stanzas using barely twenty words in different variations.

The message in this poem is simple, yet the method that the poet uses to pass that message on is very clever. He starts out with his two statements that are to be taken as fact:

> *To think*
> *I must be alone:*
> *To love*
> *We must be together.*

Interestingly, he starts with himself. He attempts to clarify his original statements in the second stanza. He may have confused himself and his readers further, but in the third verse he states the relationship between the two quite succinctly when he declares that his mind is only free enough to think when he is in love and he cannot be in love without also being in love intellectually.

The poem goes full circle in the final verse; he once again sets out the argument that he is torn between thinking and loving. He just does not seem to know what he wants any more.

Howard Nemerov
Wolves in the Zoo

THIS POEM TRIES to tell us the truth behind the bad press that wolves have been given over time. The poet is on a visit to the zoo and muses over the fate of wolves in history and mythology. His first impression of them is interesting; they look odd or out of place, 'like big dogs badly drawn, drawn wrong'. The inscription beneath their cage is defiant, and tells the poet that there is no proof of any serious wrong-doing by any wolves.

He dismisses the stories of Romulus and Remus, and of Little Red Riding Hood. He says that she and her grandmother were the real bullies in the cautionary tale. He tells us that the two species of wolf are nearly extinct because of our attitude towards them. He points out that we have this attitude instilled in us from a very young age, and we have accepted and perpetuated the mythology until wolves have become enemies of humankind along with ghosts and monsters. They became animals worthy of killing by hunters even though they are only like 'big dogs badly drawn'. There is no logic for our fear of these animals besides our growing hatred, fostered by mythology.

Now, the few survivors of our fear have ended up in zoos along with other strange creatures we don't understand. This poem urges us to think twice before allowing myth to become fact.

Julie O'Callaghan
Problems

WE JOIN THIS poem halfway through a rant. The opening line, 'Take weeds for example', is definitely not the first line of an argument. Something or someone has prompted her to launch into a tirade of complaints about seemingly small, inoffensive things. It's true that weeds can be troublesome, but to say that they will overrun your life is an example of the poet's use of hyperbole. Her portrayal of snails as devious and of slugs as thuggish hordes far overstates the reality of the situation. She appears to overestimate the seriousness of puddles of water discolouring the bathtub, and seems to take a deep breath to fume about grass growing up on driveways. Her frustration and exasperation reaches its climax when she addresses her audience as 'Hey, knuckleheads!' She seethes, not just at 'how many problems there are', but at the importance allotted to these minor inconveniences.

Julie O'Callaghan The Net

THIS POEM DETAILS the speaker's discovery that her former classmates from High School are organising a reunion. This is being done through the Lost Classmate website. Immediately we see that the speaker lacks enthusiasm for this project. She says that she is being 'hunted' to infinity. She also speaks about evading the class committee. The wild animal imagery crops up again in the second stanza when she talks about being 'coralled'. She also talks about being 'bombarded'. Her former classmates have been 'captured'. Her language seems extreme for such a simple thing.

She contrasts herself with her 'former locker partner' who

> looks forward
> to being reunited with
> her old school chums.

The word 'chums' seems to be laced with sarcasm. It could be that the speaker might not have the highest regard for her ex-classmates and is surprised that her friend doesn't feel the same way. The speaker cannot be accused of looking back through rose-tinted glasses.

In fact, she seems to be full of what may be unnecessary dread. She promises to hide out and wear a 'disguise', a false name, to see what happens without her. She ends the poem with a double meaning She tells us that she will do

> what I've always done:
> slip through the net.

This tells us a lot about her school days and indicates to us why she seems so reluctant and unenthusiastic.

Mary Oliver **The Sun**

THIS LYRIC IS similar in theme to Gerard Manley Hopkins' poem, 'Spring'. It is one sentence long. This gives the poem an exuberant, flowing tone. The poem feels as if the poet is trying to get all of her ideas about the sun out in one breath. On one level, it is a paean or homage to the sun and to nature, but later in the poem it asks deep questions about human nature and about how we treat the world. Mary Oliver is renowned as a naturalist, and as such her environmentally conscious attitude in it makes this poem very relevant in the early part of the twenty-first century.

The poem begins with a heartfelt question that twists and turns its way down the page of the poem. She exudes her marvel at the beauty and wondrous nature of the sun as it goes down 'every evening/ relaxed and easy'.

She then focuses on the beauty of the sun as it rises the following morning, 'like a red flower'. She expresses the purity of her love for the sun:

> and have you ever felt for anything
>
> such wild love –

She even calls her own homage futile. She tells us that there is not

> ... anywhere, in any language,
> a word billowing enough
> for the pleasure
>
> that fills you,
> as the sun
> reaches out,
> as it warms you

At the end of the poem she issues a warning to those who do not appreciate the beauty and wonder of the sun. She says the sun is not just a tool for humans to abuse and take advantage of and condemns those who do. This anger at the end of the poem is salutary and seems out of context with the celebratory mood of the rest of the poem. Yet, it seems to fit in the context of the world we live in today. It warns us that material things are not all that they are cracked up to be. We should appreciate what we have before we look to the new.

Marge Piercy *Will We Work Together?*

THIS LYRIC EXAMINES the relationship between a pair of lovers in bed. There has been a misunderstanding between them that needs to be clarified. The speaker in the poem is trying to bring clarity to the situation but is finding herself asking as many questions as she answers.

She addresses her angry lover, who complains that she is 'only sometimes there'. Her riposte is that when she is there, at least she is full of passion:

> *I am bright*
> *as a fireplace roaring*
> *with love, every bone in my back*
> *and my fingers is singing*
> *like a teakettle on the boil.*

These are interesting similes that she uses to describe herself (the fireplace and the teakettle). They are both full of heat and energy. They both signify attempts to put control on a natural substance (fire and water). She is telling us that she is raw energy when she is with him, only kept under control by unnatural methods.

She then declares that her love is unquantifiable. She is so full of passion that she expresses herself in ways that words cannot: 'Words / shred. Poems are refuse.'

She says that she wants their love to be a piece of classical art, something that will inspire love in others. She wants their love to be a celebration and something to be celebrated. She finishes the poem with an aspiration. She wants more than anything else for their love to be 'some useful thing.'

Sylvia Plath *Poppies in July*

DESPITE ITS TITLE, this poem isn't actually about the flowers at all. This is a deeply disturbing poem that describes Plath's state of mind as she lay in hospital, depressed and suicidal. It was written in 1962 during the breakdown of her marriage to Ted Hughes. Because of the confessional nature of Plath's poetry, it is very difficult to separate the poems from her personal life. In some cases, this can lead to students forgetting about the poem and concentrating on her life. However, this poem is certainly a deeply personal plea for help by the poet as she describes the depths to which her mind has sunk.

She begins by describing the poppy flowers as 'little hell flames' as they remind her of a fire as they dance in the breeze. They do not symbolise the comfort and warmth usually associated with flames, instead they remind her of 'hell's flames' and extreme burning, distress and despair. She speaks directly to the flowers. It appears that she is at the edge of reason as all her attention focuses on the flowers. She cannot touch them, they are out of her reach, yet she tries, she puts her hand among the flames in an act of self-harm but she can feel nothing, for 'Nothing burns'.

She is numb, devoid of feeling for the outside world and is despairing in her internal hell. She is mesmerised by the flowers, which leaves her exhausted. There is an element of violence introduced with the mention of a bloodied mouth.

The colour red that dominates the poppies dominates the poem as well. Indeed, the colour red seems to trigger a stream of consciousness in her where she makes free associations with the redness of the poppies, from the flames to 'the skin of a mouth' to the 'bloodied skirts'. The image of the blood is repeated in disgust, as if she wishes to bleed or burn just so she can prove to herself that she is still capable of feeling something. Even if that something is pain, any feeling will do.

These flowers are sending her mind in wild directions as she fails to see any beauty in them at all. She searches for the drugs associated with the poppies. She yearns for an escape, either through pain or sleep. She craves a feeling other than the numbness she feels.

She refers to the poppies' drug-like qualities; some breeds of poppies are used to make drugs like opium and heroin. However, these will numb her even more, so she wishes to be able to 'bleed or sleep'.

She drifts into a stupor even further, so that eventually her whole world becomes 'colorless. Colorless.' This haunting refrain finishes the poem and describes the void that Plath felt herself drifting into.

Sylvia Plath Child

THIS VERY SPECIAL poem about Plath's love for her child is made all the more poignant by the fact that the poet committed suicide two weeks after writing it. The opening line stands alone in the poem. Not only is it the longest line presented on the page, but it is also full of love, joy and admiration for her child. The poet recognises that having a clear eye, unclouded by the difficulties associated with life, is an 'absolutely beautiful thing'. She wants to fill her child's sight with fantastic and interesting things that children love. She wants to present her child with colour and ducks and 'The zoo of the new'. The zoo is full of the unusual and the attention-grabbing, and children love seeing wild animals close-up, which helps to broaden their imagination.

The child meditates on everything that is new. He is untouched by the outside world. He is like a little plant without signs of age or 'wrinkle'. He reflects all he sees and learns like a clear pool of water. The poet hopes that all he sees will be 'grand and classical'.

The final verse is dark and depressing. The poet is aware that she is not providing the things she had hoped for her child. He deserves the 'colour and ducks', 'The zoo of the new', but instead the child is being exposed to 'troublous / Wringing of hands' and a starless sky — a ceiling. There is no potential for adventure in the final verse, only desolation and depression. She should be offering beauty and adventure and potential to develop, but instead the final verse shows her and her child locked inside a cocoon of darkness and despair and there is no ray of hope. The poem ends in despair.

There is no padding in this poem; it is direct in its hopes and aspirations and just as clear in its grimness and melancholy. She knows to what she should aspire to fulfil the child's development needs fully, but concludes knowing she cannot respond as she feels both helpless and hopeless under 'this dark / Ceiling without a star'. The reality is a sense of desolation and this completely overshadows the mother's great intentions.

Sylvia Plath *The Arrival of the Bee Box*

SYLVIA PLATH'S FATHER, Otto, was a professor of biology at Boston University, and a devoted beekeeper. In 1962, Plath decided to follow in her father's footsteps and try beekeeping. She wrote a series of five poems about her experiences and this narrative is one of them. All five poems consisted of five-line verses and this poem is exceptional in that it ends with a single sentence, separate from the seven five-line verses.

The poem opens with the poet telling us this is of her own doing, that she is in control: 'I ordered this'. The bee box has arrived. She describes it using internal rhyme, 'Square as a chair', and a humorous metaphor, 'the coffin of a midget / Or a square baby'. We hear the constant buzz of the imprisoned bees in the onomatopoeic words 'din in it'. We are immediately faced with an image of something unusual and abnormal — a noisy, coffin-like box fit for a midget or an oddly shaped baby.

Verse 1 displays the box as strange, but verse 2 highlights the threat involved. The box is locked for safety; it is dangerous. The poet has no choice but to endure it until morning. We sense that although she is scared, she is also drawn to the bee box. She is fascinated as she cannot see inside clearly. It is left to her imagination to build a picture of what is going on behind the 'little grid'. There is a sense of confinement and imprisonment in the two simple words 'no exit'.

Unable to contain her curiosity, the poet looks through the grid in verse 3. It is 'dark, dark', 'Black on black', resembling African slaves caged up. The atmosphere created is one of constant, furious movement; 'angrily clambering' and miniature hands desperately looking for an escape. No longer is the poet an outsider, she has become a player in the drama. She has been sucked in and feels great empathy for the bees: 'How can I let them out?'. She wants to help; she has forgotten her fear and fascination and now wants to become their liberator.

However, although verse 4 begins with empathy in the first line, the second line changes the poet's mood once again: 'It is the noise that appals me most of all.' She is distressed and dismayed and now compares the bees to a Roman mob — a force to be reckoned with. Individually the bees are acceptable, but as a large, disorderly mob they are to be feared. There is no way of reasoning with their 'unintelligible syllables'. Once again there is a hint of fear, and she is an outsider.

Verse 5 sees the poet examining her part in the scene. She listens to the foreign noise and knows that she is not like Caesar, a cold ruthless leader, but recognises that she is in control, she has choices. She can return the bees, she can starve them, she is their lord and master. They are 'maniacs' and she may do with them as she likes. Just as she says she is not a Caesar in verse 5, she shows her compassionate side in verse 6 as she wonders how hungry they are. She wonders if she released them and stood back, 'turned into a tree', would they forget her and go to feast on the fragrant laburnum and cherry blossoms. We see here that she would love to liberate the bees and watch as they greedily devour the beautiful, pollen-rich flowers outside.

In verse 7 the poet is the alien in her 'moon suit'. Once the bees are freed, she is no longer part of their lives as she has nothing they need: 'I am no source of honey'. She would become unnecessary and irrelevant. She makes plans to set them free, to be their compassionate 'sweet God'. The last sentence, standing alone, promises freedom: the confinement will end, **'The box is only temporary'**. The poet is the controlling power in the poem, and in exercising her power she will do the right thing and release her captives.

In this poem Plath deals with many issues — control, liberation and confinement, power — and the choices available in life.

Adrienne Rich

NOTES ON THE poems of Adrienne Rich have not been included for copyright reasons.

William Shakespeare
Sonnet 18

SHAKESPEARE BEGINS SONNET 18 by asking if he should compare his friend to a summer's day. He decides, however, that a summer's day is changeable, and his friend is more temperate and still lovelier. He also remarks that the length of the summer is too short in comparison to the length of his subject's beauty. In the second quatrain (lines 5–8) Shakespeare continues to debate his choice of comparison. He sees that sometimes the sun shines too hot and sometimes it is clouded over.

And so in the third quatrain (lines 9–12) the poet decides not to compare his friend to a summer's day. His friend's beauty will never fade like that of the summer, he will never lose possession of what he owns because the poet has recorded this for eternity in poetry. The rhyming couplet confirms to us that for as long as men can breathe and see, this poem will regale them with the image of his truly beautiful friend, thus guaranteeing his immortality.

William Shakespeare
Sonnet 60

THE THEMES OF this poem are the ravages of time and the poet's hope to immortalise his friend in this sonnet. The sonnet opens with a simile comparing our time on earth to the waves beating against a stony beach. It seems to be an unending job as waves change and compete with one another. The neat quatrain further develops the theme, saying that birth crawls towards maturity and old age and Time conspires against you to destroy all that has been achieved in your lifetime.

The third quatrain increases the sense of malice and danger posed by time. Time is personified and is intent on destroying blossoming youth by **'digging'** deep wrinkles on a once beautiful brow and devouring all that is rare and beautiful and youthful. This quatrain is rich in active verbs and strong, vivid imagery as the speaker declares that nothing can halt Time/Death as she harvests with her deathly scythe. Just as we feel that the battle is lost and that Time is to be the victor, the final rhyming couplet catapults the sonnet in a completely different direction. The speaker vows to immortalise his friend and **'thy worth'** in spite of all that Time can try to do to destroy him. The poem ends on a note of defiance and hope as the poet hopes to put a halt to Time's campaign against youth and beauty.

Percy Bysshe Shelley
Ozymandias

HERE WE MEET an explorer who has travelled through ancient lands. The traveller tells of the sights encountered on his travels. In the middle of a desert he sees the remains of a statue: 'Two vast and trunkless legs of stone / Stand in the desert'. There is no remnant of the torso, all that remains are two huge legs. Beside the legs lies a head, half sunk into the sand. The head reveals the face of a tyrant. It displays a frown, a wrinkled lip and a look of hard, unfeeling authority. From examination of the statue the traveller deduces that the sculptor has succeeded in interpreting the pharaoh's personality and transferring it onto the statue.

On the base of the statue there is an inscription: 'My name is Ozymandias, king of kings: / Look on my works, ye Mighty, and despair!' This great pharaoh issues a challenge to all other rulers to look at the greatness of his civilisation and acknowledge their inferiority. There is nothing else remaining of this once-great kingdom except miles and miles of sand.

This poem comments on power and the greatness of time — nothing can resist time. Humans, like Ozymandias, boast of their achievements and greatness, but as time passes so too does their supremacy. Looking through the eyes of history, those who were once powerful, reigning supreme, are now reduced to sand and dust. All empires will diminish with time; nature will conquer, time will pass and civilisations will be rendered powerless and inconsequential.

Penelope Shuttle
Jungian Cows

Note: Carl Gustav Jung was born 26 July 1875, in the small Swiss village of Kessewil. He is one of the most influential figures in the practice of psychiatry and psychoanalysis. One of his theories centres around the mother archetype. All of our ancestors had mothers. We have evolved in an environment that included a mother or mother-substitute. We would never have survived without our connection to a nurturing presence during our times as helpless infants. It stands to reason that we are 'built' in a way that reflects that evolutionary environment: we come into this world ready to want mother, to seek her, to recognise her, to deal with her.

THIS CLEVER POEM describes a situation where a herd of cows in Switzerland has fallen into Jung's archetype. They are expecting a mother figure to look after them. Their names are even mythological and historical: 'Venus, Eve, Salome, or Fraulein Alberta', the god of love, the temptress of John the Baptist and a solid local girl all there, suggesting a group of divas on four legs.

They are used to being milked by the lady of the house. However, when she is not available they refuse to yield to her husband. He must adopt a disguise in order to get them to supply him with milk. These divas will not give into a milking machine so the man must become 'an echo of the woman', a surrogate mother to these temperamental heifers. He must put on a 'cotton skirt', wear 'his sweetheart's sunday-best fringed scarf' and walk 'smelling feminine and shy among the cows'.

This is a humorous take on the roles of men and women in society and the stereotypical roles that are expected of them — even by cows.

Penelope Shuttle Zoo Morning

THIS POEM EXAMINES stereotypes. It uses hyperbole to suggest that very often, those we consider to be wild can be more civilised than those who appear to be very civilised on the surface. The poet examines a range of different animals in a typical zoo and puts them in situations where you wouldn't expect to find them. It is as if the animals are putting on an act for their morning visitors in order to fit their image, something the humans who visit seem incapable of.

The elephants appear sombre and stern despite having spent the night partying away. The monkeys fit their likeness by 'gibbering and gesticulating' and abandon their night-time habits of studying and reading. Bears drop their activism and 'adopt their cute-but-not-really teddies' stance' for the visitors. The lions and tigers give up their delicate artwork in favour of snarling and looking mean. Only the snakes stay as they are, still not to be trusted. She salutes them and spells out why they go through their façade each day:

> What a life.
> But none of them would give up show-
>   business.

She turns her attention to the humans and she sees creatures who are incapable of abandoning their base instincts: 'we are not up to being us'. To give us the idea that this might not be all fantasy, she points to a sophisticated performing creature:

> In the insect house
> the red-kneed spider dances on her
>   eight light fantastics

This poem examines what a stereotype is and how assumptions can fool us into smugness. Our ideas of what or who is civilised can often be misguided.

Peter Sirr Madly Singing in the City (after Po Chü-i)

PO CHÜ-I WAS a gentleman poet and government official during the golden age of the Tang dynasty in China (772–846). He was born in Shansi, but later settled in Ch'ang-an in the north-west. He held several government posts during his lifetime, including palace librarian, and several provincial governorships. But because of his willingness to speak out openly against government policies, he was also banished several times.

Po Chü-i eventually retired to a monastery when he was in his 50s. One of his legs was paralysed at the end of his life.

This is a version, or 'after', one of his poems. It is not a direct translation but rather is influenced by the original poem.

The poem begins in celebration of finishing a 'new poem'. The speaker goes to his balcony to look over the city. He wishes to declare his news, when he gets a waft of smoke in his nostrils from the local chip shop. The smell takes him inside the 'chipper' and the rest of his senses spring to life. He sees, smells, hears, tastes and touches everything in the fish shop again. He leans out again and sees the spires of all the churches in his area, he is captivated by his locality and remembers a time when he carried a 'glass table-top'.

He is happy with his place and is ready to sing in celebration. He says that he has become part of the city. The city life, which he may have entered unwillingly, has become part and parcel of his being. He wants to exclaim his love for the city and his life from the rooftops.

William Stafford
Traveling through the Dark

THIS VERY WELL-KNOWN poem presents the speaker with a moral dilemma: does he rescue a half-dead doe, or does he look after the greater good and toss the animal over a deep ravine? He is driving his car on a treacherous winding road when suddenly he sees a deer lying in the road. Immediately, the speaker realises what he must do: 'It is usually best to roll them into the canyon'.

We understand that this is not a new situation for the speaker; the speaker has had to shove dead deer off the road into the canyon many times before. And the speaker makes it clear that to leave the deer lying in the road could cause oncoming motorists to swerve and go toppling into the canyon, which 'might make more dead.'

So, he got out of the car, which he parked just ahead of the deer carcass, and 'stumbled back of the car'. He examines the deer and finds that she has 'stiffened already' and she was 'almost cold.' But as he drags her body over to the lip of the canyon, he notices that 'she was large in the belly.' The doe is carrying a baby fawn in her pregnant belly.

The speaker can tell that the doe has a fawn inside her because 'her side was warm.' The baby was still alive. This turn of events causes the speaker to reconsider. Pushing an ordinary dead deer off the side of the cliff is one thing,

but here is a deer whose baby is alive, almost ready to be born.

He knows that if he pushes the dead doe over the cliff, he will kill the unborn fawn, so he hesitates. Despite the fact that a car could come flying around the bend any moment, the gravity of the situation catches the speaker off-guard and makes him wonder how could he just callously toss away this innocent life?

The fourth stanza describes the scene and acts as a place-holder while the speaker mulls over his alternatives. He notes the 'lowered parking lights', the engine 'purr[ing]' 'under the hood' while he 'stood in the glare of the warm exhaust turning red; / around our group I could hear the wilderness listen.' All of these images depict a scene in which the speaker has but a few seconds to decide what to do.

The fifth stanza tells us that the speaker thought 'hard' about what to do. He calls his hesitation 'my only swerving' because when he realised that the doe was with fawn, his straightforward action had to be questioned.

But he finally comes to the conclusion that he has no choice but to try to save other human lives before it was too late, so he 'pushed her over the edge into the river.'

Dylan Thomas Do Not Go Gentle into That Good Night

ALTHOUGH THIS COULD be addressed to anyone, by the end of the poem it is obvious that it is written for Thomas' sick father. In this poem he never sent, the son begs his father not to accept death quietly, but instead to fight it. While most people tell the dying that it is better to accept death peacefully and gracefully, something more provocative is at work here: that is, though death is a 'good night' in its romantic or hopeful sense of restful bedtime and peaceful darkness, one should not accept it, and instead 'rage' against this 'dying of the light.' Perhaps it is this contradiction that gives this poem its power.

The poem does not preach calm, as might be expected, but rage, rage against death, that event often equated with Nature as an ultimate physical force. This is not a villanelle expressing the pleasure of nature's cycles and seasons, a balanced acceptance of births and deaths, but a raging against that cycle, an acknowledgment that a life within nature — as all lives subject to life and death must be — is not just harmoniously repetitive, but also full of sudden pain and occasional grieving. Perhaps this is one reason for Thomas' phrase, 'good night', an expression minimising death, that event that apparently is too painful for Thomas to mention.

Day and night, or light and dark are long-standing metaphors for life and death, and while Thomas merely adopts the tradition, he also breathes new life into it. The four middle tercets describe the acts of four kinds of men — 'wise', 'good', 'wild' and 'grave' — employing words associated with light and dark. In the second stanza, the words of wise men 'forked no lightning', presumably in the darkness of the foolish. In the third stanza, the deeds of the last tide of good men were not 'bright' enough to 'dance' (sparkle) on the 'green bay.' As the water is green instead of blue, this could suggest a darker, more dangerous world.

The wild men of the fourth stanza 'who caught and sang the sun in flight' only 'grieved it on its way', that is, made matters worse, perhaps by being partially blind to the darker side of human wildness. Finally, in the fifth stanza, grave men near death, despite their 'blinding sight', that is, their presumed ability to see more clearly because they are dying, can 'blaze like meteors and be gay,' being gay or happy suggesting a state of lightness.

Thomas asks us to see rage as a kind of beam of light shooting through the darkness of death, a light that refuses death's pacification or darkening. Such a light yields a vision which exposes death in the way Thomas comprehends it: the ultimate horror. Therefore, Thomas counsels his father to make the ultimate refusal by refusing the ultimate, urges his father toward futile rebellion against what is and what cannot be stopped.

David Wheatley
Chronicle

THIS CAREFULLY CRAFTED poem is about heritage, family and roots. The poet takes a trip back to his family's town land in County Wicklow and rediscovers facts about his family and himself.

The first stanza brings us to the speaker's grandfather. He recalls a story he has heard about the man driving his 'wood-panelled Morris Minor' through the garage door. In the next stanza, he turns his attention to his own father. He recalls that his father did not carry on the family tradition of farming and instead drove a taxi. He tells us about the failure to communicate between himself and his father. He feels like a stranger in his own house and feels separated from the land that his grandfather farmed by more than just a generation.

He feels like a stranger to his own family, their relationship with **'their few poor roods'** seems alien to him. He is awkward in this rural setting and is unsettled by it. This displacement is hereditary. His father, too, felt out of touch with the rural life and was chastised by his own father for having the temerity to move to Bray, which, while still within the boundaries of County Wicklow, was never going **'to be properly *Cill Mhantáin*.'**

The speaker in the poem has come back here as he is making his way to a school in his home county. He visits a graveyard in Hacketstown, just over the border. Despite their fierce family pride in their county, they find themselves displaced, just as the speaker does himself; just as his father did before him, as did the previous generations.

This poem tells us about family pride and how local pride, rather than bringing people together, can put even more distance between them.

Richard Wilbur **The Writer**

THE POET OBSERVES his daughter immersed in a world of her own as she struggles to write a story. He compares her efforts to those of a ship. She is sitting at the **'prow'** and the noise from her typewriter reminds him of a chain being pulled over the side of a ship. A cargo, some of it heavy, weighs her down as she continues her journey. The poet wishes his daughter well on her passage or journey of exploration. All falls silent and even the house appears pensive until the clamour begins again and stops at intervals.

The poet's mind once again wanders and he considers the room his daughter is working in. Two years previously, a starling was trapped in there. Every effort was made to help it find its way back outside and yet still it took over an hour of hard struggle and toil for the bird to soar to freedom. The poet did all he could to aid the bird, but did it quietly and without intruding. The bird tried and failed many times as the poet unobtrusively stood back and hoped for success. He tells us how his spirits soared when success was achieved.

The poet wishes the same for his daughter. He stands in the background hoping, wishing and urging her on, but only she can soar. He wishes for her what he wishes for the bird, **'only harder'**.

Richard Wilbur **A Summer Morning**

THIS CAREFULLY CRAFTED poem tells of a cook and a gardener working in a big house. They are the ones who really live in the house, even though they do not own it and are mere servants to their employers.

From reading between the lines, the employers seemed to have inherited the house without any respect for the house itself or the wealth at their disposal. The cook is able to predict that they will not be rising for breakfast because of the state they arrived home in the previous evening. The cook has a quiet morning ahead of herself and intends to not only enjoy it but to relish the peace of the house. She has everything in its proper ordered place. She is able to take in the precious sounds of nature outside her window.

She is also able to hear the Gardener at work outside. He too is able to get on with the work he obviously enjoys without any interference from his 'young employers'. Again, he appreciates the grandeur of what is before him and does his best to give the Big House the respect that it deserves.

The poet finishes the poem by bringing the two characters together. He points out that there is a difference between possession and ownership. Anybody can own something, it is down to economics and inheritance, but possession requires something more intuitive, a sense of being in touch with the needs of the place itself: 'Possessing what the owners can but own.'

William Carlos Williams *This Is Just To Say*

THIS CONCISE POEM is loved and hated by critics in equal measure. Traditionalists will say that it is not a poem at all, it is more like a note left on a fridge, others will point out that it is one of the first and most powerful symbolist poems, full of suggestion and subtlety.

The poet's words need little explanation. However, there is some ambiguity and inference in the poem. Williams himself claimed that what made this a poem was its regular metre, but it doesn't actually have that. His line breaks are interesting. The first syllable in each line is an up-beat, which gives the poem a sense of mischief. The sounds, especially the broad vowels, make the plums sound very luxurious. Finally, there is a sense in the poem that when he says 'Forgive me', he doesn't really mean it. He seems to be teasing by pointing out the positive qualities of the plums. Perhaps, he is obeying the saying that it easier to seek forgiveness than permission.

William Wordsworth *She dwelt among the untrodden ways*

THIS SHORT, SIMPLE lyric celebrates the life while also lamenting the death of a girl called Lucy. The poet does not complicate the poem with information about who she was, how he met her or even how she made him feel. He avoids the standard approach of detailing her qualities and why he loved her. Instead, he feels that it is adequate that we know simply that her death impacted upon him. He presents to us simple and clear snippets. Lucy lived in an isolated place beside the fresh springs of the River Dove. Few knew her or knew of her so she never received praise and very few loved her. We do not know how, or even if, this affected Lucy, but because the poet declines to mention one way or the other, we are left to presume it did not really distress or unsettle her.

In stanza 2 the poet compares her to the small and beautiful delicate violet hiding behind a mossy stone. He says she is 'as fair as a star' even though she is not shining brightly for all to see.

In stanza 3 we discover that Lucy has died — how, why or when are not divulged. There is no comment, even about her lying in her grave: Is she at peace? Did she live a full life? Was she fulfilled? These lines pose more questions than answers. Even the poet's last exclamation

and, oh,
The difference to me!

does nothing to help us to understand his state of mind. Lucy has returned to nature and it has really impacted upon the poet. That is all we learn. Possibly the hurt is too raw to describe or perhaps he honours her in death just as she lived in life — privately and beyond comment or criticism.

William Wordsworth
From The Prelude: Skating [ll 425–463]

AN AUTOBIOGRAPHICAL POETIC work, *The Prelude* was written by Wordsworth over several decades. Following his death, his widow renamed it 'The Prelude: growth of a poet's mind'. The poem highlights some of the formative moments throughout the poet's life. It provides a series of snapshots tracing the poet's journey from boyhood to maturity and understanding.

The poem opens on a frosty evening in Wordsworth's childhood. In an act of defiance, he stays outside with his friends and engages in horseplay rather than going home. The poet reflects that though this was a happy time for all, somehow it meant more to him. He describes it as 'a time of rapture!' The scene is brought to life with sights and sounds of stampeding untiring youngsters, all focused on having fun.

Despite all the chaos and fun, however, the poet heeds another call. The sounds become echoes as the poet distances himself from the crowd and strays into the shadowy banks. He is no longer part of the gang — the 'confederate'. He is a solitary figure as he strives to soak in all nature's bounty. He moves from chaos and action, movement and sound into a quieter, more tranquil dreamlike state. A window in his consciousness is opened and through it floods visions of nature. Yet he does not feel in true communion with nature, he feels removed from the scene: 'I stood and watched'.

William Wordsworth
It is a beauteous evening, calm and free

THIS IS A PETRARCHAN sonnet divided into an octet and a sestet.

The octet describes to the reader an amazingly beautiful scene witnessed by Wordsworth and his daughter in France around 1802. We are presented with a vision of a beautiful, calm evening. It was as quiet as a nun's 'breathless' adoration of God. The sun was setting and the poet feels a spiritual communion with God. Wordsworth senses the great power of God intensely. In the sestet the poet ponders his daughter's different reaction to the greatness of the scene he has just experienced. He calls to her 'Dear Child! dear Girl!' and knows that although she is with him physically, she is not experiencing the scene in the same meditative and spiritual way that he is. He does not, however, reprimand her for this. Instead, he envies her. While he has internalised things and given everything great intellectual thought, she has acted spontaneously. The child does not have to process the scene analytically for it to be of value for her. Wordsworth recognises that she is close to God at all times because of her innocence and open acceptance of the beauty around her.

Enda Wyley Poems for Breakfast

THIS POEM STARTS with the speaker and her fellow poet in the house, waking with a start and perhaps the cold; 'Another morning shaking us.' The house itself seems to be shaking. In fact, it could be said that the house becomes like a character in the poem. The house seems to be in minor neglect. The plants are thirsty and frail, the cat is hungry and the window is chipped.

When the postman arrives, the post is something that is passed over, being brought to attention by the clinking of the dog's collar. They make their way through their minor chaos, arbitrary books as well as 'cold half-finished mugs of tea, / last week's clothes at the bed's edge.'

What brings real wonder to their lives is their rediscovery of some of their favourite poems. They leave the books that contain them open using the 'pepper pot, marmalade jar, a sugar bowl' to keep them ready for reading and consumption. Indeed, it is the word 'consumption' that best explains the title. They consume the poems like others would their daily cereal. These poems go to live with them for the rest of their day. If breakfast is said to be the most important meal of the day, then the 'poems for breakfast' that they devour with obvious relish are incredibly important for them.

The poems give them focus, but it also gives them a common start. It seems to be an affirmation of their love and the life that they wish to have together:

these days that we wake together in – our door forever opening.

W. B. Yeats The Wild Swans at Coole

THIS POEM OPENS with a beautiful autumnal scene. Yeats is admiring the beauty of the Coole Park estate owned by his good friend and mentor Lady Augusta Gregory. The rhythm is slow and reflective as the October sun sets and another year is drawing to a close. Yeats is 51 years of age, and in the autumn of his life he is taking stock.

He sees 59 swans on the brimming water. It is 19 years since he first set eyes on the swans and he remembers that first vision. The image of the swans is one of greatness, strength, noise and activity. Line 14 interrupts this stream of thought as the poet admits his own state of mind. 'And now my heart is sore.' This is in complete contrast to the harmony and contentment surrounding him. In the 19 years since Yeats first saw the swans, everything has changed. Nineteen years ago he feels he was light-hearted and walked with a 'lighter' step. As he reflects, he again turns his attentions to the swans and he envies them. After all these years they do not show signs of fatigue or wear and tear. The swans swim loyally side-by-side in a display of togetherness and companionship. They appear to have stood still in time, and Yeats craves this sense of eternal contentment.

There is, however, an uneven number of swans, and maybe the thought of one, alone, has triggered Yeats to consider his own romantic status. The first time Yeats saw the swans, 19 years previously, he was recovering from the disappointment of a marriage-proposal rejection from his life-long love, Maud Gonne. Now, looking at the swans, he admires in them the qualities he most yearns for. To be 'unwearied', to be loved and enjoy companionship, and to feel a sense of freedom is all Yeats yearns for. Life has failed him, but this does not detract from his admiration of the swans.

The poem ends pessimistically as Yeats thinks of the day he will discover the swans have all flown away and left him. They may move on and bring delight to others, but he will remain, feeling nostalgic desolation.

- -

W. B. Yeats *An Irish Airman Foresees His Death*

THIS POEM TELLS us about Major Robert Gregory, son of Yeats' great friend Lady Gregory from Coole Park, Co. Galway. Robert Gregory died in action in January 1918 as a member of the Royal Flying Corps. Yeats laments the death of his dear friend's son and portrays him as a brave and confident soldier who foresees his own death.

In this poem the speaker is the voice of Robert Gregory. He intuitively knows that he will meet his destiny among the clouds. He admits that he is not committed to the conflict of the war (the First World War) as he neither hates the enemy nor loves those he protects. He is from Kiltartan Cross, a place far removed from the battleground. He loves the local people there and it is irrelevant to them whether the war is won or lost; the outcome will not make them richer or poorer. Gregory further confesses that he joined the Royal Flying Corps not through any compulsion of law. What drove him towards the turmoil of war was a 'lonely impulse of delight', a mysterious calling which forced him to take stock of his life.

It became clear to him that the past had been 'A waste of breath' and that the future held only the same. To enlist and die in the skies was the most attractive option when all was considered,

*In balance with this life,
this death.*

Yeats admires Robert Gregory for his ability to calmly detach and succumb to a heroic impulse calling him to live for the moment and disregard the past and the future.

Approaching the unseen poem: some suggestions

1 *Read* through the poem once, then read it again slowly.
2 If you are still unsure about the meaning of the poem, *read the questions* set on it as they will often help you to work out the theme of the poem.
3 Read the poem *again*.
4 If the poem is punctuated, *break the poem into sentences* and read these sentences one at a time.
5 Try understanding *each part* of the poem first and then come back to the whole poem.
6 *Make notes* in the margins as you are doing this.
7 You must approach the *oral aspect* of the poem. Make sure you hear the rhythms and sounds of the poem in your head.
8 When *analysing* the *rhythm* of a particular poem, always consider the following elements:
   i) **Metre:** notice the regular pattern of stressed and unstressed syllables. Words more heavily stressed are usually central to the poem's meaning.
   ii) **Rhyme:** notice repetition of similar sounds in endings of words. Work out if the poem has a discernible rhyme scheme or not.
   iii) **Lines:** consider the use of end-stopped versus run-on lines. Look out for caesurae, which are breaks within lines.
   iv) **Punctuation:** consider how punctuation influences pausing, and thus the rhythm and effect of the poem.
   v) **Sound imagery:** consider use of sound techniques, such as alliteration, assonance and onomatopoeia, all of which influence the rhythm of the poem.
9 Remember that *variation* in any of the above elements is usually meant to achieve a certain effect.
10 Try using the **SIFT** method, which involves analysing the **S**ense, **I**ntention, **F**eeling and **T**one of the poem.
11 In considering the **sense**, you should explain to yourself briefly what the poem is about.
12 Identify the poet's **intention** or purpose in writing the poem.
13 When you comment on the **feelings** that the poem evokes, you should refer to poetic language and techniques such as metaphors and images, use of sound effects and structural considerations.
14 Finally, you need to identify the **tone** of the poem, which needs to be consistent with the poet's intentions.
15 Now start to answer the questions. The mark allocation for each question will give you an indication of the length of answer required. Take your time and think before you write, but if you change your mind about an answer, don't hesitate to cross out and rewrite. Examiners far prefer to see a correct, somewhat untidy answer than a beautifully neat, incorrect one.
16 Finally, read through the poem and the questions *again* followed by your answers to make sure there is nothing you have missed.

Paper 1 of the Leaving Certificate English exam tests your ability to:

1. **Comprehend** (understand);
2. **Compose** (write).

Section 1
- There are three texts. These can be newspaper reports, stories, letters, photographs or even advertisements.
- Each text is followed by Question A and Question B.
- Students must answer Question A (Comprehending) from one text and Question B (Composing) from either of the two remaining texts. **You must not answer Question A and Question B from the same text.**

Section 2
You are required to choose and write a composition from a list of ideas, titles and themes, some related to Section 1.

Criteria for assessment
The tasks set for candidates in both Paper 1 and Paper 2 will be assessed in accordance with the following criteria:

| Clarity of purpose | 30% |
(Ability to display a clear and purposeful engagement with the task set)

| Coherence of delivery | 30% |
(Ability to sustain the response in an appropriate manner over the entire question)

| Efficiency of language use | 30% |
(Management and control of language to achieve clear communication)

| Accuracy of mechanics | 10% |
(Correct spelling and grammar appropriate to the required or chosen register)

Approaching the exam paper

Timing: Paper 1
- You have 170 minutes to answer Paper 1.
- Section 1 carries 100 marks.
- Section 2 carries 100 marks.

A suggested breakdown of your time:

15 minutes: Read through the full paper from start to finish. Decide which questions you intend to answer.

30 minutes: Section 1 – Question A: Comprehending

30 minutes: Section 1 – Question B: Composing

80 minutes: Section 2 – Composing

15 minutes: Read through all your answers from start to finish.

Writing Skills
We use language for many reasons and there are various types of language to suit different situations. It is important that students understand which type of language is appropriate to any given situation.

In preparation for Paper 1 the student must understand five types of language. It is important that students can identify and write in each of these modes.

1. Language of narration.
2. Language of information.
3. Language of persuasion.
4. Language of argument.
5. The aesthetic use of language.

However, in the examination over recent years students have been asked to write under a number of different headings:

1. Letter-writing.
2. Writing instructions.
3. Speech-writing.
4. Describing an image or photograph.
5. Diary-writing.
6. Creative writing.
7. Summarising.
8. Writing a newspaper article.
9. Writing a review.
10. Writing a personal opinion.

⓫ Writing a commentary.

⓬ Writing an interview.

Guidelines for letter-writing

Letter-writing appears regularly in the exam paper, especially as a Question B in Section 1, Paper 1.

While it is important to lay out your letter correctly, the bulk of the marks will be allocated on the body of the letter.

There are two types of letter: informal and formal.

1 Informal letters

Informal letters are written to family and friends in a personal and chatty way.

Layout of an informal letter

4 Rue Mouffetard,
Paris 75006,   ← ***Your Address***
France.

27 July 2009   ← ***Date***

Casual greeting

Hi Guys,

I made it! I am finally settled here in Paris. Nicole and her family seem really nice and I think I'll have a good time over the next few weeks on this exchange.

I'm not as lonely as I thought I'd be, probably because the family has planned something for us to do every day. What are we going to do with Nicole when she comes to Ireland?? We don't have an Eiffel Tower or an Arc de Triomphe to show her. Mum – get your thinking cap on quickly and plan some exciting things for us to do. We are going to EuroDisney on Tuesday and I can't wait. Remember the fun we had in Funderland in Dublin at Christmas? Well I imagine this is going to be even better.

The plan is that we stay here in Paris for the rest of this week and then go down to Nice on the coast to their family home for the next week – POSH!!! I hope to get a great tan and will do loads of shopping and find gorgeous presents for everyone. I'm sending you some photos Mrs Du Bois took of us on our sightseeing tour of the city.

Relaxed conversational language

Missing you loads,   ← ***Informal ending***
Love, Marie.

2 Formal letters

In the exam you may be asked to write:
- a letter of complaint;
- a letter of enquiry / requesting information;
- a letter of application;
- a letter of invitation;
- a letter to the editor of a newspaper.

There is a very specific layout to be followed when writing a formal letter. Your letter should be *structured, organised and to the point*. The language should be standard English. The tone should be *businesslike* and *polite*. Avoid abbreviations and slang.

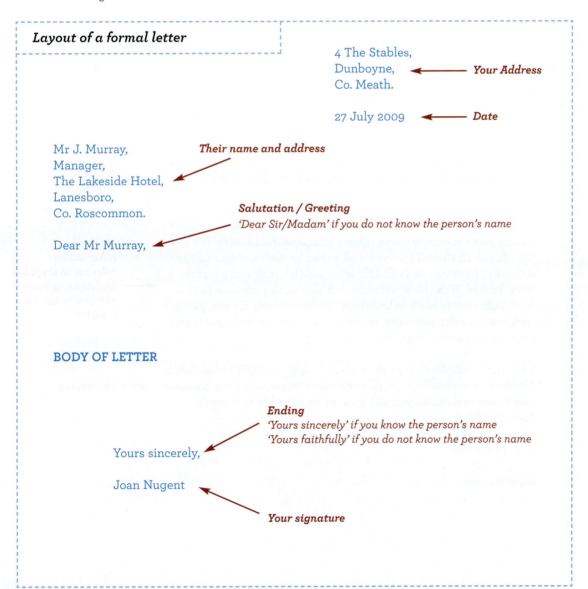

Layout of a formal letter

4 The Stables,
Dunboyne,
Co. Meath. ⟵ *Your Address*

27 July 2009 ⟵ *Date*

Mr J. Murray, ⟵ *Their name and address*
Manager,
The Lakeside Hotel,
Lanesboro,
Co. Roscommon.

Salutation / Greeting
'Dear Sir/Madam' if you do not know the person's name

Dear Mr Murray, ⟵

BODY OF LETTER

Ending
'Yours sincerely' if you know the person's name
'Yours faithfully' if you do not know the person's name

Yours sincerely, ⟵

Joan Nugent ⟵ *Your signature*

4 The Stables,
Dunboyne,
Co. Meath. ← *Your Address*

27 April 2009 ← *Date*

Mr R. Mahon, — *Their name and address*
Veterinary Surgeon,
Animal Rescue Centre,
Main Street,
Dunboyne,
Co. Meath.

Dear Mr Mahon,

I wish to apply for a part-time position in the Animal Rescue Centre for the duration of my summer holidays (June to September) and possibly weekends during term time. ← *State the purpose of your letter*

I am seventeen years old and will be sitting my Leaving Certificate this June in St Mary's Secondary School where I have been a student for the past five years. ← *Personal information*

I am very interested in working with animals and I hope to study to qualify as a veterinary nurse when I complete my Leaving Certificate. I believe I am very well suited to such a career as I love animals; I have two dogs and three cats, a fish tank and a budgie. I have worked in the local pet shop and also work part-time in the local kennels. My work in both jobs involves caring for and playing with the animals; grooming, feeding and cleaning out kennels and cages. I am hardworking, honest and diligent. ← *Information relevant to the job highlighting your suitability for the position*

I will have completed my exams on 25th June and will be available for work immediately. I am also enclosing references from previous employers and I hope you will give my application favourable consideration. ← *Conclusion*

Yours sincerely,

Joan Nugent

4 The Stables,
Dunboyne,
Co. Meath.

27 April 2009

The Manager,
'Nice Bites',
Main Street,
Navan,
Co. Meath.

Dear Sir / Madam,
I am writing in relation to an unsatisfactory meal I purchased in your café ◄—— *State the purpose of your letter*
on Saturday last, 23 July 2009.

    I entered your café at 7 p.m. having read your menu displayed outside. I was however disappointed to be presented with a totally different menu once I was seated. A waiter informed me that the menu displayed outside was out of date and that your staff 'hadn't got around to changing it'.

    Although disappointed I chose from the new menu and sat back waiting for my meal. A half hour passed and although the restaurant was not very busy I still had not been served. When I enquired about my order the waiter disappeared into the kitchen and was not seen again for the duration of my visit.

    Finally at 7.45 p.m. my meal arrived. The burger was fine, but I had ordered a baked potato and side salad, and it came accompanied by chips and onion rings. I tried to catch the attention of the waiting staff to rectify this but gave up and ate only what I had ordered – the burger.

    As I was paying I explained to the cashier, Ruth, that I was dissatisfied and did not want to pay for what I had neither ordered nor eaten. She was sympathetic but said that she could not charge for just the burger and that I had to pay for the full meal. I asked to speak to a manager but no one was available.

Outline the complaint

    I am enclosing my receipt for €12.95 which I paid in full. I would be grateful if you could refund this amount to me in cash. I would also recommend that your waiting staff undergo more training on both dealing with customers and taking orders. I would also like to point out that the menu displayed outside your café still has not been changed and I suggest that this be done immediately to prevent more customers being disappointed before they even taste your food.

Conclusion and recommen-dations

Yours faithfully,

Joan Nugent

Sample letter to the editor

You may be required to write to the editor of a newspaper. People usually write to a newspaper to agree or disagree with an article or letter previously printed in the newspaper, or to highlight a topic about which they may feel strongly. The writer usually uses his/her own personal experiences as well as facts and figures to substantiate his/her viewpoint.

Madam,
I would like to add my support to your journalist Brendan Joyce who represented the views of young people living in cities and towns in his article 'Good for Something'. I am tired of the teenager-bashing that goes on every day in newspapers, on TV and in conversations in general. I would like to congratulate Brendan Joyce for his observations on young people and I recommend that adults stop and have a good think before they label all young people 'wasters'. My friends and I, all under eighteen, spent our summer holidays working and saving to support ourselves when we hopefully start college in September. We don't have time for drinking, wandering the streets in search of trouble or indeed lazing in front of the TV, as many adults tend to believe. We need more 'Reality Journalism' and less 'Reality TV'.
    Yours etc.,
    J.P.
    Sligo

Sir,
Last Thursday, August 4th, I booked by email with Discount Air a return flight to Hamburg six weeks in advance of travel. The only fare available cost me €450 – and Discount Air calls itself a low-fare airline. Be warned.
    Yours etc.,
    P. Murray,
    Dublin

Sir,
Having travelled on the Luas for the first time last Thursday, 20th July, I have to admit I was very impressed with our newest form of city travel.
    There is no doubt but that this service will improve the lives of many thousands who live near the route and stops. It has enhanced life in Dublin in a most positive way and was well worth the months of disruptions.
    I appeal to the Corporation and the planners to expand this service and improve the lives of many more who are prisoners in their cars as they chug along the clogged arteries of Dublin every morning and evening trying to get to and from work.
    The Taoiseach recently announced that there could be no expansion due to lack of funds, yet the government can find money for state banquets and state jets. I implore the guardians of our state to get their priorities in order and spend our money wisely!
    Yours etc.,
    Mary Mc Murray,
    Dublin 12

Guidelines for writing instructions

In the Leaving Certificate exam you may be asked to give simple yet detailed information on how to perform a task. You are required to give clear information without any personal opinions.

1. On a *rough work* page jot down all that the task requires. (Main steps to be taken, equipment needed, time scale, etc.)
2. *Organise* these under headings.
3. Give a *brief* introduction.
4. Explain any technical details or *jargon*.
5. Use numbered, *step-by-step instructions*.
6. Use *simple, direct* language.
7. *Highlight any dangers* or downsides that the reader should be aware of.

How to set a solid fuel fire

Open fires are not as popular nowadays as they once were. The modern house is now usually equipped with a clean and efficient gas fire or oil-fired central heating. However a roaring open fire is not difficult to create.

You will need:
A fireplace designed to hold a solid fuel fire
Dry burning fuel – turf / coal / wood
Small thin pieces of wood / sticks
Firelighter
Old sheets of newspaper
Matches or lighter

Procedure:
1. Protect yourself and your surroundings by wearing an apron and rubber gloves.
2. Gently remove any ashes remaining in the grate and place in a metal fireproof bucket or box. Remember to be careful as there may be sparks and warm cinders from previous fires.
3. Place the firelighter in the centre of the grate.
4. Crumple up the sheets of newspaper into tight balls and place around the firelighter.
5. Arrange sticks in a criss-cross way over the newspaper.
6. Light the firelighter and allow the flames to grow.
7. Place a small amount of fuel loosely on top at first.
8. Once the fire is burning well add more fuel a little at a time. Avoid putting too much on at any one time as this will smother the flame and the fire will go out.
9. For safety always place a fireguard in front of the fire and keep children away from the fireplace.

Guidelines for writing a speech or debate

1. Decide on the *purpose* of your speech. Are you trying to convince, to persuade, to inform, to praise, to ask for help or support, or to entertain your audience? Whatever the reason for the speech, you should start by making a clear and confident statement of your purpose.
2. *Brainstorm:* write down all the points, words, people and facts you know associated with your title.
3. *Prioritise:* put your most important points first and *support* your points with statistics and facts. It is also useful and interesting to include personal anecdotes to strengthen your argument.
4. When writing a speech or debate you must be aware of your *audience.* You should begin by addressing your audience. Regularly during your speech you should refer to them, appeal to them to agree with your points, and of course, in your conclusion, thank them for their support and attention.
5. Addressing your audience is not enough. You must adopt the appropriate *register.* Your language, tone and approach will differ depending on your audience. Imagine giving a speech on litter in your locality. Your speech to the County Council would be very different from your speech to the local primary school students.
6. Your *introduction* should capture the audience's attention. A good opening will allow the audience to know what to expect. *Challenge* the audience with a question, deliver a *quotation* from a respected source or shock the audience with an unexpected statistic.
7. If you are writing a debate *acknowledge* the opposition's arguments. Be aware of opinions that are contrary to yours and deal with them in a clear and logical way, using plenty of examples to support your view and dispute the opposing standpoints. Avoid emotional language and slang, and avoid offending the audience or indeed the opposition. Your presentation of the evidence should win the support of the listeners so there is no need to 'rant and rave'.
8. In *conclusion* you should sum up your main points, making one final statement of purpose, appeal to the audience to support your point of view and thank them for their attention.

Guidelines for describing an image or picture

1. Start off with a *general* statement: 'This is a photograph / book cover / CD cover /poster . . .'
2. Mention the *shape* of the image and describe the border or frame if there is one.
3. You may choose to begin by describing the *background.* What do you see behind the main features of the photograph? Is it a country scene or an urban setting, is it inside a studio or out in the great outdoors?
4. Next describe the *foreground.* What is nearest the observer? Start with the centre and then describe what is to the right and the left. Point out what is the main focus of the image.
5. Discuss what you see in *detail.* Describe colours, shapes, expressions on faces, time of day or night, lighting, weather, etc.
6. Where is the *camera* and *photographer*? Is this a wide-angle picture, a close-up or an aerial photo?
7. What is the *purpose* of the image? Is it part of an advertisement or an image to be used for promotional reasons, is it modern or an image from history, is it informative or is it aiming to arouse sympathy or anger or support?

Guidelines for writing a diary

1. A diary is a *personal account recording daily events*. The writer is telling about his/her own environment and experiences. The writer sometimes addresses the diary as if it were a close friend – 'Dear Diary'.

2. In the Leaving Certificate exam students may be asked to write *two to three diary entries* as part of Section 1, Question B, worth 50 marks; or a full composition structured as a diary, worth 100 marks in Section 2, Composing.

3. What is written in a diary is rarely intended to be read by anyone other than the author, so the tone is very *open and honest*. The style can be revealing and reflective, divulging personal feelings the writer may not tell anyone else. The language is chatty and conversational.

4. Remember that this is still a *narrative*. You still have a story to tell or a message to deliver.

5. Most diaries include a date, a salutation ('Dear Diary'), a description of something that has occurred that day and the writer's *feelings* on this incident.

Guidelines for creative writing

Writing a short story or narrative is not as simple as merely telling a story. The writer must engage the reader in the opening paragraphs and entice him/her to read on. Writing a good short story is a skill which does not come naturally to everyone. The following points are guidelines to assist the writer to develop his/her own style.

An original idea

When you choose a title from the list in Paper 1, Section 2: Composing, the idea for what you intend to write may be based on an essay you have already written or it may come 'out of the blue'. It might be something that has happened to you or someone you know, or it might be something you have read about or seen on television. Whatever the idea, it must inspire you; you must feel excited about it. If it is not of interest to you, your audience will detect this and you will fail to capture their interest and attention. This central idea is your theme.

Characters

1. The characters in your story should be believable; the reader should feel that these are real people even though they may be fictional.

2. A short story usually revolves around one main character whose problem or dilemma is of interest to the reader.

3. Too many characters in a story means the reader cannot get to know any one very well and you, the writer, will not have an opportunity to develop them all fully.

4. You should show the story through the eyes of your central character. You may be that character (first person narrative) or you might tell the story as a narrator (third person narrative). The first person can be easier to write as you endeavour, through the use of 'I', 'me' and 'my', to express emotions naturally as if they were your own.

5. Avoid long descriptions of your characters, the general rule to follow is 'Show, don't tell'. A writer can bring the character to life by *showing* the reader what he/she is like rather than *telling*.

6. Paint the picture rather than describing it. For example, to write 'He was a bully who intimidated everyone he met', is far less effective than showing the reader an occasion when the character uses menacing language to terrify others, allowing the reader to hear exactly what is said and draw their own conclusions.

7. Three elements the writer may use to make the characters real and believable are Name, Personality and Appearance.

Setting or background

1. It is very difficult to write about life on the moon if you have never experienced it. In the same way you should not attempt to describe life in New York or Dublin or the desert if you know little or nothing about that environment. It is wise to choose a setting you know; it doesn't even need to be somewhere real as long as you can picture it clearly in your mind.
2. Do not ignore lighting. Is it day or night? Daylight or dusk? Summer sunshine or a dull, grey, winter's evening? Describing the lighting evokes the atmosphere.
3. Allow your readers to hear the sounds, experience the smells, and notice the movements in an effort to help them envisage the scene.

A good opening

1. Start slowly.
2. Set the scene and outline the main problem in the first few paragraphs.
3. Do not tell all in the first paragraph.
4. Introduce your central character as soon as possible.
5. Interest and encourage your readers to read on. Grab their attention by presenting them with a situation which makes them have to read on to discover what the main character will do.

The story

To hold the reader's attention you must not try to take in too much. Keep the time span relatively short as you will not realistically fit in a full life story in 500–1,000 words or in the time allowed. Stick to the main storyline and avoid telling extra stories within the story. Only mention what is directly linked to your plot or information, which will help to develop the characters.

The ending

Your ending is a winding-up of the story. You do not need to have a happy 'they all lived happily ever after' ending, as this can be unrealistic. You can have your character learning a lesson in difficult circumstances but moving on through life with new hope. Experiment with different endings to your stories — the cliffhanger, the 'happily ever after', the stark reality. Avoid the 'it was all a dream' scenario as the reader is left feeling robbed and betrayed, and also avoid the ending where everyone dies or leaves having learnt nothing or taken anything from the experience.

Common mistakes in story writing

- Story-line too ordinary.
- Story-line too far-fetched.
- Nothing happens.
- Too much 'padding' or descriptions.
- Too many characters.
- Not getting to know the characters in any depth.
- Trying to cover too much.
- No shape / no paragraphs / not divided into beginning, middle and end.
- Time span too long.
- Not enough dialogue.
- Telling the reader instead of showing.
- Flat ending — nothing is resolved.
- Cheat ending — 'They all die' / 'It was all a dream'.

Guidelines for summarising and paraphrasing

A written summary should always paraphrase first, rather than just repeating what was said. You must learn to paraphrase before you summarise.

1. PARAPHRASING

To paraphrase is to rewrite something using different words without changing the original meaning. This is what is usually meant by the phrase 'in your own words'. The paraphrase should be clearer and more easily understood than the original. It is usually similar in length to the original.

To paraphrase

1. Read the text carefully. Underline, or note, any important words.
2. Look at any difficult words, and try to find alternative words for them.

3 Try to find different ways of indicating time or place.

4 Rewrite each sentence. Try to simplify the sentence structure and the vocabulary without changing the meaning.

5 Revise what you have written, comparing it to the original. Your paraphrase should *clarify* the original.

6 Do not forget to include appropriate reference information at the end of your paraphrase, especially regarding facts.

2. SUMMARISING

A summary is much shorter than the original text. It should communicate the main idea of the text and the main supporting points, written in your own words, in a very brief form. The summary should give someone who has not read the original a clear and accurate overview of the text. A formal summary should also include the author, title, year of publication and source of the original.

Writing a summary requires a thorough understanding of the content of the text, and the ability to paraphrase.

To summarise

1 Record the author, title, year of publication and source of the text.

2 Skim the text. Note any sub-headings or try to divide the text into sections.

3 Read the text carefully. Use a dictionary if necessary, and be prepared to read very difficult texts more than once.

4 Pay special attention to the first and last paragraphs. Try to identify the main idea or argument.

5 Identify the topic sentence in each paragraph. This is frequently the first sentence in the paragraph.

6 Identify the main support for the topic sentence.

7 Write the topic sentence of your summary. Include the author's name, the title of the text, the year of publication and the author's main idea or argument.

8 Try to write one or two sentences for each paragraph. Include the main idea (usually a paraphrase of the topic sentence) and

the main support for the topic sentence (also paraphrased).

9 Revise and rewrite.

10 Proofread and make corrections as required.

Guidelines for writing a newspaper article

The first thing prospective reporters must know is that newspaper articles are written differently depending on their format or purpose. Newspaper articles can be divided into three categories: news articles, feature stories and columns.

HOW TO WRITE A NEWS ARTICLE

Pure news articles are the most structured type of newspaper article. A specific format must be followed in writing this type of article. The purpose of this article is to convey the facts of an event to an interested reader.

Guidelines for writing a news article

1 As with all newspaper articles, it should be set off with a headline. The headline should not be a summary of the article; instead it should serve the purpose of getting the reader's attention.

2 The story should start with a 'lead paragraph' which is the summary of the story. Do not tease at the beginning or summarise at the end as you sometimes see on television news. Lay all your cards out on the table. The lead paragraph should include the *who, what, when, where and why* of the story.

3 After the lead paragraph comes explanation and amplification, which deals with highlighting details. Use discretion in choosing which details to include. Some details may not be as important as others. Put them in order of importance from greatest to least. Don't feel the need to include everything you know, but do include everything you feel is important.

4 If the average reader will be confused, fill in the gaps with background information.

When in doubt, give the information.

5. Do not use the first person. If you feel that it is absolutely necessary, think about writing a feature story or a column instead (see below).

6. *No bias.* Personal prejudices should not find their way into the article. Again, use of an opinion-editorial or column forum is recommended for personal opinions.

7. When possible, use quotes to flavour the article. However, don't use quotes for the sake of using quotes — make sure they are relevant. Also, make sure the quotes aren't a grammatical embarrassment — avoid run-ons especially.

HOW TO WRITE FEATURE STORIES

Features are interesting stories about people, places and events. They aren't as concerned with conveying basic facts as in conveying a mood, feeling, or theme. Unlike writing news articles, there are no hard and fast rules for composing features. Features are common in newspapers and even more common in magazines.

Guidelines for writing feature stories

1. Many feature stories are biographical sketches of individuals. Often interviews with public figures (athletes or entertainers) or compelling people (such as a homeless person) can make for interesting feature stories.

2. Unlike in a news article, the feature writer is allowed much creativity in the story's composition. The order of presentation is based solely on the criteria of what makes for the most interesting read.

3. Pretend you are telling a story. Draw on storytelling techniques from other media, such as movies, theatre, fiction and music. This may include visualisation of the scene you are creating. Sounds, smells, and even textures can be a viable means of expression. Paint a picture with words.

4. Metaphors and comparisons are fair game in feature stories. Your impressions can be given.

5. Although personal insights are allowed in a feature, strive for objectivity. Tell both sides of the story. If you are featuring a homeless man include comments critical of the police for enforcing loitering violations, give a police spokesperson a chance to respond.

HOW TO WRITE A COLUMN

A column, or opinion-editorial (op-ed), is the most open-ended of newspaper articles. It is a chance to express your opinion. There are not many rules to writing this type of article. *The most important thing is to have all your facts correct.* Always keep in mind that it is difficult to persuade readers by offending or insulting them.

A final piece of advice

Become a vigorous reader of newspapers. Read pure news articles, features and columns and note what makes them effective. Good writers are always good readers.

Guidelines for writing a review

BEFORE WRITING
What are you reviewing?
- Film
- Concert/event
- CD
- Video/DVD
- Book
- Restaurant
- Theatre
- Game
- Art exhibition

The medium that you are reviewing should directly affect how you approach it. In a review, detail is very important, so make sure that the peculiarities of the medium are shown; for example, with a DVD, are there special features on it? With a concert, what were the facilities like? What was the atmosphere like?

Who are you reviewing for?
Who is your audience? Will they understand lingo like 'techno' or 'gig', etc.? Is your review

written for a tabloid or broadsheet, or for a magazine or radio, etc.?

Read plenty of reviews
The best writers are the best readers!

WRITING THE REVIEW

1. **Give a headline.** If the review is for a newspaper or magazine, keep the headline short and to the point.
2. **Name the material.** Identify what you are dealing with as early as possible, for example: '*Booked!* by Tom Humphries is a new collection of articles by the *Irish Times* journalist.'
   or
   'The Red Hot Chilli Peppers headlined another sell-out gig at Slane.'
   or
   '*O* by Damien Rice has just been released to critical acclaim.'
   or
   'Mike Myers and Eddie Murphy are back for another whirlwind adventure in *Shrek 2*.'
3. **Summarise the story** but do not give away any twists or the ending.
4. **Give plenty of opinion.** Don't be afraid to be emotive. Let your feelings be known.
   'The best part of the book was when . . .'
   'My favourite character was . . .'
   'I felt let down by the performance of X in the role of Y.'
5. **Give detail of one part of the book, etc.** Dedicate one paragraph to a detailed analysis of one element of the media or event you are reviewing.
6. **Give your verdict or final evaluation.** Would you recommend it to somebody else? Give a mark out of ten or a star rating.

Guidelines for writing a personal opinion piece

BEFORE WRITING
What are you asked to do?
This type of writing is often asked for in the exam papers. It usually asks you to write about your feelings on a certain topic or it can ask you about how a topic affects you and its importance in your life.

WRITING THE PIECE

1. **You do not have to tell the truth.** Use your imagination if you wish. The person marking the exam does not know who you are or anything about you and your opinions. Do not be afraid to make things up in order to make the writing more interesting. However, do not let your piece get too far-fetched. Keep it realistic.
2. **Don't be afraid of your feelings.** Do not be afraid to use emotive language. Tell the reader clearly and directly what you feel on the topic.
3. **Vary your language when you are describing your feelings.** Get used to using a thesaurus and find as many words as you can to describe each of your basic emotions.
4. **Be exact,** for example:
   'The very first time I felt that way was on the 17th of August, the day of my Leaving Certificate results.'
   This allows the reader to identify with the events you describe and your feelings towards them.
5. **Introduce your topic directly and early.**
6. **Give good examples to back up your feelings.**
7. In your final paragraph, **summarise** by stringing together all the points that you have made to justify your position.

Guidelines for writing a commentary piece

BEFORE WRITING

You could be asked to write a commentary piece for radio or television. In this piece you will be asked to describe a period of action. The most obvious types of commentaries are sports events, state funerals or nature programmes of the David Attenborough-type. They will each need a different approach. It is important to pay clear attention to various radio and television commentaries.

WRITING THE PIECE

1. Remember that you are the eyes of your audience.
2. You must provide the details that they cannot see.
3. Provide details of colour and exact descriptions of clothing and movement.
4. Do not be afraid to use your opinions.
5. Keep your sentences short so you do not lose your audience.
6. Put enthusiasm into the tone of a sporting commentary.
7. Keep a funeral or nature commentary sombre and steady.
8. Remember to give details of names and scores as appropriate.

Guidelines for writing an interview or a question-and-answer piece

This format will be familiar to anybody who reads newspapers or magazines or those who listen to radio or watch television.

1. There are always at least two people involved: the interviewer and the interviewee.
2. Give an introduction to the interview, for example 'The Taoiseach has been in the news recently after the recent strike action taken by teachers. I met him in the Gresham Hotel to discuss his feelings on the issue.'
3. Structure your piece so that the interviewer's name comes first, then his/her question. Underneath this you can put the interviewee's name and his/her answers, for example:

   Irish Times   Taoiseach, what do you think . . .

   Taoiseach   I think . . .
4. The interviewee cannot be expected to give a good answer unless they are asked a good question — stick to relevant and interesting questions.
5. Be aware of the audience for the piece.
6. Do not ask questions that can be answered with a yes or no.
7. Do not give one-word answers. Do not be afraid to give too much information; be afraid to give too little.
8. Do not be afraid to make the questions interesting and provocative. Be controversial if appropriate.
9. Do not be afraid to be humorous, but make sure you stick to the topic.
10. If you have a choice of interviewee, make sure it is somebody of interest to the audience that has been identified. For example, if you are asked to write an interview with a rock star for a tabloid newspaper, ensure that it is somebody that the readers of a tabloid would know, not just an obscure person known only to you and your friends.

Questions based on exam papers

Section 1, Question B

Letters

1. Write a letter to your favourite pop star or celebrity inviting him or her to come to the launch of a charity to help the homeless. In your letter you should explain how you intend to raise money for the charity.

2. Write a letter to the owner of a hotel complaining about a bad experience.

3. Imagine you are a refugee in Ireland. Write a letter home telling your family how refugees are treated and how you feel about this. (100–150 words)

4. Imagine your friend has recently moved to Dublin to attend college. Write a letter to him or her enquiring about college life in Dublin.

5. 'What is it about the *Titanic* that continues to grip our interest nearly 100 years after she sank on that 'Night to Remember'?'
Write a letter to David Robbins, author of a review of a new book on the *Titanic* giving your answer to the above question, which he asks in his review. (150–200 words)

6. Write a letter to the editor of a sports paper or magazine giving your views on boxing.

7. You are a student at a school for racing apprentices. Write a letter home to your parents describing your first week in the school.

Personal opinion

1. Write the answer you would give to the question: 'What does entertainment mean to you?'

2. Write about the changes you would like to make to your room, or to your home, or to the area in which you live.

3. Imagine you were asked to give an interview during your final term in school. Write the answers you would give to Question 1: What positive memory will stay with you as you grow older? and Question 2: What hopes do you have for the world? Can you see yourself making any difference to the world, however small?

Newspaper articles

1. Computer games — do they have a good or a bad effect on young people? Write an article for a newspaper expressing your view on this question.

Review

1. Write a review of your favourite film or TV programme or radio programme.

Commentary / Speech / Debate

1. Imagine you are a radio or TV commentator for a sporting or non-sporting event. Write the commentary you would give on one important moment during that event.

Diary

1. Write two or three diary entries recording your own or your family's experiences during the first week of the changeover to the euro.

2. Compose the diary entries that a girl, Phoebe, who has moved to Dublin, might write in her first month at college.

Sample paper 1: War
Section 1: Comprehending (100 marks)

WAR: TEXT 1

Birdsong

The German enemy has rescued Stephen Wraysford, a British captain during the First World War, after an explosion buries him underground for many days.

They helped Stephen to the bottom of the rope and gave him water. They lifted him up, and Levi walked with his arm round him to the end of the tunnel while Lamm and Kroger went back into the darkness to bring out the body of Jack Firebrace.

Levi guided Stephen's slow steps up the incline towards the light. They had to cover their eyes against the powerful rays of the sun. Eventually they came up into the air of the German trench. Levi helped Stephen over the step.

Stephen breathed deeply again and again. He looked at the blue and distant sky, feathered with irregular clouds. He sat down on the firestep and held his head in his hands.

They could hear the sound of birds. The trench was empty. Levi climbed on to the parapet and raised a pair of binoculars. The British trench was deserted. He looked behind the German lines, but could see nothing in front of the horizon, five miles distant. The dam had broken, the German army had been swept away.

He came down into the trench and sat next to Stephen. Neither man spoke. Each listened to the heavenly quietness.

Stephen eventually turned his face up to Levi. 'Is it over?' he said in English.

'Yes,' said Levi, also in English. 'It is finished.'

Stephen looked down to the floor of the German trench. He could not grasp what had happened. Four years that had lasted so long it seemed that time had stopped. All the men he had seen killed, their bodies, their wounds. Michael Weir. His pale face emerging from his burrow underground. Byrne like a headless crow. The tens of thousands who had gone down with him that summer morning.

He did not know what to do. He did not know how to reclaim his life.

He felt his lower lip begin to tremble and the hot tears filling his eyes. He laid his head against Levi's chest and sobbed.

They brought up Jack's body and, when the men had rested, they dug a grave for him and Joseph Levi. They made it a joint grave, because the war was over. Stephen said a prayer for Jack, and Levi for his brother. They picked flowers and threw them on the grave. All four of them were weeping.

Then Lamm went looking in the dugouts and came back with water and tins of food. They ate in the open air. Then they went back into the dugout and slept.

The next day Stephen said he would have to rejoin his battalion. He shook hands with Kroger and Lamm, and then with Levi. Of all the flesh he had seen and touched, it was this doctor's hand that had signalled his deliverance.

Levi would not let him go. He made him promise to write when he was back in England. He took the buckle from his belt and gave it to him as a souvenir. Gott mit uns.

Stephen gave him the knife with the single blade. They embraced again and clung on to each other.

Then Stephen climbed the ladder, over the top, into no man's land. No hurricane of bullets met him, no tearing metal kiss.

He felt the dry, turned earth beneath his boots as he picked his way back towards the British lines. A lark was singing in the unharmed air above him. His body and mind were tired beyond speech and beyond repair, but nothing could check the low exultation of his soul.

FROM *BIRDSONG* BY SEBASTIAN FAULKS

N.B. Candidates may NOT answer Question A and Question B on the same text. Questions A and B carry 50 marks each.

Question A

(i) Describe the reception Stephen receives from the Germans upon his rescue. (10)

(ii) What are Stephen's feelings when he hears that the war is over? (20)

(iii) Describe, using evidence from the passage, what life was like in the trenches during the First World War. (20)

Question B

Write out the script of a news reporter for television reporting on the end of a war. (50)

WAR: TEXT 2

When the killing finally stopped

On 2 November 1944, more than three years after the first gassing experiments at Auschwitz, an order arrived from Heinrich Himmler: 'I forbid any further annihilation of Jews.' On his orders, all but one of the crematoria were dismantled, the burning-pits covered up and planted with grass, and the gas pipes and other equipment shipped to concentration camps in Germany. The single remaining crematorium was for the disposal of those who died natural deaths and for gassing about two hundred surviving members of the Sonderkommando.

The final solution was formally over. Although tens of thousands of Jews and others would go on dying of neglect and brutality, the systematic killing had ended. Why Himmler made this decision is not certain. One possible reason was that the Reich was desperate for labour, even Jewish workers. Evidence suggests, however, that Himmler foresaw the disaster that awaited the Third Reich and was desperately trying to save his own skin by compiling a record of what he might have termed 'leniency'. Indeed, his order to stop the killing contained a further, ingratiating directive instructing that 'proper care be given to the weak and the sick'.

Less than three months later, on 17 January 1945, the last roll call was conducted at Auschwitz. The Germans counted 67,012 prisoners at the main camp and the satellite camps. This amounted to less than half the peak population of 155,000 tabulated during the previous August. Many had already been sent westwards to camps in Germany, and more had died. Now, with the artillery of the approaching Red Army thundering on the horizon, the Germans ordered the evacuation of all but about 6,000 inmates who were too infirm to make the trip by train or on foot.

The 58,000 or so evacuees struggled westwards in agony. Even those who were put aboard trains suffered privation. Many thousands died of starvation or exposure in the unheated wagons. Many had to march all the way to Germany in freezing cold. Staggering along in rags, barefoot or on wooden clogs, sustained only by a starvation diet, thousands fell by the wayside and were shot by their SS guards. One march lasted for more than 16 weeks and claimed the lives of all but 280 of the 3,000 who began it.

Those left behind at Auschwitz suffered too. Without food, water, or heat, sick and despairing, they died by the hundreds each day. The SS guards disappeared bit by bit until finally the inmates had the camp to themselves. On 27 January 1945, the Russians arrived. It was a 'beautiful, sunny winter's day,' a survivor wrote in his diary. 'At about 3.00 p.m., we heard a noise in the direction of the main gate. We hurried to the scene. It was a Soviet forward patrol – Russian soldiers in white caps! There was a mad rush to shake them by the hand and shout our gratitude. We were liberated!'

By that time, about 2,800 people remained alive at Auschwitz. The soldiers fed the survivors, tended to the sick, and buried the dead. Thousands upon thousands had died before these at Auschwitz, but this mass burial was the 'first dignified funeral' ever held there, an inmate observed.

FROM THE *THIRD REICH AT WAR*
EDITED BY MICHAEL VERANOV

N.B. Candidates may NOT answer Question A and Question B on the same text.
Questions A and B carry 50 marks each.

Question A

(i) From your reading of the above passage why did Himmler issue an order forbidding 'any further annihilation of Jews'? (20)

(ii) What is your understanding of the term, used in the second paragraph 'the final solution'?

(iii) What happened to prisoners who were fit enough to be evacuated from Auschwitz as the Russian 'Red' army approached? (10)

(iv) What happened to the 6000 prisoners who were too ill to be evacuated? (10)

Question B

Imagine you are a newspaper reporter who has been sent to report on the discovery of a death camp in the aftermath of the Second World War. Write the headline you would use and a short and informative article. 100–150 words (50)

WAR: TEXT 3

Here are some images relating to war. Look at them and then answer the questions.

N.B. Candidates may NOT answer Question A and Question B on the same text.
Questions A and B carry 50 marks each.

Question A

(i) In your opinion do these images represent an exciting or a frightening view of war? (15)

(ii) Choose the image that best captures what war is really about. Explain your choice. (20)

(iii) Write a description of the image you have chosen in (ii) above. (15)

Question B

Imagine you have been awarded the Victoria Cross Medal for Bravery. Write the letter you receive from the authorities informing you of your award. (50)

Sample paper 2: Memories

Section 1: Comprehending (100 marks)

MEMORIES: TEXT 1

Delusions

When I was nine, I started turning into John Wayne. At first it wasn't that obvious – just a hint of a swagger and a US marshal badge pinned to my chest during every waking moment. Which made bathtime pretty painful.

But the more John Wayne movies I saw, the more he took over my life. I started insisting people call me The Duke. Or Marion. I spent hours mastering the lasso. By the time I was 10, I could corral any guinea pig that'd stay still for more than two minutes – three if the rope still had washing on it. I started chewing tobacco, and when I couldn't get tobacco, I'd lick ashtrays. I'll never forget swaggering out of How the West Was Won with Wayne's distinctive rolling gait and wondering if he walked like that because he too had a plastic holster that stuck to his leg and made his shorts ride up. I asked the usherette about this in his distinctive drawl. She didn't understand, probably because my front three teeth were missing so it was more of a drool. I didn't care. I went to the nearest rocky outcrop and threw myself with a fearless cry on to a passing Comanchero. Luckily for me, bikies were quite tolerant in those days.

The most exciting hours of my adolescence were the ones I spent watching The War Wagon, Hellfighters, True Grit and A Midsummer Night's Dream. (That last one was a mistake. When I read in the review about the Duke wearing tights, I rushed straight out and bought a ticket.)

I'm not sure now what finally broke the spell. News that Wayne had started to wear a girdle, perhaps, and Mum's refusal to lend me one. Or perhaps it was the lousy service I got in my local Vietnamese restaurant once I took to wearing that green beret.

Whatever it was, one day I realised I was no longer John Wayne. I couldn't be, because I was Dustin Hoffman. I'd just seen The Graduate and, in two hours, my life had changed. Here at last was a hero without a hair on his chest. Even more exciting, the close-ups showed that, like me, he didn't even have follicles in that area.

I was captivated. A hero I could emulate, even in rooms with mirrors. Plus, I mused as I left the cinema with Dustin's distinctive anaemic slouch, a hero who shared my bad posture and love of high-pitched singing. (The moment I first heard Simon and Garfunkel I knew they'd had plastic holsters.)

I emulated Dustin in every way I could. I spent days in deep introspection. It wasn't hard because I already knew the required facial expression. It was the one John Wayne used when he looked down and saw he had an arrow in his leg.

The years passed and I waited for another screen hero to occupy my psyche. It didn't happen. I did drive a car that displayed the number 007 for a few months, but only because the trip meter was broken. I did say 'I'll be back' a few times at one stage, but only because I was negotiating which part of the school fete donkey I'd be.

Screen heroes have come and gone, and I've remained strangely unaffected. Until recently. I didn't even notice what was happening at first. I thought the hair loss was just the result of genetics and wearing a cowboy hat too young. I thought my swelling midriff was just the result of too many calories. (Nobody told me that when you chew tobacco you're not meant to swallow it.)

Okay, I have been watching a lot of TV lately, but only because they've been showing so many John Wayne and Dustin Hoffman movies. And I have developed a big appetite for bacon, cheese slices, doughnuts and ribs, but not always in the same meal.

So you can imagine how surprised I was at dinner the other night when, just after I mistakenly ate a cheese slice with the wrapper on and said 'Doh', the kids gave a loud wail. 'Oh no,' they cried, 'Dad's turning into Homer Simpson.' I was indignant. Bitterly so. In my mind I formulated a carefully structured argument listing my many intellectual, artistic, humanist and cultural qualities. As dessert arrived I opened my mouth and let them have it.

'Mmmmm,' I said, 'chocolate chip.'

FROM *SELF-HELPLESS*
BY MORRIS GLEITZMAN

N.B. Candidates may NOT answer Question A and Question B on the same text.
Questions A and B carry 50 marks each.

Question A

(i) 'But the more John Wayne movies I saw, the more he took over my life.' In what ways did John Wayne take over the author's childhood? (20)

(ii) Apart from John Wayne what other screen heroes did the writer copy and how did he imitate them? (15)

(iii) In what way is the writer becoming more and more like Homer Simpson? Is he happy with the transformation? (15)

Question B

Write the answer you would give to the question: Where would you like to be in five years' time? (50)

MEMORIES: TEXT 2

Rich teas

A lunch is being held in honour of a French writer who is in Dublin to organise a writers' festival. The conversation turns inevitably to food and, as often happens with a large group around a table, the general conversation breaks down into sub-plots of chat. After a while, the visiting writer notices the animation of your neighbours at the table and wants to know what is the reason for all this excitement. He seems puzzled when you tell him – biscuits.

But he need not have been so surprised. Marcel Proust unlocks his past not with a rare steak or a slice of pâté de foie gras but with a small teacake, a madeleine. Sweet dreams are our key to memory. The naming of biscuits was for the Irish guests at the table a guided tour through childhood – the sugared crumbs, a trail of recollection. Marietta was there at the beginning of the path. The round coin of austerity with its suggestion of poorly heated parish halls and convent parlours and prudent excess. Or else the dismembered Marietta biscuits reduced to the scale of the doll's world, sustaining Sindy or Barbie through those endless afternoon teas of the winter months, miniature dramas played out with droplets of milk in scratched red plastic cups and the occasional scolding from the director when Barbie fouled her twin set with great boulders of biscuit. Butter redeemed Marietta's puritan plainness. Spread on two biscuits that were then put together, the butter that oozed through pinpricks on the surface like inquisitive earthworms carried with it the promise of luxury and a faint intimation of decadence.

Digestive biscuits in their gritty wholesomeness were associated like all things that are good for you with the sickroom. In the same category as coarser breakfast cereals, they suggested disciplined recovery from mumps or the measles or a bad flu. Hot lemon drinks and the tentative crumbling of the plain digestive biscuit broke up the sick-day routine of endlessly reread *Treasure* and *Tiger* and *Jag* comics from the last school garden fête – where it always rained despite the promise of Gallic summer in fête. Chocolate on digestive biscuits was always confusing, like a category confusion in logic, so that these biscuits were consumed with something like lingering guilt, as if you were found stuffing yourself with Belgian chocolates on a health farm.

Rich Tea and Morning Coffee. The decorous abandon of late morning, the fountain trickle of talk radio and the house huge with the silence of the children gone to school or a day snatched from work, yawning with possibility. The biscuits that adorn the dark tables of meetings never seem to have the same effect, as if the suggestion of leisure is scotched by the seriousness of purpose, the tea going cold and the biscuits, more worry beads than sweetmeats, dismembered by fidgety fingers. Afternoon Tea Assorted. The panic of want as the unexpected arrival of a neighbour or a relative (*Just thought*

I'd say hello, Margaret) means turmoil in the kitchen. The only biscuits left are four Lincolns, soft with age, and shards of cream cracker. Behind the welcoming smiles are urgent, whispered commands to go to Donnelly's and buy a packet of biscuits. While your bike carries you to the shop, your mother is back at the house talking to the neighbour-relative as if she was an accomplice in a robbery, distracting the police officer's attention with bogus requests for directions to go to Blackhall Place or Constitution Hill. As the tray arrives with the tea and the biscuits are spread in a bountiful landslide on the plate (not too large, of course, otherwise the biscuits thin into insignificance), the complimentary guest (*How big you are now! What class are you in?*) secretly appraises the offering. Excessive plainness in the biscuit is a subtle affront, the Marietta snub. Chocolate fingers or Bourbons suggest a social ambitiousness that needs to be watched. Away from the grand manoeuvres of the Good Room, there is, however, the campfire of gossip in the warm kitchen where biscuits are dunked and time dissolves in the Great Plains of a weekday afternoon and the doilys stay in the sideboard.

With Empire came the lure of the exotic. Kimberley, Mikado, Coconut Creams. A late Victorian map of plenty, handlebar moustaches and steamships plotting passages for the cargo of raw materials and spices from the four corners of the earth. But our minds soon tired of the *Look and Learn* immensity of overseas possessions and began to focus in on the one abiding passion of childhood – demolition. The trick was to use your front teeth like a barber's razor, removing the two white banks of coconut, leaving the thin stream of strawberry in the middle, resting on its biscuit base. A similar gopher-like application was used to remove the coconut mound in another biscuit from its base: the cleaner the cut, the keener the triumph. Chocolate Snack biscuits were other contenders for the demolition derby. Here, the aim was to remove chocolate in a series of quick, decisive bites until only the biscuit was left, pale, slightly moist, the cream fragment of bone exposed by the energetic dig. The pleasure was in removing whole sides of chocolate in one carefully aimed

nip. If only a piece came away, or the top section had to be scraped off, there was a vague sense of irritation, an irritation that returns in adult life when taking off wallpaper, obstinate islands of ancient paste interrupting the triumphant march of the paper stripper. Chocolate mallows involved more delicate surgery. Here, the fine chocolate membrane had to be removed from the sticky dome underneath while leaving the dome intact. Only when the marshmallow lay exposed, vividly white, could the next operation begin: the severing of the marshmallow from its base. As the sweet oyster dissolved in your mouth, the final act was to eat the base itself, moist now and striated with the ploughed ridges of teeth marks.

FROM *TIME TRACKS* BY MICHAEL CRONIN

N.B. Candidates may NOT answer Question A and Question B on the same text. Questions A and B carry 50 marks each.

Question A

(i)   Why are biscuits so important to the writer? (10)

(ii) Of what do Marietta and Digestive biscuits remind the writer? (10)

(iii) Which of the biscuits did the writer most enjoy eating? Explain your answer. (10)

(iv) What comparisons does the writer draw between childhood and adulthood in this piece of writing? (20)

Question B

In the above piece of writing the writer gives a detailed account of how he ate a Chocolate Mallow. Write detailed instructions on how to do one of the following:

(i)   Make a cup of tea.

(ii) Peel an orange.

(iii) Set the video recorder to record a film from TV.

MEMORIES: TEXT 3

Here are some images looking back in time. Look at them and then answer the questions.

N.B. Candidates may NOT answer Question A and Question B on the same text. Questions A and B carry 50 marks each.

Question A

(i) Select one of the images and explain what it reveals about the mood of the characters or the scene. (15)

(ii) Write a caption for each of the images. (20)

(iii) Which of the images do you like best and why? (15)

Question B

Write the dialogue / conversation that you imagine takes place in any one of the images. (50)

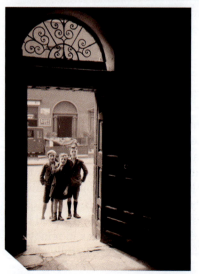

Sample paper 3: Music
Section 1: Comprehending (100 marks)

MUSIC: TEXT 1

Ride On
True you ride the finest horse
I have ever seen
Standing sixteen-one or two
With eyes wild and green
And you ride the horse so well
Hands light to the touch
And I could never go with you
No matter how I wanted to

Chorus
Ride on, see ya
I could never go with you
No matter how I wanted to
And when you ride into the night
Without a trace behind
Run the claw along my gut
One last time
I'll turn to face an empty space
Where you used to lie
And smile for the spark that
Lights the night
Through a teardrop in my eye

Chorus
Ride on, see ya
I could never go with you
No matter how I wanted to
No matter how I wanted to

People often ask me about this song but, purely and simply, it is a song of parting. The parting of lovers, the parting of emigrants from their homeland and friends, the parting when illness or accident takes the life of a loved one. I have been asked to sing this song at many funeral services and, somehow, it always feels right.

Christy Moore recorded this song on his Ride On album in 1984 and it was my first hit. I will always be grateful to him for giving me the start with what would have been then regarded as a most unlikely song-writing voice. Christy obviously recognised 'Ride On' as a song of parting when, on its release, he dedicated it to the memory of the great Luke Kelly.

I am often asked about the line 'Run the claw along my gut one last time' (in the same way as I'm asked about the line 'I am the geek with the alchemist's stone', from my song 'The Bright Blue Rose'). These dramatic lines jolt the listener into a deeper engagement, or at least this was my intention in employing such devices. That is not to say that they were not a natural part of the flow of expression but, while most writers would edit them out, I feel that a song, like life, depends on the decisions one makes and these decisions were not taken lightly. Some people may think that I just throw paint at the canvas, but there is exactitude and detail in the placing of every word and phrase until I am satisfied that the lyric is absolutely watertight. It has always bothered me that the previously mentioned line from 'Ride On' has often been changed to 'Run your claw along my gut one last time', which clearly denotes an intention to cause pain, when the pain I envisioned is simply the pain of living life. The pain of parting and separation that no life can escape. Life is hard, Ride on.
FROM 'RIDE ON' IN *RIDE ON* BY JIMMY MCCARTHY

N.B. Candidates may NOT answer Question A and Question B on the same text.
Questions A and B carry 50 marks each.

Question A
(i) Why is Jimmy McCarthy grateful to Christy Moore? (15)
(ii) What does Jimmy McCarthy say about the line 'Run the claw along my gut one last time'? (15)
(iii) Do you think that Jimmy McCarthy takes his song-writing seriously? Give examples to back up your argument. (20)

Question B
Write a short article for a magazine on the importance of music in your life.

MUSIC: TEXT 2

Music

To claim that you can stroll into a back street Irish pub, or a pub way out in the wilds, and stumble on spontaneous sessions of wonderful music, sounds like a myth. On the whole, it isn't. You can come across champion performers almost anywhere. One reason for this is that almost every Irish musician is hyped as a champion.

Traditional Irish music lives on partly because it takes easily to being blended with more up-to-date stuff. The Irish music scene has produced some wonderfully creative combinations of traditional music with rock, punk, classical, cajun, native American and the like. One of the most alluring sounds in the country, apart from 'I'm paying for the drinks', is that of a woman singing unaccompanied in the native language. In this 'sean-nos' (old-style) form of song, the voice is used more as an impersonal instrument than as an expression of individual personality. You let the tradition sing through you rather than aim for originality, and keep personal emotion to the minimum. Irish musicians dislike flashy self-presentation, and some fiddlers have been known to play with their backs to the audience. Even if Irish musicians have an audience, they sometimes tend to behave as though they're not there.

A lot of Irish music comes to us only from the oral tradition, collected and written down by scholars who roamed the countryside in search of tuneful old codgers. One such expert asked an old woman where she had found a particular song, to be told that she had heard it sung by a blind harper from a village over the mountain. And where had he got it from? inquired the expert. From his old uncle, she replied, who had been a roving tinker. And where had he got it from? He got it from the radio.

In fact, there's a serious point behind the joke. A lot of what people regard as traditional Irish songs aren't traditional at all, and some of them aren't even Irish in origin. The words of 'Danny Boy' weren't written by an Irish composer. Genuine Irish singers and musicians wouldn't be found dead performing the sentimental drivel which some visitors think of as typically Irish.

Another story is told in Ireland of three fiddlers at a musical festival. The first stepped up wearing an expensive black suit and carrying a Stradivarius violin in a richly ornamented case made of Florentine leather. He took the violin out with exquisitely manicured fingers, placed it under his chin with a flourish, and drew the bow across it. And by God he was useless.

Then up stepped a second fiddler, a bit of a Flash Harry in a sequined suit and spotted bow tie, carrying a well-polished, moderately expensive fiddle. He placed it under his chin, swept back his oiled locks, bared his teeth to the audience in a glittering smile and began to play. And by God he was useless.

A third fiddler then shuffled to the front: a bent, wheezing little fellow in a beer-stained jacket with matchstick-thin legs and his behind hanging out of his trousers. He had no violin case, just a battered old instrument he had played since he was a lad. By this time the audience had lost patience and was barely listening. But the little old man fixed the fiddle under his grizzled chin with a shaking hand, and began slowly, tenderly, to play.

And by God he was useless too.

FROM *THE TRUTH ABOUT THE IRISH* BY TERRY EAGLETON

N.B. Candidates may NOT answer Question A and Question B on the same text. Questions A and B carry 50 marks each.

Question A

(i) Do you think that the writer likes traditional Irish Music? Why do you think this? (15)
(ii) What does the writer say about originality in paragraph 2? Does he see this as a good or a bad thing? (15)
(iii) What does the writer say about appearances in traditional music? (20)

Question B

Imagine you are an American tourist and have gone to see your first traditional music session. Write a letter home explaining what it felt like. (50)

MUSIC: TEXT 3

N.B. Candidates may NOT answer Question A and Question B on the same text.
Questions A and B carry 50 marks each.

Question A

(i) Choose the image of Irish music that you think is the one that most young people would relate to. Describe that image. (15)

(ii) Which type of music pictured below or over the page appeals most to you? Explain your choice. (15)

(iii) Write a short note on the typical audience for each type of music. (20)

Question B

Write a review of your favourite song, album or concert for your school magazine. (50)

Sample paper 4: Sport
Section 1: Comprehending (100 marks)

SPORT: TEXT 1

All aboard for the chicks with sticks revolution

Camogie, despite itself perhaps, has undergone a huge change. In those estates which teem with kids, GAA clubs and soccer clubs have always thrived, while sport for girls has always been something of an afterthought, if even that. Now, perhaps because of a change in the safety of the environment and a change in the expectation levels of girls and their parents, camogie has been in there competing for customers. Girls still play basketball and soccer and Gaelic football, but more and more of them walk around with hurleys in their hands.

Some clubs just can't get enough coaches for their mini leagues. It's intriguing and thrilling to watch. Girls are as different from boys in team situations as cats are from dogs. A dog will fetch sticks without thinking about it. A dog will pull a sled through snow without question. Just happy to be there. That's boys, the incessant tail-waggers of the sporting world. Girls have to see the point of everything.

'You're going to run out there, jab-pick the ball and solo back and handpass,' says the coach.

'Yeah? Why?' comes the answer.

But they love it. Their play is an extension of their personality, their intensity, and the will to win is sometimes frightening. And camogie was there all along? . . . I asked three twelve-year-olds this week what they were going to be when they got older. One surgeon (Clare), two professional hurlers (Fionnuala and Carol).

Camogie has problems, though. It's a competitive world out there and the game has more skills to be learned than any other you can think of. Takes time. Needs money. Requires patience. Gaelic football has gobbled up the imagination of much of its natural constituency. Soccer too. Fixture lists are often chaotic, with not enough games being played in summer, while minor grade is at under-16 so the sport haemorrhages good kids too early. And the game needs, not to be gender specific about it, a make-over, not to make it look like something it isn't, but for its image to begin to reflect what it has become.

Next year is the centenary of the association, and camogie is looking to put as much life into its image as it has into its game. To that end, the association has formed a committee, the average age of which is twenty-seven and which will be electrifying the sport's image over the next year or so.

This isn't unusual. Sports market themselves all the time for the better.

It's a world full of sharks out there, and the tragedy of camogie is that it has suffered for too long from its image of being something for big girls with fat ankles to do between Macra dances. It has no face, no stars, no real impact on those who don't play it or know it.

How radical are they going to be? Well, try 'Chicks with Sticks!' as a slogan. The working group (I repeat, average age twenty-seven, not a Macra dance between them) will be moving at last towards a stronger GAA/camogie alliance, with all the benefits that would bring. That alliance on a national level will change both the GAA and camogie forever.

Tests have shown that, once you've tried a GAA club with a thriving and vibrant camogie section, you'll never go back to the old 'men stewing in their own bitterness' model. The GAA club at its best is part of the community, not a men's retreat house.

Having a camogie section means the club represents the community better and opens itself up to new perspectives and new ways of thinking. We have a strange way of thinking about sport in this country. Largely, we view it the wrong way around. A Sonia O'Sullivan happens despite ourselves, really. Then we start rewarding elite athletes to make up for our earlier negligence. We don't target girls for sporting development and we don't reward them. We don't cover enough girls' sports on

Monday mornings. Oddly, we don't view women as a market for sport.

It's shocking that, despite the huge impact camogie has on ordinary, day-to-day life in Ireland, the senior inter-county leagues and championships in the sport are still available for sponsorship, and no one has taken those competitions by the neck, tagged their name to them and committed the rest of their spend to telling the stories and revealing the person-alities.

Girls don't stand up laneways and throw rubber balls against walls anymore. You hardly ever see them skipping. They are housebound and baby-sat by the Gameboy and the TV. But, let loose, the chicks with sticks get to play on teams and grow and express themselves strenuously.

Girls have discovered camogie for themselves. They are waiting now for the rest of the world to discover them.

Life begins at 100.

FROM *BOOKED!* BY TOM HUMPHRIES

N.B. Candidates may NOT answer Question A and Question B on the same text.
Questions A and B carry 50 marks each.

Question A

(i)   What does the author say about the differences between boys and girls when it comes to sport? Do you agree with him?(10)
(ii) What does the author say about the way in which sportspeople have been treated in Ireland? (10)
(iii) How does camogie intend to move forward? Do you think it will work? (10)
(iv) What does the author say about women's input into GAA clubs? (20)

Question B

Imagine you are a reporter for a sports magazine. You have been asked to write an interview with a famous sportswoman.
Write six questions and the answers you would expect to get. (50)

SPORT: TEXT 2

There's only one red army

Back to Rovers. The first we knew that my father had a new woman in his life was when he arrived to pick Eoghan up at Connolly Station to bring him to a match and the woman was with him. She is still with him. It's a few years ago. The incident hurt my mother very much. We were playing Bray Wanderers that day and drew 1–1 with a late goal from a Scottish guy called Barry Cliff. Harry crossed the ball to him, Fago had put Harry away down the wing.

It hurt my mother because following Rovers had been part of what we were as a family. My father's introduction of his new woman into this private space showed that he was determined to confront us with her. He wasn't going to go away and live his life elsewhere. He would continue to follow Rovers and he would subsume it into his new life.

My mother coped with it as people learn to cope with what is.

My father was back at the games. It seemed ridiculous to ever have expected he would be able to keep away from The Showgrounds. None of us talked much to him then. But we managed to discover a language which could re-admit him to our lives. The language of Sligo Rovers. The problem of what you say to a father who has deserted you was solved. When you met him, you had ninety minutes of the Sunday gone by to discuss and ninety minutes of the Sunday coming to anticipate. Under that shelter you could talk.

My father even calls to the house sometimes on his way to home matches. Himself and my mother exchange a few words and when the conversation understandably palls, they can always be rescued.

- Is Ian Gilzean fit enough?
- Was Johnny Kenny better a couple of seasons ago?
- Why did we let Gavin Dykes go?
- Do you remember Pat McCluskey, Gabriel Ojo, Johnny Brooks, Kevin Fallon, David Pugh?

And when they begin to remember together players from the past who they saw together in The Showgrounds before I was born, I realise that there is no judgement I can make on these two people who have known each other for so much longer than I know either of them.

My father's partner comes to the games. I don't think she has much of a choice. Herself and my mother often sit in the same pubs after the game. They don't like each other. But they each recognise that this is how things have turned out and they can't stop the other person having a drink wherever they want to. It's messy but at back it's decent, like a lot of the new difficult real Ireland.

The family from the 1975 photo is still in The Showgrounds, except it has been dispersed throughout the ground. Myself, Eoghan and Colm in The Shed, My mother and Maura in the main stand, my father in the stand facing them. Our lives have changed in ways we could not have imagined then, but there is a constant fortnightly ninety minutes which has remained the same.

FROM *THERE'S ONLY ONE RED ARMY*
BY EAMONN SWEENEY

N.B. Candidates may NOT answer Question A and Question B on the same text.
Questions A and B carry 50 marks each.

Question A
(i) What part does soccer play in the family's life? (10)
(ii) How has sport helped to heal problems in the author's family? (15)
(iii) What does the writer mean by the line: 'My mother coped with it as people learn to cope with what is.'? (10)
(iv) How does the family treat the father's partner? Discuss this. (15)

Question B
Imagine you are a supporter of a team which is not doing well. Write your diary entries for the last three matches of the season. (50)

SPORT: TEXT 3

N.B. Candidates may NOT answer Question A and Question B on the same text. Questions A and B carry 50 marks each.

Question A

(i)   What do the images suggest to you about the effort that goes into sport? (10)

(ii) Which image is your favourite? Describe the image. Explain your choice. (20)

(iii) In your opinion what makes a great sportsperson? Give an example and reasons for your choice. (20)

Question B

Imagine you are a radio commentator. Write your radio commentary for the most important moment during a match or a sporting event.(50)

Important words and terms for the study of English

Alliteration	When two or more words starting with the same letter or sound are placed consecutively, e.g. 'Not a cute card or a kissogram'.
Ambiguity	When words have one or more meanings and this meaning is not made clear. In poetry this can often be intentional.
Anthology	A collection of literature by various writers.
Assonance	Internal rhyme, especially the repetition of vowel sounds in words close to each other, e.g. 'of clay and wattles made'.
Ballad	A poem or song that tells a story.
Caricature	An exaggerated portrait.
Cliché	A phrase that has been over-repeated, e.g. 'It rained cats and dogs'.
Climax	The point of greatest intensity in the work.
Closure	The way a poem ends.
Compare	Examine similarities between two things.
Conceit	When an interesting and unlikely connection is made between two seemingly very different things.
Contrast	Point out differences between two things.
Couplet	Two consecutive lines that have the same metre and rhythm, e.g. 'Pour away the ocean and sweep up the wood. For nothing now can ever come to any good.'
Define	Give a clear and exact meaning.
Describe	Give a detailed account.
Dialect	A local variation of a language, see 'Kidspoem/Bairnsang' by Liz Lochhead.
Dramatic monologue	A poem written in a specific situation where a character is speaking directly to somebody else, e.g. in 'For Heidi with Blue Hair' by Fleur Adcock.
Elegy	A poem which mourns the dead, e.g. 'Funeral Blues' by W. H. Auden.
Epigram	A short witty poem often written with simple rhyme.

Epigraph	A relevant quotation at the start of a poem or a book.
Epiphany	A moment of revelation.
Euphemism	Substitution of milder words for ones that may have been more crude or blunt.
Evaluate	Analyse the arguments that have been put forward.
Fable	A legendary story with a moral.
Free verse	A poem without rhyme.
Hyperbole	Use of exaggeration in poetry, e.g. 'Ride ten thousand days and nights'.
Illustrate	Make clear; explain with examples.
Image	A picture in words.
Irony	a) When something is said in such a way that the opposite of the true meaning is meant. b) When somebody says something that has deeper meaning for what is about to happen to them. This is often obvious to the reader but not to the speaker (dramatic irony).
Lyric	A short personal poem, often with musical qualities.
Metaphor	When a comparison is made without using 'like' or 'as', e.g. 'And time itself's a feather / Touching them gently'.
Mood	The feeling a reader gets from a poem.
Myth	A traditional story that has ancient religious or supernatural ideas or a widespread but false idea.
Octet	An eight-line verse. In a Petrarchan sonnet it is the first eight lines.
Ode	A poem that is written in celebration.
Onomatopoeia	Words whose sounds accentuate their meaning by sounding like what is being described, e.g. 'slap', 'clip-clop'.
Outline	Describe without detail.
Oxymoron	A figure of speech where seemingly opposite ideas are brought together.
Paradox	A statement that at first appears inconsistent but is really true.
Parody	A close but mocking imitation of a well-known work.
Pathetic fallacy	This occurs when human feeling is given to nature, e.g. 'The winter evening settles down'.
Pathos	Evoking pity.
Persona	When the poet uses a voice in the poem that is not his own, e.g. the voice of Bruce Ismay in 'After the *Titanic*' by Derek Mahon.

Personification	When a poet gives voice to non-human characters.
Poetic licence	Permission given to writers that allows them to tamper with true facts.
Prose	Ordinary language written without metre or rhythm.
Pun	Wordplay where words may have the same sound but different meanings.
Quatrain	Four-line verse.
Repetition	Repeating sounds, words, lines or verses for poetic effect.
Rhetorical question	A question where the answer is already known.
Rhyme	Identical or close similarity of sounds in the final syllables of two or more words.
Rhyming scheme	The pattern of rhyme in a poem.
Rhythm	How sounds or words move within a poem. The critic Neil Astley has called it the 'essence of poetry'.
Run-on line	Also known as enjambment, this occurs when a sentence or phrase continues past the end of one line and into the next.
Sarcasm	Bitterly ironic statement.
Satire	Act of attacking a silly or evil act by using mockery.
Sentimentality	Presentation of a feeling in an over-the-top way.
Sestet	A six-line verse or the final six lines in a sonnet.
Simile	A comparison using the words 'like' or 'as', e.g. 'Silence between them like a thread to hold / And not wind in.'
Sonnet	A fourteen-line poem.
Stanza	Verse.
Subject matter	The details that a poet writes about in order to express his/her theme.
Symbol	Word or image which represents something other than itself.
Syntax	The arrangement of words in a sentence.
Tercet	Three-line verse.
Theme	The main idea in a poem.
Tone	The attitude of the poet as conveyed through his/her poem.
Trace	Explain stage by stage.
Verse	A subsection of a poem.
Voice	The person speaking in the poem, not necessarily the poet, see Persona, above.

Past Examination Questions
(Ordinary level)

Poems also prescribed for Higher Level

Patrick Kavanagh
Shancoduff (page 56)

1 (a) How does the poet show that he likes Shancoduff, his home place?
Support your answer by reference to the poem. (10)

(b) Where in the poem does he show that life in Shancoduff can be harsh?
Support your answer by reference to the poem. (10)

(c) On balance, do you think that Shancoduff would be a likeable or a harsh place to live in? Give a reason for your answer. (10)

(Ordinary Level 2003)

2 Answer ONE of the following: [Each part carries 20 marks]

(i) Imagine Patrick Kavanagh puts his farm up for sale. Write the advertisement that might appear in the local newspaper. Base your advertisement on the poem.

OR

(ii) 'They are my Alps and I have climbed the Matterhorn...'
Why, in your opinion, does Kavanagh refer to the Alps and the Matterhorn in this poem?

OR

(iii) What do you think is the cattle-drovers' view of Kavanagh's way of life?
Refer to the poem in your answer.

Denise Levertov
What were they like? (page 72)

1 (a) What impression does the poet give us of the people of Vietnam? Refer to the poem in your answer. (10)

(b) From the six answers given in the second part of the poem, choose an answer that

for you creates the clearest picture of the horrors of war. Explain your choice. (10)

(c) Did you like this poem? Give a reason for your answer. (10)

2 Answer ONE of the following: [Each part carries 20 marks]

(i) The shape of this poem is unusual – a set of questions followed by a set of answers. Do you think it is a good way to write the poem? Explain your answer.

OR

(ii) Imagine you were asked to make an anti war video in which this poem is spoken. Describe the music and images you would use as a background to the reading of the poem.

OR

(iii) Do you think the title of the poem, What Were They Like?, is a good one? Explain your view.

(Ordinary Level 2005)

Patricia Beer
The Voice (page 10)

1 (a) What picture of the poet's aunt emerges from this poem?
Refer to the poem in your answer. (10)

(b) In your opinion, what part did the parrot play in the aunt's life? Explain your answer by referring to the words and events in the poem. (10)

(c) Which of the following statements best describes your response to the poem? Give a reason for your answer.
- *I found the poem amusing*
- *I found the poem sad*
- *I found the poem both amusing and sad*
(10)

2 Answer ONE of the following: [Each part carries 20 marks]

(i) Imagine that the poet was asked to make a speech at the 'funeral' of the parrot. Write out the speech that you imagine she might deliver.

OR

(ii) 'Nature's creatures should not be kept in cages for our amusement.'

Write a short piece outlining your views on this topic. You should refer to the poem to support the points you make.

OR

(iii) Imagine you were asked to make a short film or video using one moment or event from this poem. Describe the moment or event you would choose and explain the kind of film or video you would make.

(Ordinary Level 2006)

Howard Nemerov

Wolves in the Zoo (page 98)

1 (a) What, in your opinion, is the poet's attitude to wolves? Give a reason for your answer, based on the poem. (10)

(b) Why do you think the poet talks about 'Little Red Ridinghood and her Gran'? Explain your answer. (10)

(c) Choose two lines from the poem that especially appeal to you. Explain your choice. (10)

2 Answer ONE of the following: [Each part carries 20 marks]

(i) 'This poem tells us a lot about the attitude of human beings to wild animals.'
Would you agree with this statement? Give reasons for your answer based on the poem.

OR

(ii) A company is publishing a book of nature poetry for young adults called Our Animals – Our Friends. You have been invited to choose a poem for publication. Explain why you would or would not choose Wolves in the Zoo for inclusion.

OR

(iii) You are a wolf in the cage in the zoo. Describe your thoughts and feelings. You may use the material in the poem to support your response.

(Ordinary Level 2007)

Robert Frost

Out, Out– (page 34)

1 (a) Which words and phrases in the first twelve lines (ending at '…when saved from work') help to give you a clear picture of the place where the poem is set? Explain your choice. (10)

(b) Describe the boy's reaction when he realised that his hand had been badly damaged by the saw. (10)

(c) Do you think the poet shows sympathy for the boy? Explain your answer. (10)

2 Answer ONE of the following: [Each part carries 20 marks]

(i) Write the diary entry of the boy's sister, in which she records her experiences and feelings on the day the accident happened.

OR

(ii) People have said that this is a very dramatic poem. Do you agree? Explain your answer.

OR

(iii) Which of the following statements best describes your response to the poem?
- *I found the poem cruel because…*
- *I found the poem dramatic because…*
- *I found the poem sad because…*
Give reasons for your answer.

(Ordinary Level 2007)

Maya Angelou

Phenomenal Woman (page 4)

1 (a) From your reading of Stanza 1 (lines 1–14) what, according to the poet, is her secret for women? (10)

(b) 'Men themselves have wondered
What they see in me.'
What answer does the poet give to the men in Stanza 3 (lines 31–46)? (10)

(c) Having studied the poem, do you think the poet is a 'Phenomenal woman'? Explain your answer. (10)

2 Answer one of the following: [Each part carries 20 marks]

(i) Did you enjoy reading this poem?

Write a piece where you give your views in response to this question.

OR

(ii) This poem is about self-confidence. Choose two examples from the poem which you feel reveal this quality of self-confidence in a special way. Give reasons for your answer.

OR

(iii) If you were to write a poem entitled 'Phenomenal Man', what qualities would you give that man?
(In writing your answer, you may, if you wish, present the male qualities as the female ones are presented in the last 9 lines of the poem,
'I say,
It's in the...
That's me.')

(Ordinary Level 2008)

Derek Mahon
Antarctica (page 84)

1 (a) A friend asks you to tell him/her what this poem is about. Write what you would say. (10)

(b) Choose some words and phrases which you think create the sense of the terrible climate experienced by the explorers. Explain your choices. (10)

(c) 'I am just going outside and may be some time.'
How does the poet show that Oates (the speaker of the first line of the poem) is moving further and further away from his companions in the tent?
Explain your answer. (10)

2 Answer ONE of the following: [Each part carries 20 marks]

(i) Imagine that you are one of Oates's companions. Write what you would say to him in order to persuade him not to leave the tent.

OR

(ii) You are Edward Oates. Write the diary entry you would like to leave behind to explain your conduct in walking out into the snow to die.

OR

(iii) 'The final four lines are the finest lines in the poem.'
Do you agree with this statement?
Explain your answer.

(Ordinary Level 2008)

Paul Durcan
Going Home to Mayo, Winter, 1949 (page 30)

1 (a) What is the poet's attitude to Dublin city in this poem? Explain your answer. (10)

(b) His attitude to Mayo is very different. How is this shown in the poem?(10)

(c) What do we learn about the relationship between father and son from the poem? Explain your answer. (10)

2 Answer ONE of the following: [Each part carries 20 marks]

(i) Using one of these as an opening, write about the overall mood of the poem:
  – *I think this is a happy poem because...*
  – *I think this is a sad poem because...*

OR

(ii) Imagine that the poet keeps a diary. Write his diary entry at the end of his first day at his father's mother's house.

OR

(iii) Pick out a couple of your favourite lines or images from the poem and explain why you like them.

(Ordinary Level 2008)

Adrienne Rich
Aunt Jennifer's Tigers (page 114)

1 (a) Why in your opinion does the poet's aunt choose the theme of tigers for her screen? Give a reason for your answer, based on your understanding of the poem.(10)

(b) The massive weight of Uncle's wedding band
Sits heavily upon Aunt Jennifer's hand.
What impression do you get of Aunt Jennifer's marriage from these lines? Explain your answer. (10)

(c) Choose one of the following phrases which in your opinion best reveals the poet's attitude towards her aunt:

– she admires her
– she pities her
Explain your choice. (10)

② Answer ONE of the following: [Each part carries 20 marks]

(i)   This poem is full of movement and colour. Choose some words and phrases of both movement and colour which especially appeal to you.
Explain your choices.

OR

(ii) 'Adrienne Rich's poems are very gloomy'. Write a piece in which you agree or dis agree with this statement. Your response should include some reference to one or both of the other Rich poems on your course.

OR

(iii) In this poem, the poet speaks for her Aunt Jennifer. Write a piece in which Aunt Jennifer tells her own story. You may use the material in the poem to support your response.

(Ordinary Level 2008)

ACKNOWLEDGMENTS

We would like to thank the following for their support to the authors in this project:

Mark, Kate and Mark Óg, Mike and Maureen Clancy, Niall, Mary, Molly and Dara O'Connell, Michael Clancy, Mark, Peggy, Shane, Mary and Jim and Elaine Crehan.

Fiona, Tadhg and Mallaigh, Jack and Rose McCarthy, Eric, Donal and Rosanna McCarthy, Sheila O'Shea and Toni Hickey, Jimmy and Rosanne, Helen and Vinny and the staff of Coláiste Dún Iascaigh.

Anthony Murray, Aoileann O'Donnell and Helen Thompson, Gill & Macmillan.

PERMISSIONS

The author and publisher are grateful to the following for permission to reproduce copyrighted material:

'For Heidi with Blue Hair' by Fleur Adcock, *Poems 1960-2000* (Bloodaxe Books, 2000);

'Phenomenal Woman' by Maya Angelou reproduced from *The Complete Collected Poems* by Maya Angelou, by permission of Virago Books, an imprint of Little, Brown Book Group;

'It Ain't what you do, it's what it does to you' by Simon Armitage, *ZOOM!* (Bloodaxe Books, 2007);

'Funeral Blues' from *Collected Shorter Poems* by W.H. Auden, Faber and Faber Ltd;

'The Voice' by Patricia Beer is reproduced by kind permission of Carcanet Press Limited;

'Filling Station', 'The Fish' and 'The Prodigal' from *The Complete Poems 1927-1979* by Elizabeth Bishop. Copyright © 1979, 1983 by Alice Helen Methfessel. Reprinted by permission of Farrar, Straus and Giroux, LLC;

'Child of Our Time', 'Love' and 'This Moment' by Eavan Boland are reproduced by kind permission of Carcanet Press Limited;

'Valentine' is taken from *Mean Time* by Carol Ann Duffy published by Anvil Press Poetry in 1993;

'Going Home to Mayo, Winter 1949'. Copyright © Paul Durcan. Reproduced by permission of the author c/o Rogers, Coleridge & White Ltd, 20 Powis Mews, London, W11 1JN;

'The Tuft of Flowers', 'Mending Wall' and 'Out-Out–' from *The Poetry of Robert Frost* edited by Edward Connery Lathem. Copyright 1916, 1928, 1930, 1934, 1939, 1969 by Henry Holt and Company, copyright 1936, 1944, 1951, 1956, 1958 by Robert Frost, copyright 1964, 1967 by Lesley Frost Ballantine;

'The Hug'. Copyright 1988 Tess Gallagher. Reprinted from *Amplitude: New and Selected Poems* with the permission of Graywolf Press, Saint Paul, Minnesota;

'Daniel's Duck' by Kerry Hardie reproduced by kind permission of the author and The Gallery Press, Loughcrew, Oldcastle, County Meath, Ireland. From *The Sky didn't fall* (2003);

'A Constable Calls' from *North* by Seamus Heaney, Faber and Faber Ltd; 'A Call' by Seamus Heaney from *The Spirit Level*, Faber and Faber Ltd; 'The Underground' by Seamus Heaney from *Station Island*, Faber and Faber Ltd;

'Shancoduff' and 'A Christmas Childhood' by Patrick Kavanagh are reprinted from *Collected Poems*, edited by Anoinette Quinn (Allen lane, 2004), by kind permission of the Trustees of the Estate of the late Katherine B. Kavanagh, through the Jonathan Williams Literacy Agency;

'A Glimpse of Starlings' and 'Night Drive' by Brendan Kennelly, *Familiar Strangers: New & Selected poems 1960-2004* (Bloodaxe Books, 2004);

'Thinking of Mr D.' and 'Mirror in February' by Thomas Kinsella are reproduced by kind permission of Carcanet Press Limited;

'The Explosion' by Philip Larkin from *High Windows*, Faber and Faber Ltd; 'Ambulances' by Philip Larkin from *The Whitsun Weddings*, Faber and Faber Ltd;

'What were they like?' by Denise Levertov reproduced by permission of Pollinger Limited and New Directions Publishing Corporation;

'Kidspoem/Bairnsang' by Liz Lochhead is reproduced by permission of Polygon, an imprint of Birlinn Ltd (www.birlinn.co.uk);

'Badger' © Michael Longley – 1973;

'Meeting Point' by Louis MacNeice from *Collected Poems* published by Faber and Faber Ltd. Reproduced by kind permission of David Higham Associates;

'Grandfather', 'After the Titanic' and 'Antarctica' by Derek Mahon reproduced by kind permission of the author and The Gallery Press, Loughcrew, Oldcastle, County Meath, Ireland. From *Collected Poems* (1999);